MARVEL UNIVERSE ULTIMATE SPIDER-MAN VOL. 1. Contains material originally published in magazine form as MARVEL UNIVERSE ULTIMATE SPIDER-MAN #1-4. First printing 2012. ISBN# 978-0-7851-6149-3. Published by MARVEL WORLDWIDE, INC., a subsidiary of MARVEL ENTERTAINMENT, LLC. OFFICE OF PUBLICATION: 135 West 50th Street, New York, NY 10020. Copyright © 2012 Marvel Characters, Inc. All rights reserved. $9.99 per copy in the U.S. and $10.99 in Canada (GST #R127032852); Canadian Agreement #40668537. All characters featured in this issue and the distinctive names and likenesses thereof, and all related indicia are trademarks of Marvel Characters, Inc. No similarity between any of the names, characters, persons, and/or institutions in this magazine with those of any living or dead person or institution is intended, and any such similarity which may exist is purely coincidental. **Printed in the U.S.A.** ALAN FINE, EVP - Office of the President, Marvel Worldwide, Inc. and EVP & CMO Marvel Characters B.V.; DAN BUCKLEY, Publisher & President - Print, Animation & Digital Divisions; JOE QUESADA, Chief Creative Officer; TOM BREVOORT, SVP of Publishing; DAVID BOGART, SVP of Operations & Procurement, Publishing; RUWAN JAYATILLEKE, SVP & Associate Publisher, Publishing; C.B. CEBULSKI, SVP of Creator & Content Development; DAVID GABRIEL, SVP of Publishing Sales & Circulation; MICHAEL PASCIULLO, SVP of Brand Planning & Communications; JIM O'KEEFE, VP of Operations & Logistics; DAN CARR, Executive Director of Publishing Technology; SUSAN CRESPI, Editorial Operations Manager; ALEX MORALES, Publishing Operations Manager; STAN LEE, Chairman Emeritus. For information regarding advertising in Marvel Comics or on Marvel.com, please contact Niza Disla, Director of Marvel Partnerships, at ndisla@marvel.com. For Marvel subscription inquiries, please call 800-217-9158. **Manufactured between 9/17/2012 and 10/22/2012 by SHERIDAN BOOKS, INC., CHELSEA, MI, USA.**

10 9 8 7 6 5 4 3 2 1

MARVEL ULTIMATE SPIDER-MAN

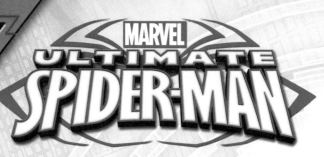

WRITERS

MAN OF ACTION, DAN SLOTT, EUGENE SON, JACOB SEMAHN, ELLIOTT KALAN & FRANK TIERI

ARTISTS

NUNO PLATI, TY TEMPLETON AND RAMON BACHS & RAUL FONTS

COLOR ARTISTS

NUNO PLATI & WIL QUINTANA

LETTERERS

VC'S JOE CARAMAGNA, CLAYTON COWLES & JOE SABINO

ASSISTANT EDITOR

ELLIE PYLE

ASSOCIATE EDITOR

TOM BRENNAN

EDITOR

STEPHEN WACKER

Collection Editor: **Cory Levine**
Assistant Editors: **Alex Starbuck & Nelson Ribeiro**
Editors, Special Projects: **Jennifer Grünwald & Mark D. Beazley**
Senior Editor, Special Projects: **Jeff Youngquist**
Senior Vice President of Sales: **David Gabriel**
SVP of Brand Planning & Communications: **Michael Pasciullo**
Head of Marvel Television: **Jeph Loeb**

Editor In Chief: **Axel Alonso**
Chief Creative Officer: **Joe Quesada**
Publisher: **Dan Buckley**
Executive Producer: **Alan Fine**

WHILE ATTENDING A DEMONSTRATION IN RADIOLOGY, HIGH SCHOOL STUDENT PETER PARKER WAS BITTEN BY A SPIDER THAT HAD ACCIDENTALLY BEEN EXPOSED TO RADIOACTIVE RAYS. THROUGH A MIRACLE OF SCIENCE, PETER SOON FOUND THAT HE HAD GAINED THE SPIDER'S POWERS...AND HAD, IN EFFECT, BECOME A HUMAN SPIDER! FROM THAT DAY ON, HE HAS ENDEAVORED TO BECOME THE...

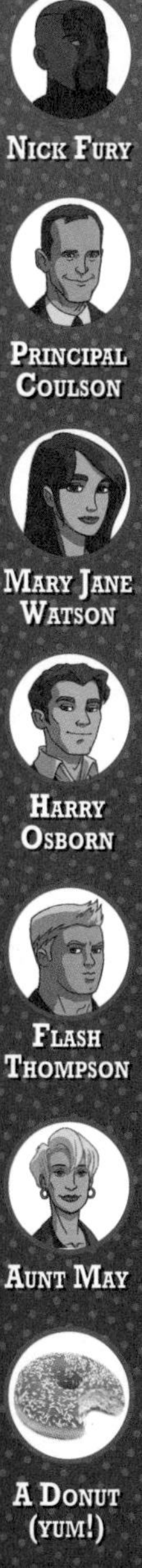

NICK FURY
PRINCIPAL COULSON
MARY JANE WATSON
HARRY OSBORN
FLASH THOMPSON
AUNT MAY
A DONUT (YUM!)

MARVEL ULTIMATE SPIDER-MAN™

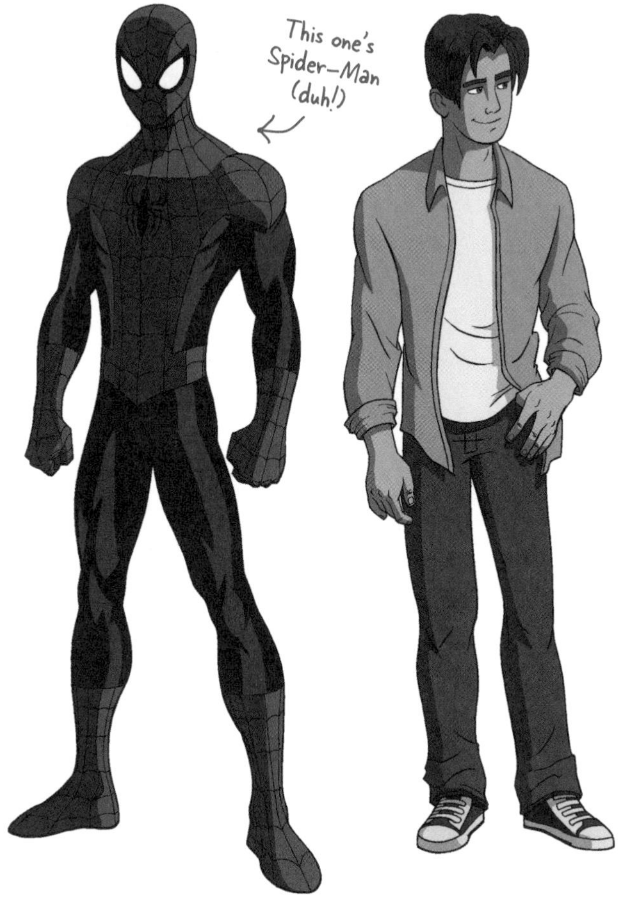

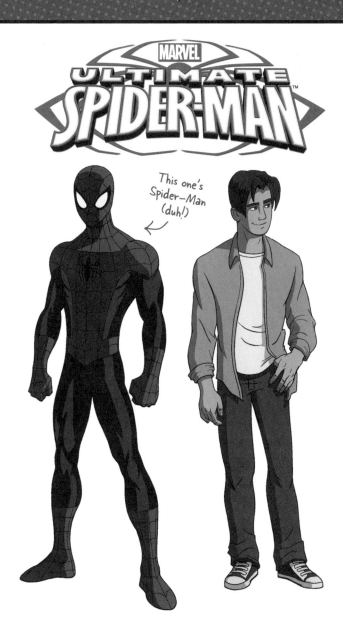

This one's Spider-Man (duh!)

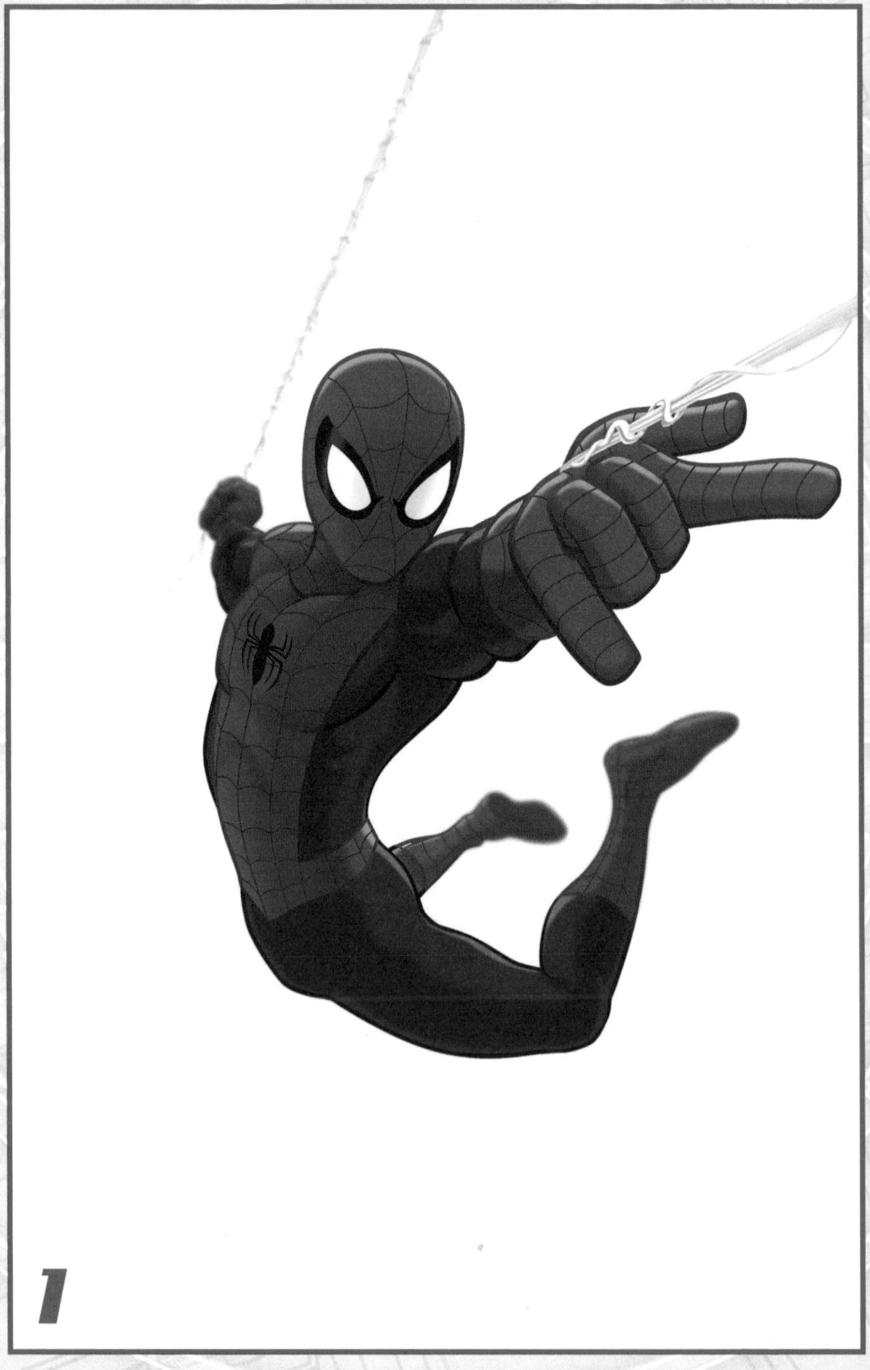

1

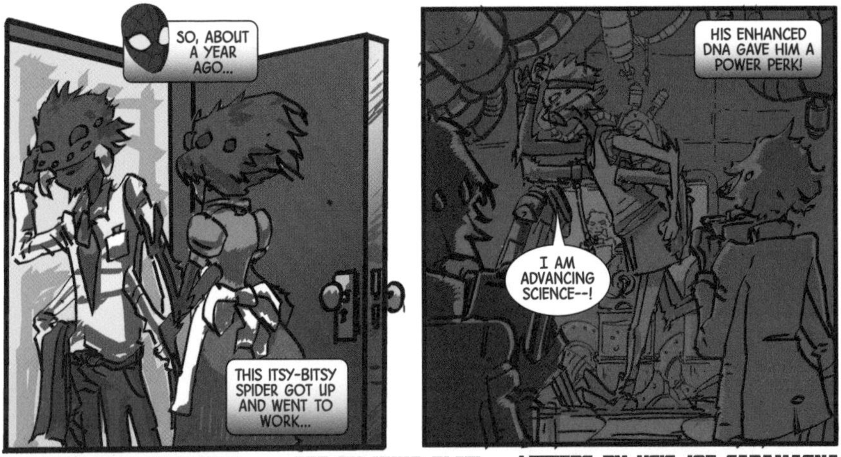
SO, ABOUT A YEAR AGO...
THIS ITSY-BITSY SPIDER GOT UP AND WENT TO WORK...
HIS ENHANCED DNA GAVE HIM A POWER PERK!
I AM ADVANCING SCIENCE--!

WRITTEN BY MAN OF ACTION ART BY NUNO PLATI LETTERS BY VC'S JOE CARAMAGNA

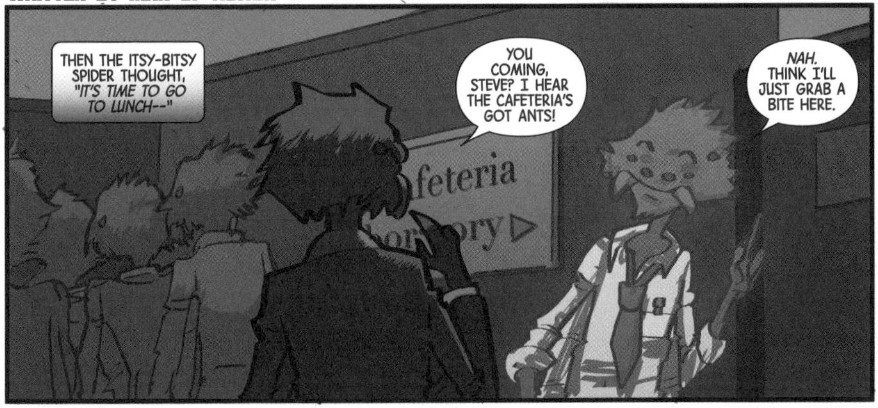
THEN THE ITSY-BITSY SPIDER THOUGHT, "*IT'S TIME TO GO TO LUNCH--*"
YOU COMING, STEVE? I HEAR THE CAFETERIA'S GOT ANTS!
NAH. THINK I'LL JUST GRAB A BITE HERE.

ASSISTANT EDITOR: ELLIE PYLE ASSOCIATE EDITOR: TOM BRENNAN EDITOR: STEPHEN WACKER

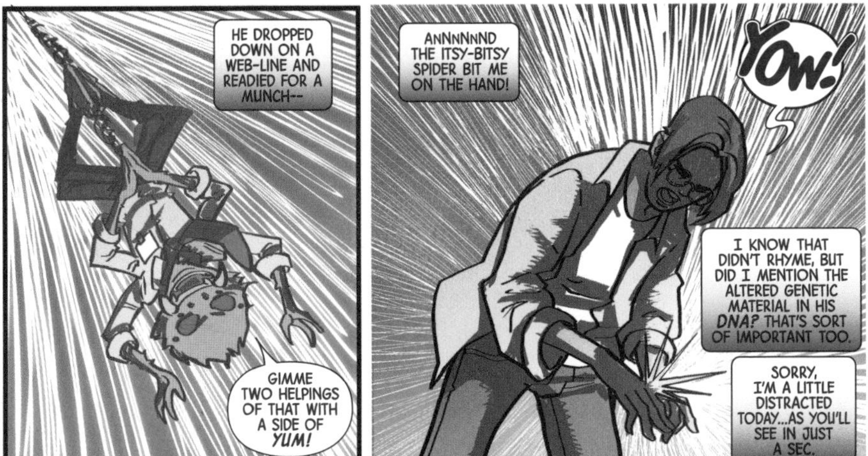
HE DROPPED DOWN ON A WEB-LINE AND READIED FOR A *MUNCH--*
GIMME TWO HELPINGS OF THAT WITH A SIDE OF *YUM!*
ANNNNNND THE ITSY-BITSY SPIDER BIT ME ON THE HAND!
YOW!
I KNOW THAT DIDN'T RHYME, BUT DID I MENTION THE ALTERED GENETIC MATERIAL IN HIS *DNA?* THAT'S SORT OF IMPORTANT TOO.
SORRY, I'M A LITTLE DISTRACTED TODAY...AS YOU'LL SEE IN JUST A SEC.

ALONSO, QUESADA, LOEB, BUCKLEY, FINE – THE BOSSES

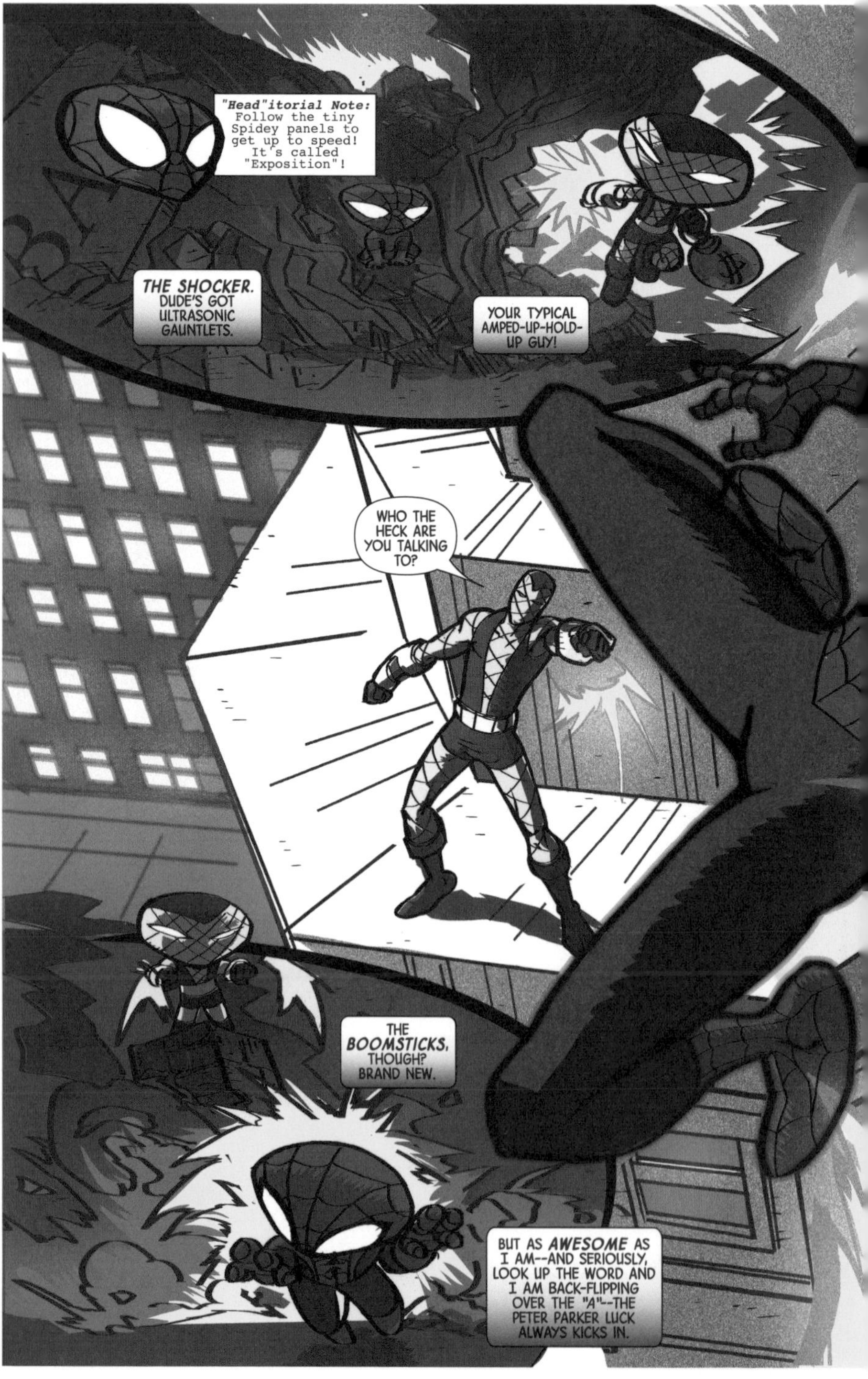
"Head"itorial Note: Follow the tiny Spidey panels to get up to speed! It's called "Exposition"!
THE SHOCKER. DUDE'S GOT ULTRASONIC GAUNTLETS.
YOUR TYPICAL AMPED-UP-HOLD-UP GUY!
WHO THE HECK ARE YOU TALKING TO?
THE BOOMSTICKS, THOUGH? BRAND NEW.
BUT AS AWESOME AS I AM--AND SERIOUSLY, LOOK UP THE WORD AND I AM BACK-FLIPPING OVER THE "A"--THE PETER PARKER LUCK ALWAYS KICKS IN.

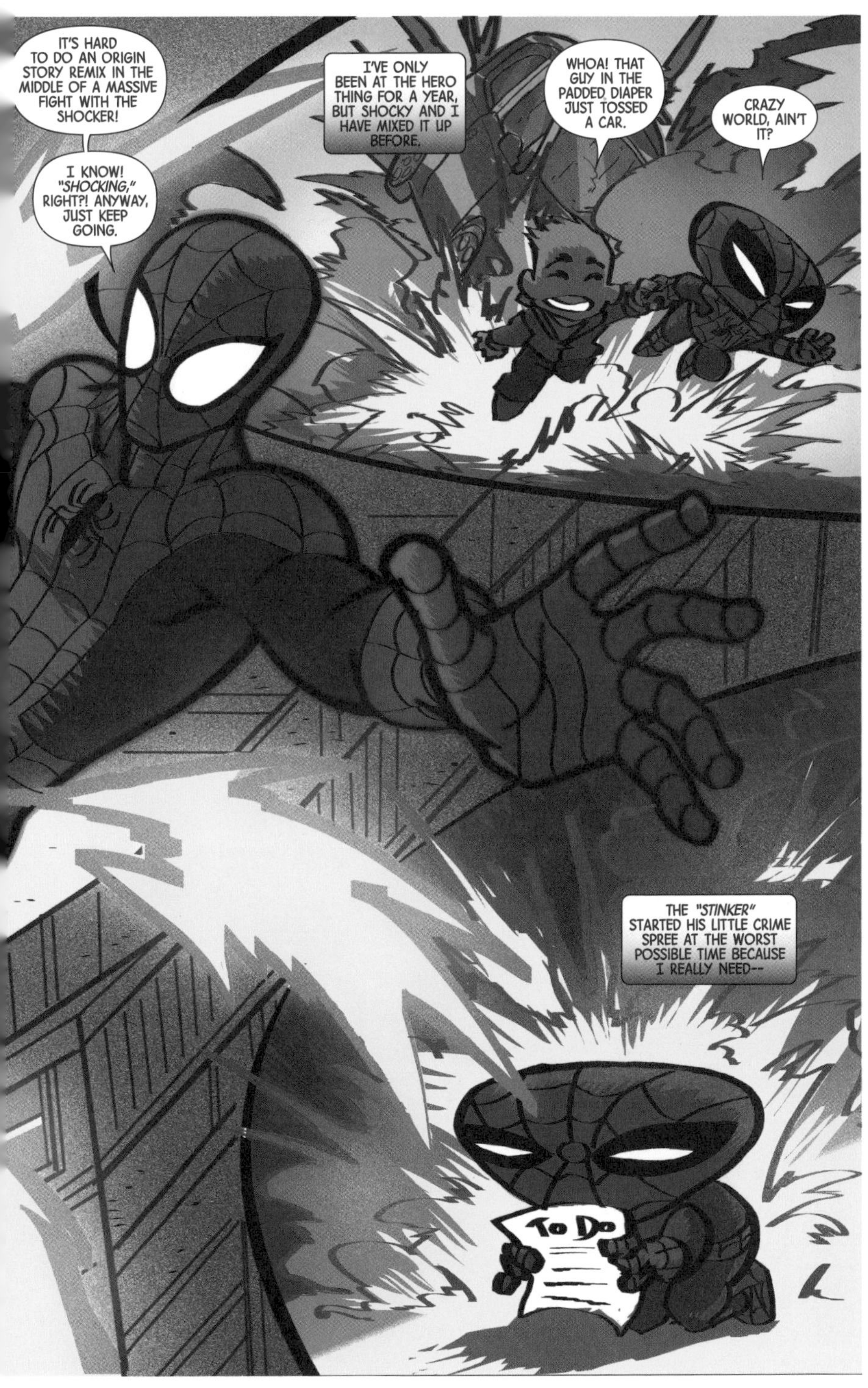

IT'S HARD TO DO AN ORIGIN STORY REMIX IN THE MIDDLE OF A MASSIVE FIGHT WITH THE SHOCKER!
I KNOW! "SHOCKING," RIGHT?! ANYWAY, JUST KEEP GOING.
I'VE ONLY BEEN AT THE HERO THING FOR A YEAR, BUT SHOCKY AND I HAVE MIXED IT UP BEFORE.
WHOA! THAT GUY IN THE PADDED DIAPER JUST TOSSED A CAR.
CRAZY WORLD, AIN'T IT?
THE "STINKER" STARTED HIS LITTLE CRIME SPREE AT THE WORST POSSIBLE TIME BECAUSE I REALLY NEED--
TO DO

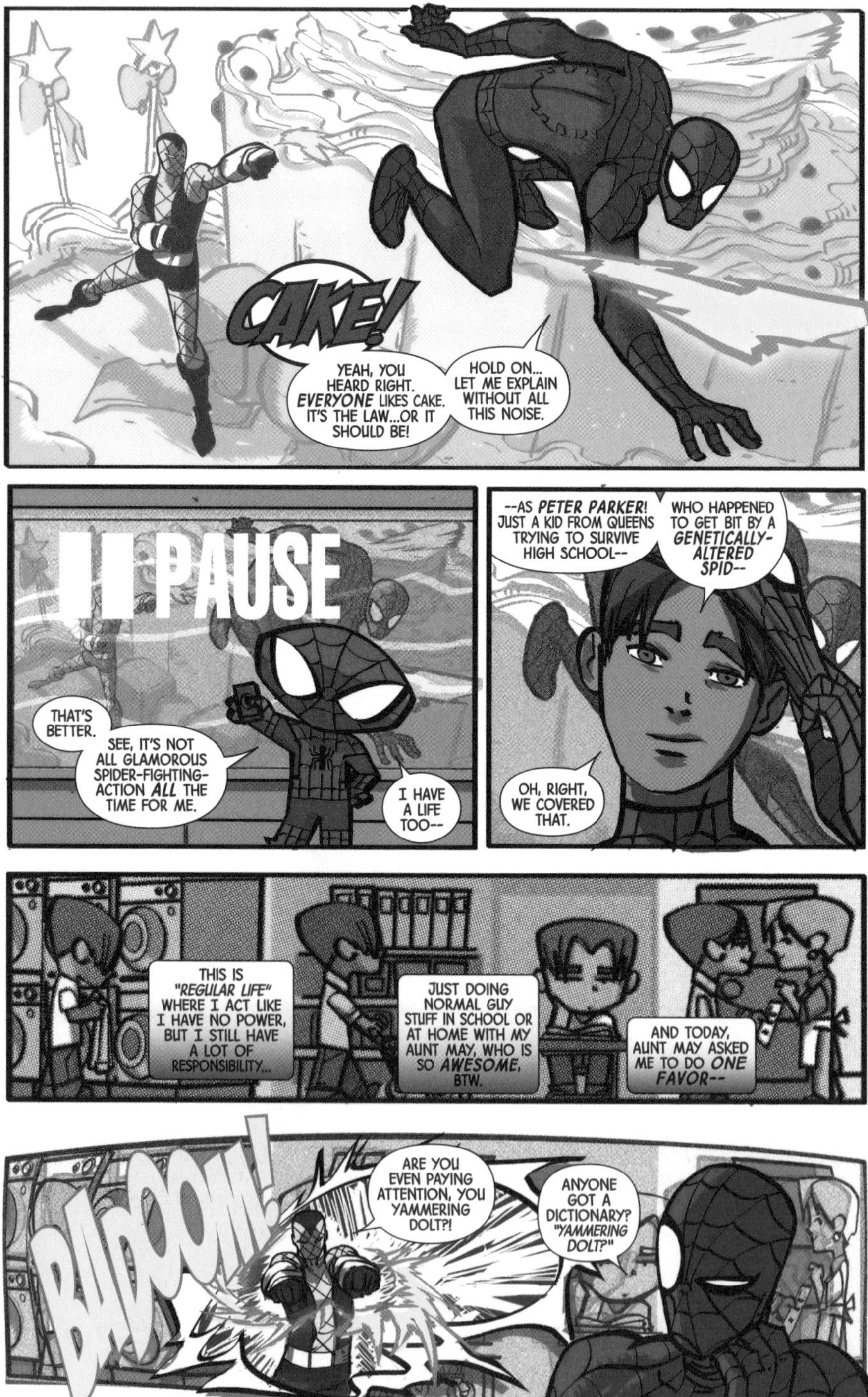
CAKE!
YEAH, YOU HEARD RIGHT. EVERYONE LIKES CAKE. IT'S THE LAW...OR IT SHOULD BE!
HOLD ON... LET ME EXPLAIN WITHOUT ALL THIS NOISE.
PAUSE
THAT'S BETTER.
SEE, IT'S NOT ALL GLAMOROUS SPIDER-FIGHTING-ACTION ALL THE TIME FOR ME.
I HAVE A LIFE TOO--
--AS PETER PARKER! JUST A KID FROM QUEENS TRYING TO SURVIVE HIGH SCHOOL--
WHO HAPPENED TO GET BIT BY A GENETICALLY-ALTERED SPID--
OH, RIGHT, WE COVERED THAT.
THIS IS "REGULAR LIFE" WHERE I ACT LIKE I HAVE NO POWER, BUT I STILL HAVE A LOT OF RESPONSIBILITY...
JUST DOING NORMAL GUY STUFF IN SCHOOL OR AT HOME WITH MY AUNT MAY, WHO IS SO AWESOME, BTW.
AND TODAY, AUNT MAY ASKED ME TO DO ONE FAVOR--
BADOOM!
ARE YOU EVEN PAYING ATTENTION, YOU YAMMERING DOLT?!
ANYONE GOT A DICTIONARY? "YAMMERING DOLT?"

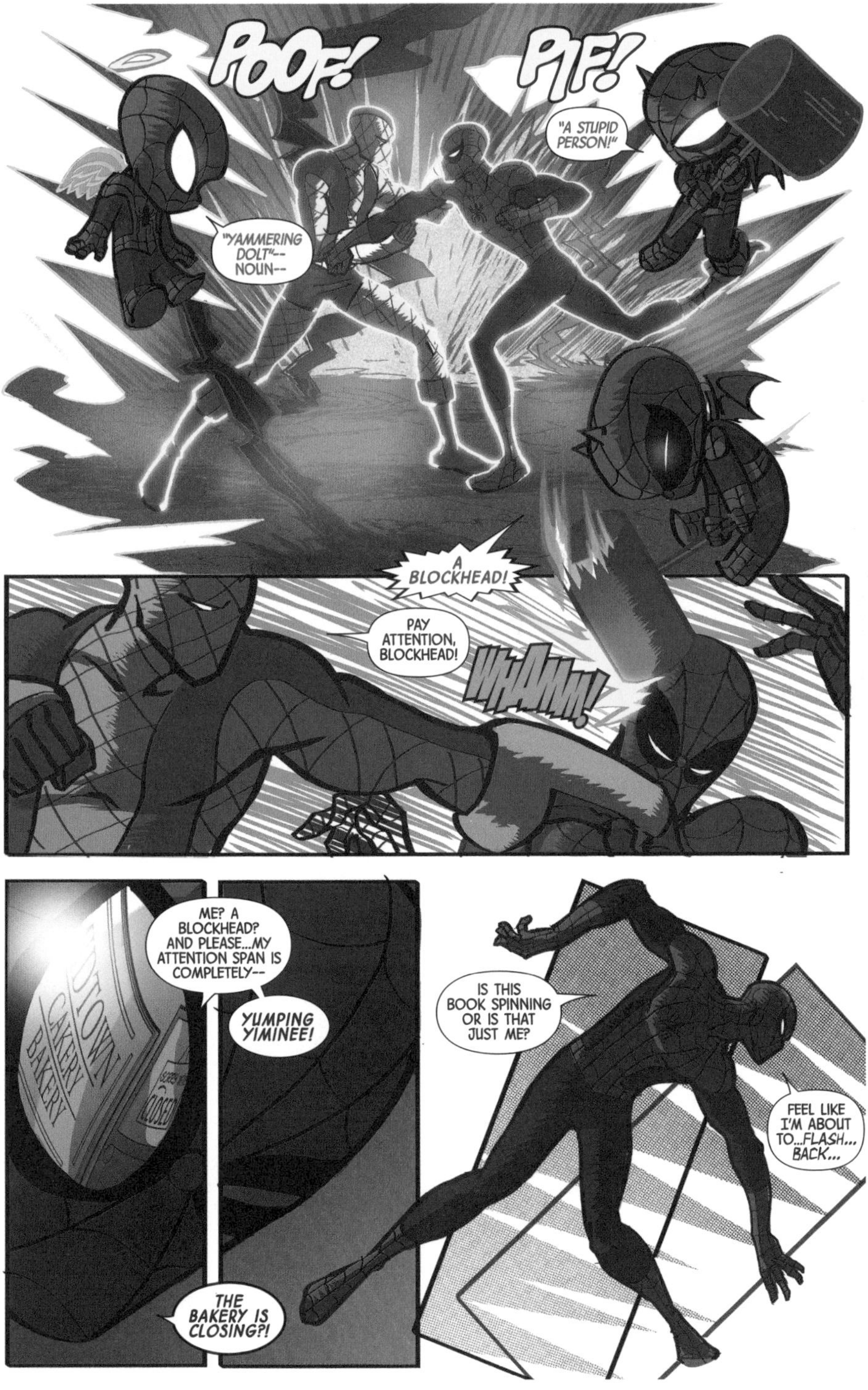
POOF!
PIF!
"A STUPID PERSON!"
"YAMMERING DOLT"-- NOUN--
A BLOCKHEAD!
PAY ATTENTION, BLOCKHEAD!
WHAMM!
ME? A BLOCKHEAD? AND PLEASE...MY ATTENTION SPAN IS COMPLETELY--
YUMPING YIMINEE!
THE BAKERY IS CLOSING?!
IS THIS BOOK SPINNING OR IS THAT JUST ME?
FEEL LIKE I'M ABOUT TO...FLASH... BACK...

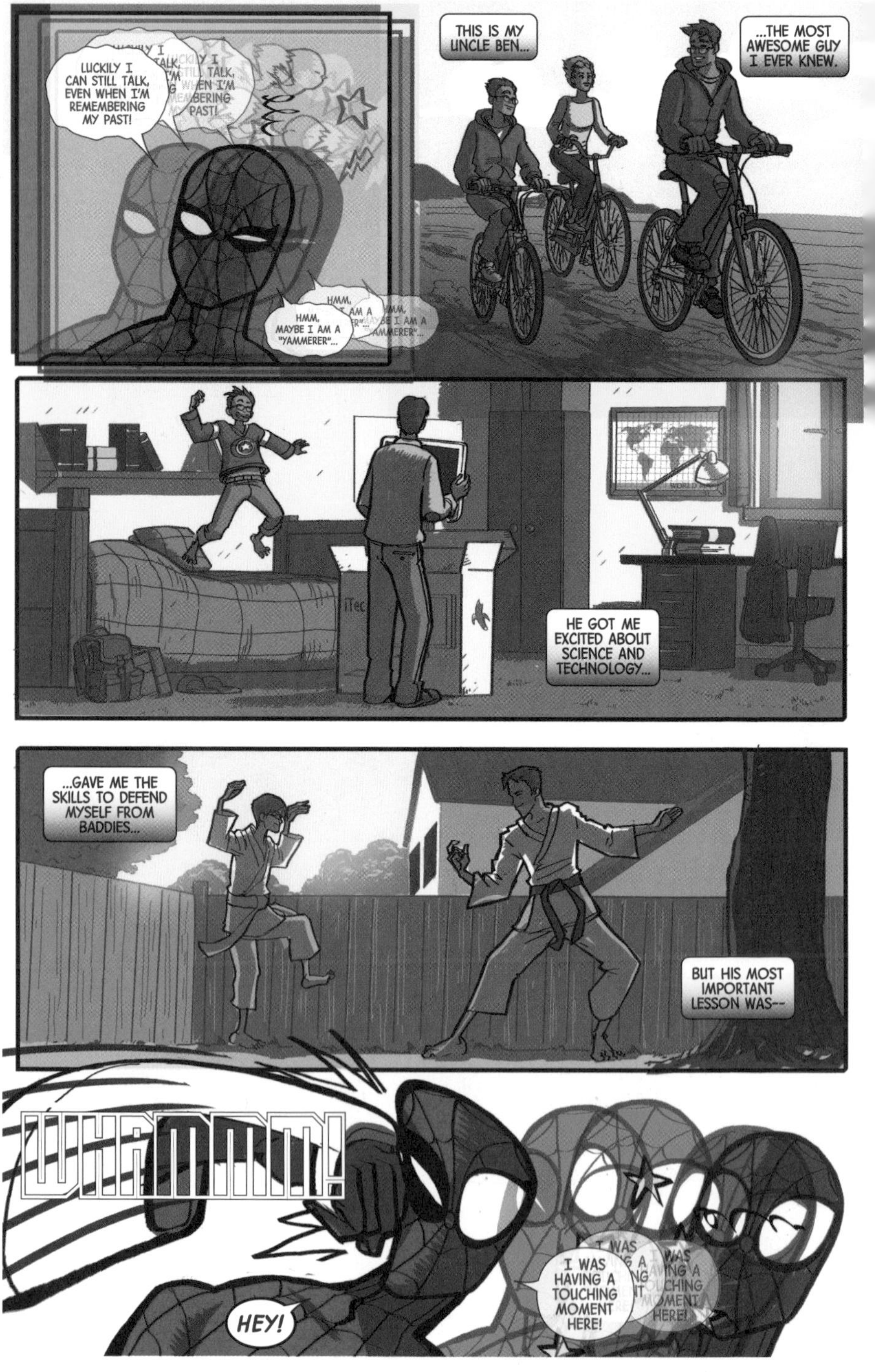
LUCKILY I CAN STILL TALK, EVEN WHEN I'M REMEMBERING MY PAST!
HMM, MAYBE I AM A "YAMMERER"...
THIS IS MY UNCLE BEN...
...THE MOST AWESOME GUY I EVER KNEW.
HE GOT ME EXCITED ABOUT SCIENCE AND TECHNOLOGY...
...GAVE ME THE SKILLS TO DEFEND MYSELF FROM BADDIES...
BUT HIS MOST IMPORTANT LESSON WAS--
WHAMMM!
HEY!
I WAS HAVING A TOUCHING MOMENT HERE!

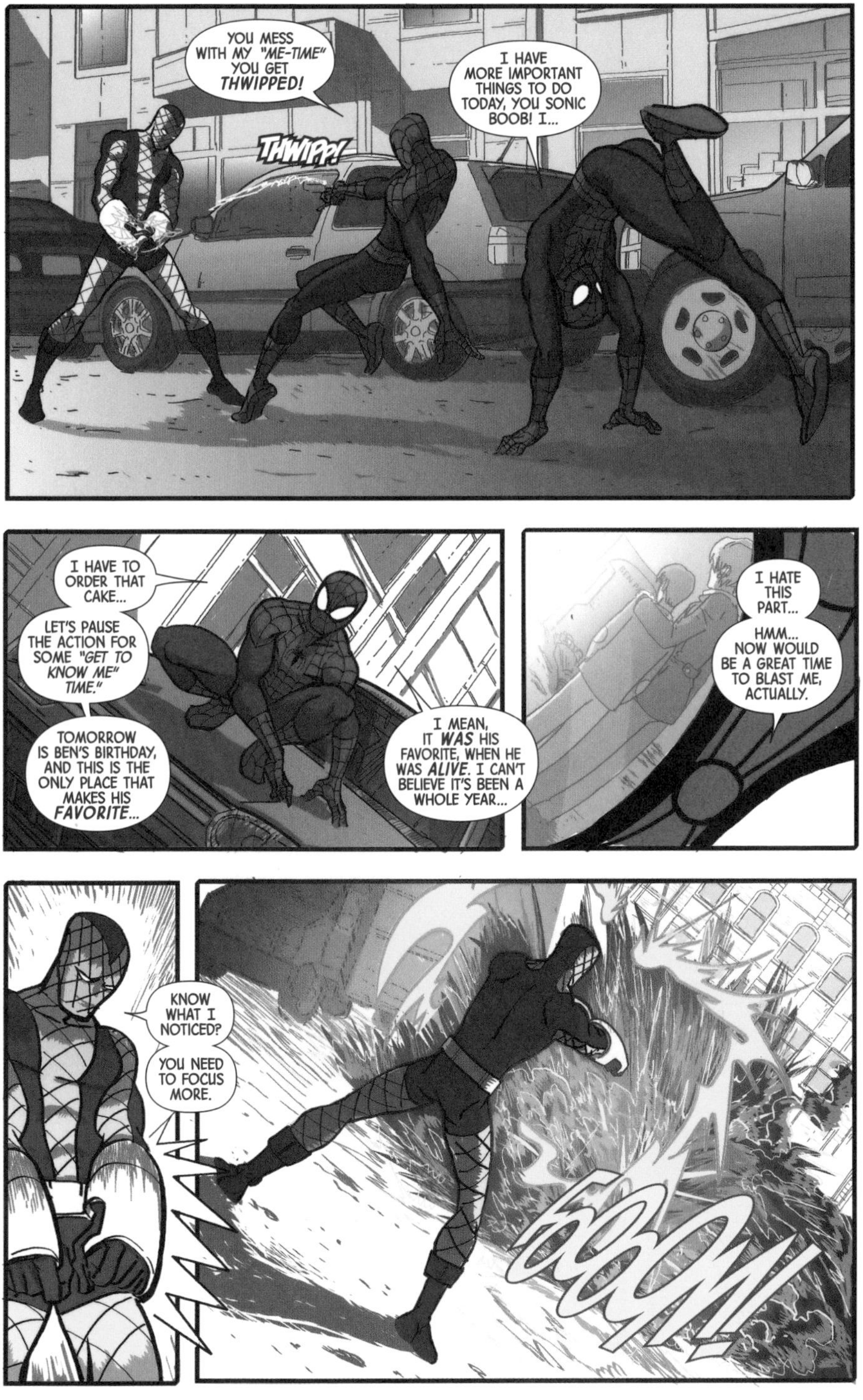
YOU MESS WITH MY "ME-TIME" YOU GET THWIPPED!
THWIPP!
I HAVE MORE IMPORTANT THINGS TO DO TODAY, YOU SONIC BOOB! I...
I HAVE TO ORDER THAT CAKE...
LET'S PAUSE THE ACTION FOR SOME "GET TO KNOW ME" TIME."
TOMORROW IS BEN'S BIRTHDAY, AND THIS IS THE ONLY PLACE THAT MAKES HIS FAVORITE...
I MEAN, IT WAS HIS FAVORITE, WHEN HE WAS ALIVE. I CAN'T BELIEVE IT'S BEEN A WHOLE YEAR...
I HATE THIS PART...
HMM... NOW WOULD BE A GREAT TIME TO BLAST ME, ACTUALLY.
KNOW WHAT I NOTICED?
YOU NEED TO FOCUS MORE.
BOOM!

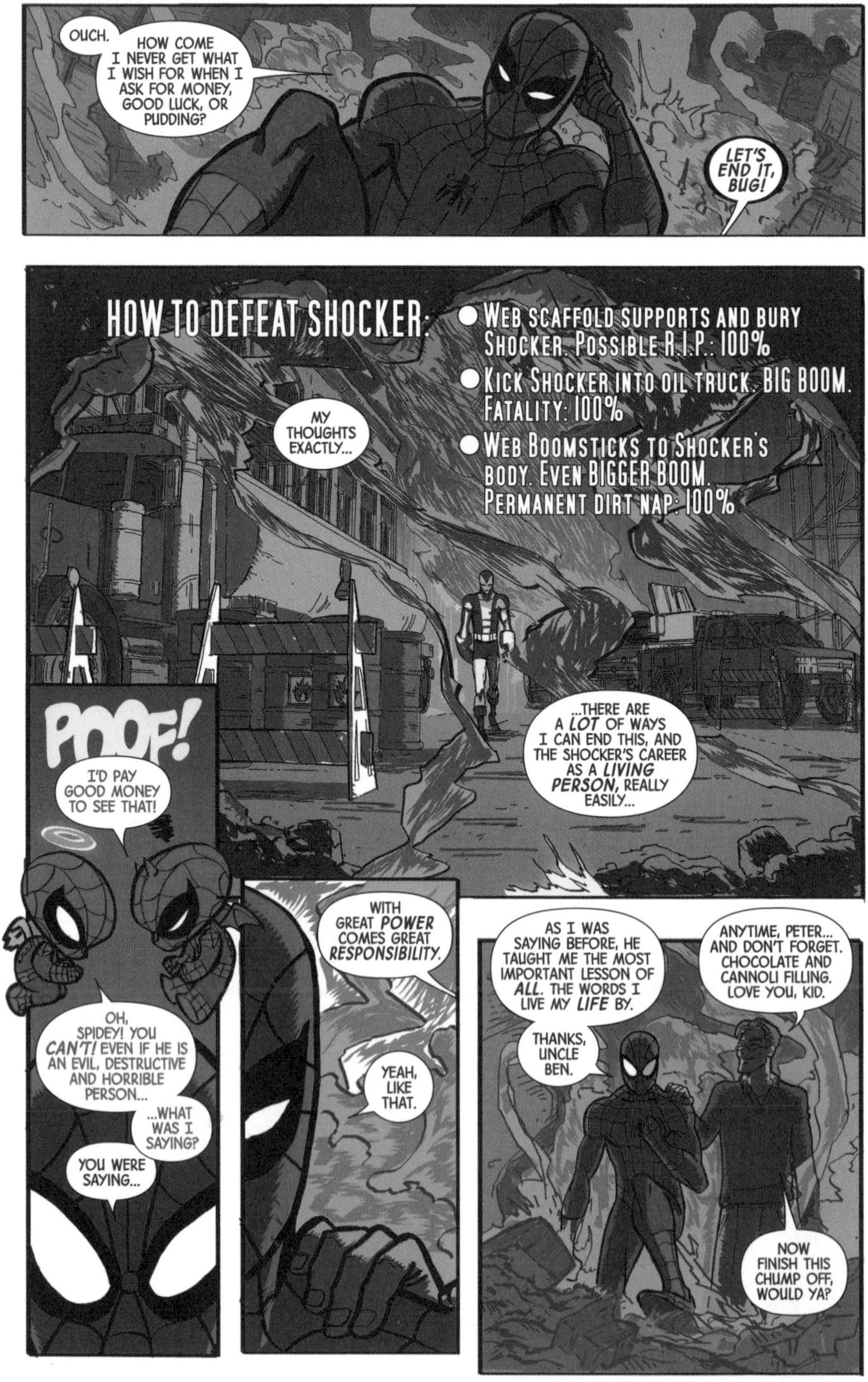
OUCH.
HOW COME I NEVER GET WHAT I WISH FOR WHEN I ASK FOR MONEY, GOOD LUCK, OR PUDDING?
LET'S END IT, BUG!
HOW TO DEFEAT SHOCKER:
Web scaffold supports and bury Shocker. Possible R.I.P.: 100%
Kick Shocker into oil truck. BIG BOOM. Fatality: 100%
Web Boomsticks to Shocker's body. Even BIGGER BOOM. Permanent dirt nap: 100%
MY THOUGHTS EXACTLY...
...THERE ARE A LOT OF WAYS I CAN END THIS, AND THE SHOCKER'S CAREER AS A LIVING PERSON, REALLY EASILY...
POOF!
I'D PAY GOOD MONEY TO SEE THAT!
OH, SPIDEY! YOU CAN'T! EVEN IF HE IS AN EVIL, DESTRUCTIVE AND HORRIBLE PERSON...
...WHAT WAS I SAYING?
YOU WERE SAYING...
WITH GREAT POWER COMES GREAT RESPONSIBILITY.
YEAH, LIKE THAT.
AS I WAS SAYING BEFORE, HE TAUGHT ME THE MOST IMPORTANT LESSON OF ALL. THE WORDS I LIVE MY LIFE BY.
THANKS, UNCLE BEN.
ANYTIME, PETER... AND DON'T FORGET. CHOCOLATE AND CANNOLI FILLING. LOVE YOU, KID.
NOW FINISH THIS CHUMP OFF, WOULD YA?

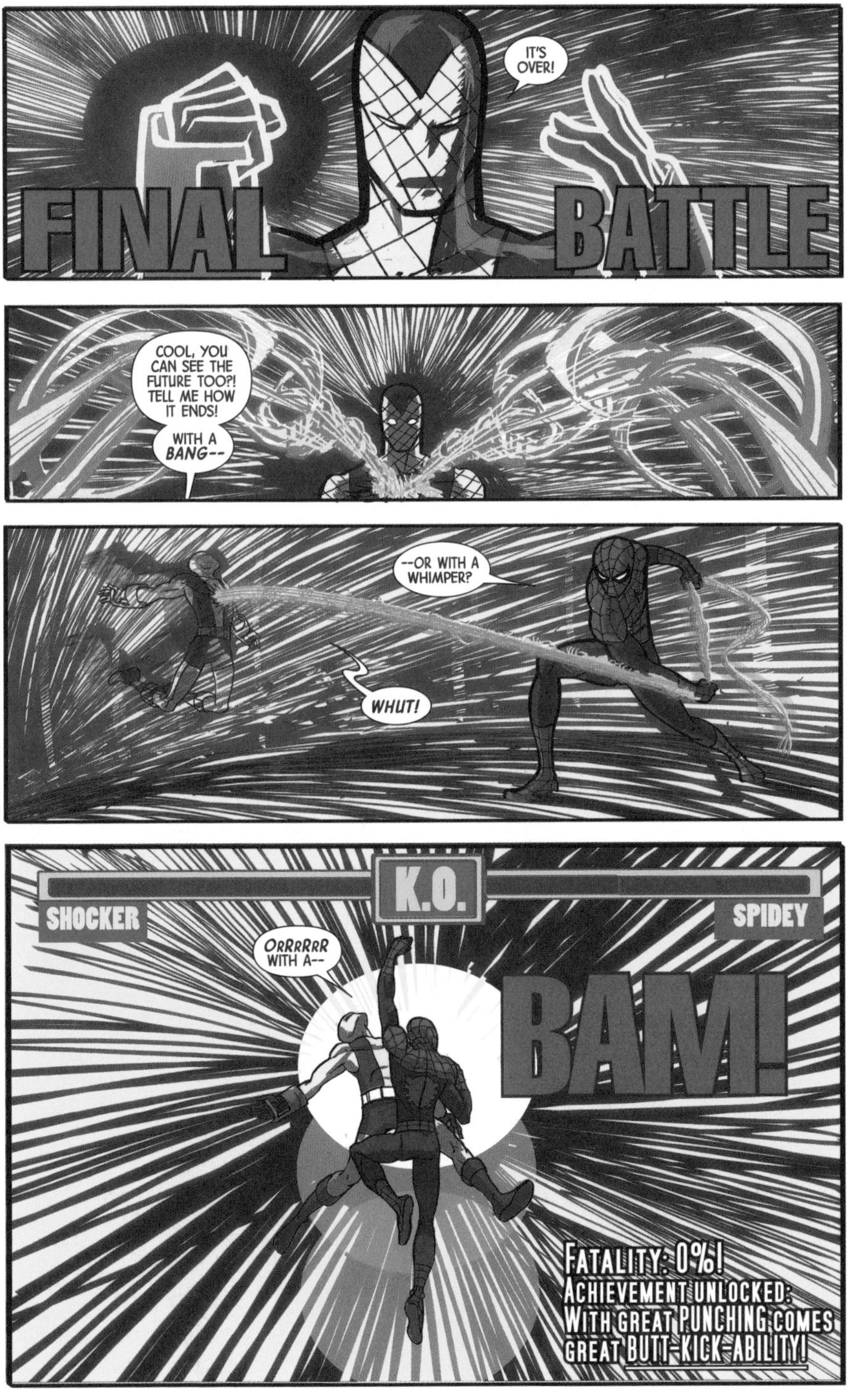
IT'S OVER!
FINAL BATTLE
COOL, YOU CAN SEE THE FUTURE TOO?! TELL ME HOW IT ENDS!
WITH A BANG--
--OR WITH A WHIMPER?
WHUT!
K.O.
SHOCKER
SPIDEY
ORRRRRR WITH A--
BAM!
FATALITY: 0%!
ACHIEVEMENT UNLOCKED:
WITH GREAT PUNCHING COMES
GREAT BUTT-KICK-ABILITY!

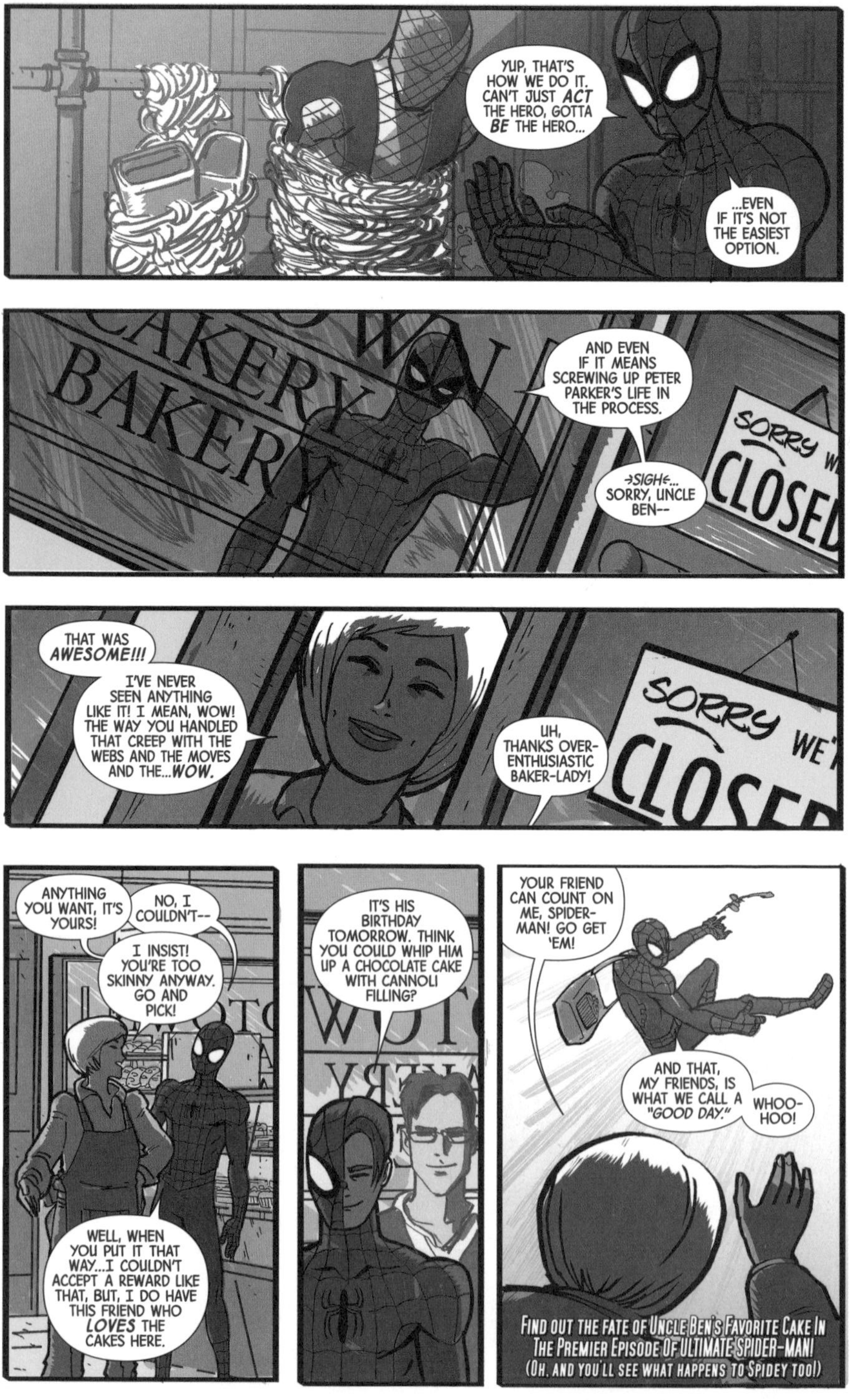
YUP, THAT'S HOW WE DO IT. CAN'T JUST *ACT* THE HERO, GOTTA *BE* THE HERO...
...EVEN IF IT'S NOT THE EASIEST OPTION.
BAKERY
AND EVEN IF IT MEANS SCREWING UP PETER PARKER'S LIFE IN THE PROCESS.
SORRY WE CLOSED
→SIGH←... SORRY, UNCLE BEN--
THAT WAS *AWESOME!!!*
I'VE NEVER SEEN ANYTHING LIKE IT! I MEAN, WOW! THE WAY YOU HANDLED THAT CREEP WITH THE WEBS AND THE MOVES AND THE...*WOW.*
SORRY WE' CLOSE
UH, THANKS OVER-ENTHUSIASTIC BAKER-LADY!
ANYTHING YOU WANT, IT'S YOURS!
NO, I COULDN'T--
I INSIST! YOU'RE TOO SKINNY ANYWAY. GO AND PICK!
WELL, WHEN YOU PUT IT THAT WAY...I COULDN'T ACCEPT A REWARD LIKE THAT, BUT, I DO HAVE THIS FRIEND WHO *LOVES* THE CAKES HERE.
IT'S HIS BIRTHDAY TOMORROW. THINK YOU COULD WHIP HIM UP A CHOCOLATE CAKE WITH CANNOLI FILLING?
YOUR FRIEND CAN COUNT ON ME, SPIDER-MAN! GO GET 'EM!
AND THAT, MY FRIENDS, IS WHAT WE CALL A "*GOOD DAY.*"
WHOO-HOO!
FIND OUT THE FATE OF UNCLE BEN'S FAVORITE CAKE IN THE PREMIER EPISODE OF ULTIMATE SPIDER-MAN!
(OH, AND YOU'LL SEE WHAT HAPPENS TO SPIDEY TOO!)

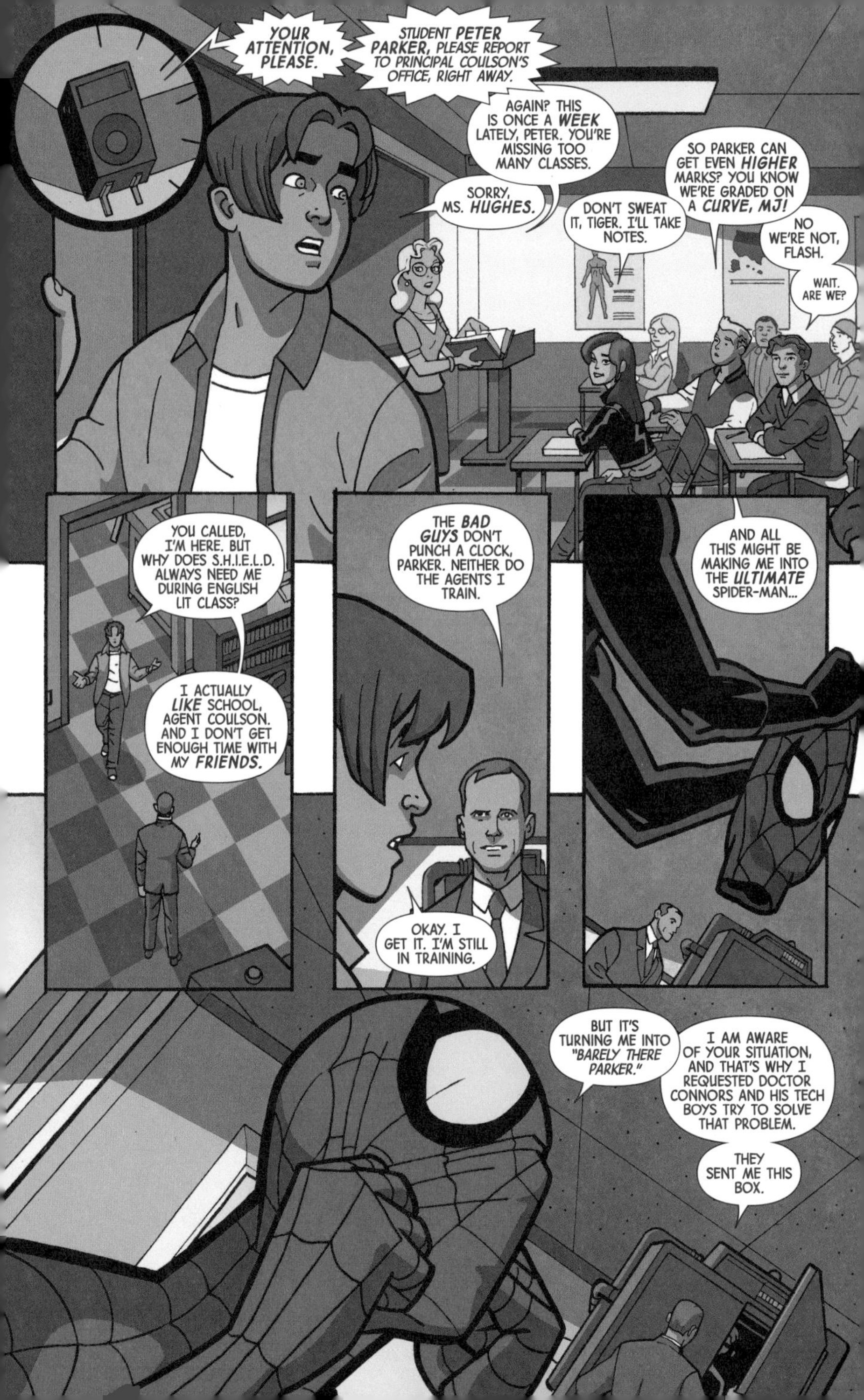
YOUR ATTENTION, PLEASE.
STUDENT PETER PARKER, PLEASE REPORT TO PRINCIPAL COULSON'S OFFICE, RIGHT AWAY.
AGAIN? THIS IS ONCE A WEEK LATELY, PETER. YOU'RE MISSING TOO MANY CLASSES.
SORRY, MS. HUGHES.
DON'T SWEAT IT, TIGER. I'LL TAKE NOTES.
SO PARKER CAN GET EVEN HIGHER MARKS? YOU KNOW WE'RE GRADED ON A CURVE, MJ!
NO WE'RE NOT, FLASH.
WAIT. ARE WE?
YOU CALLED, I'M HERE. BUT WHY DOES S.H.I.E.L.D. ALWAYS NEED ME DURING ENGLISH LIT CLASS?
I ACTUALLY LIKE SCHOOL, AGENT COULSON. AND I DON'T GET ENOUGH TIME WITH MY FRIENDS.
THE BAD GUYS DON'T PUNCH A CLOCK, PARKER. NEITHER DO THE AGENTS I TRAIN.
OKAY. I GET IT. I'M STILL IN TRAINING.
AND ALL THIS MIGHT BE MAKING ME INTO THE ULTIMATE SPIDER-MAN...
BUT IT'S TURNING ME INTO "BARELY THERE PARKER."
I AM AWARE OF YOUR SITUATION, AND THAT'S WHY I REQUESTED DOCTOR CONNORS AND HIS TECH BOYS TRY TO SOLVE THAT PROBLEM.
THEY SENT ME THIS BOX.

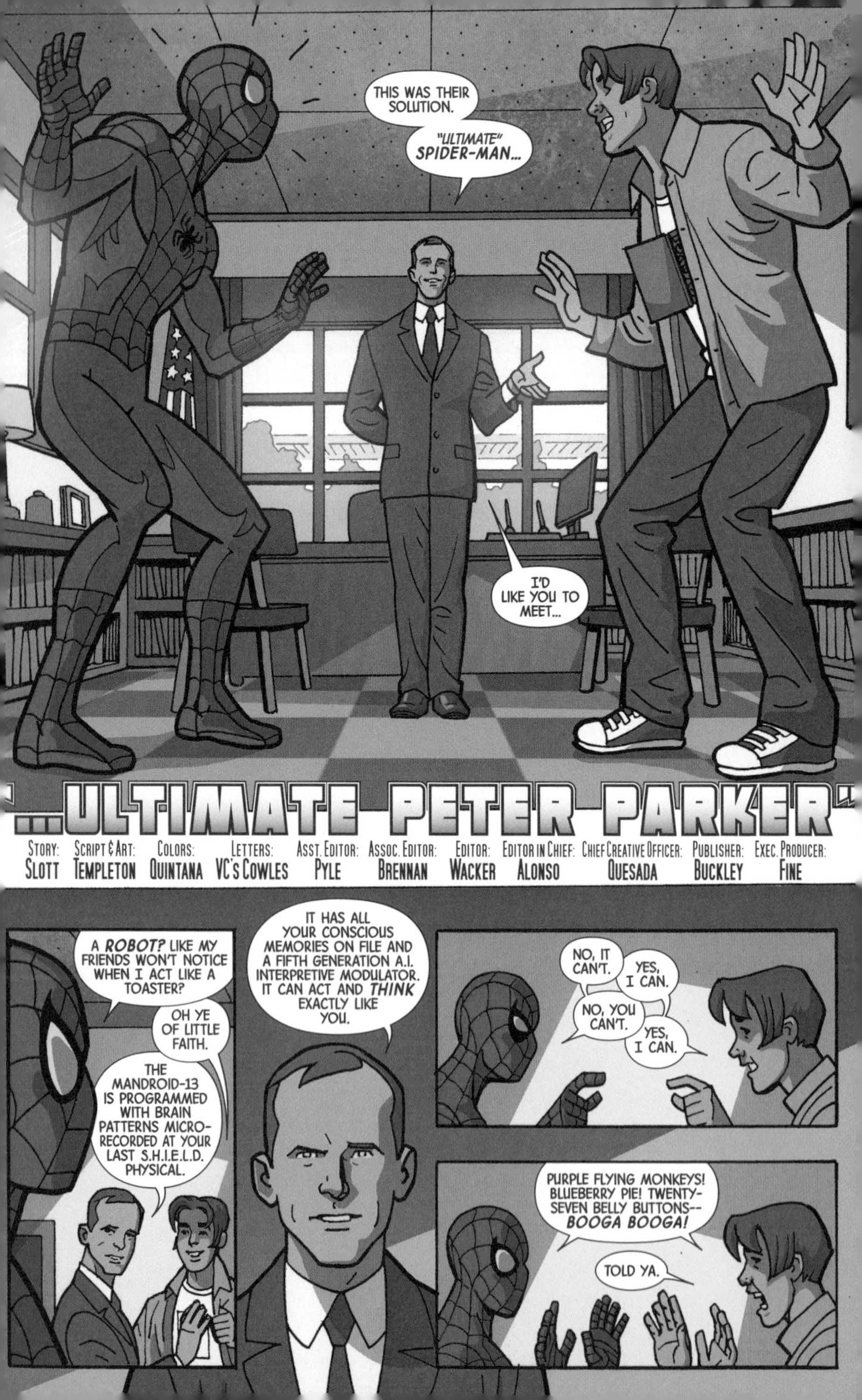
THIS WAS THEIR SOLUTION.
"ULTIMATE" SPIDER-MAN...
I'D LIKE YOU TO MEET...
"...ULTIMATE PETER PARKER"
STORY: SLOTT SCRIPT & ART: TEMPLETON COLORS: QUINTANA LETTERS: VC's COWLES ASST. EDITOR: PYLE ASSOC. EDITOR: BRENNAN EDITOR: WACKER EDITOR IN CHIEF: ALONSO CHIEF CREATIVE OFFICER: QUESADA PUBLISHER: BUCKLEY EXEC. PRODUCER: FINE
A ROBOT? LIKE MY FRIENDS WON'T NOTICE WHEN I ACT LIKE A TOASTER?
OH YE OF LITTLE FAITH.
THE MANDROID-13 IS PROGRAMMED WITH BRAIN PATTERNS MICRO-RECORDED AT YOUR LAST S.H.I.E.L.D. PHYSICAL.
IT HAS ALL YOUR CONSCIOUS MEMORIES ON FILE AND A FIFTH GENERATION A.I. INTERPRETIVE MODULATOR. IT CAN ACT AND THINK EXACTLY LIKE YOU.
NO, IT CAN'T.
YES, I CAN.
NO, YOU CAN'T.
YES, I CAN.
PURPLE FLYING MONKEYS! BLUEBERRY PIE! TWENTY-SEVEN BELLY BUTTONS--BOOGA BOOGA!
TOLD YA.

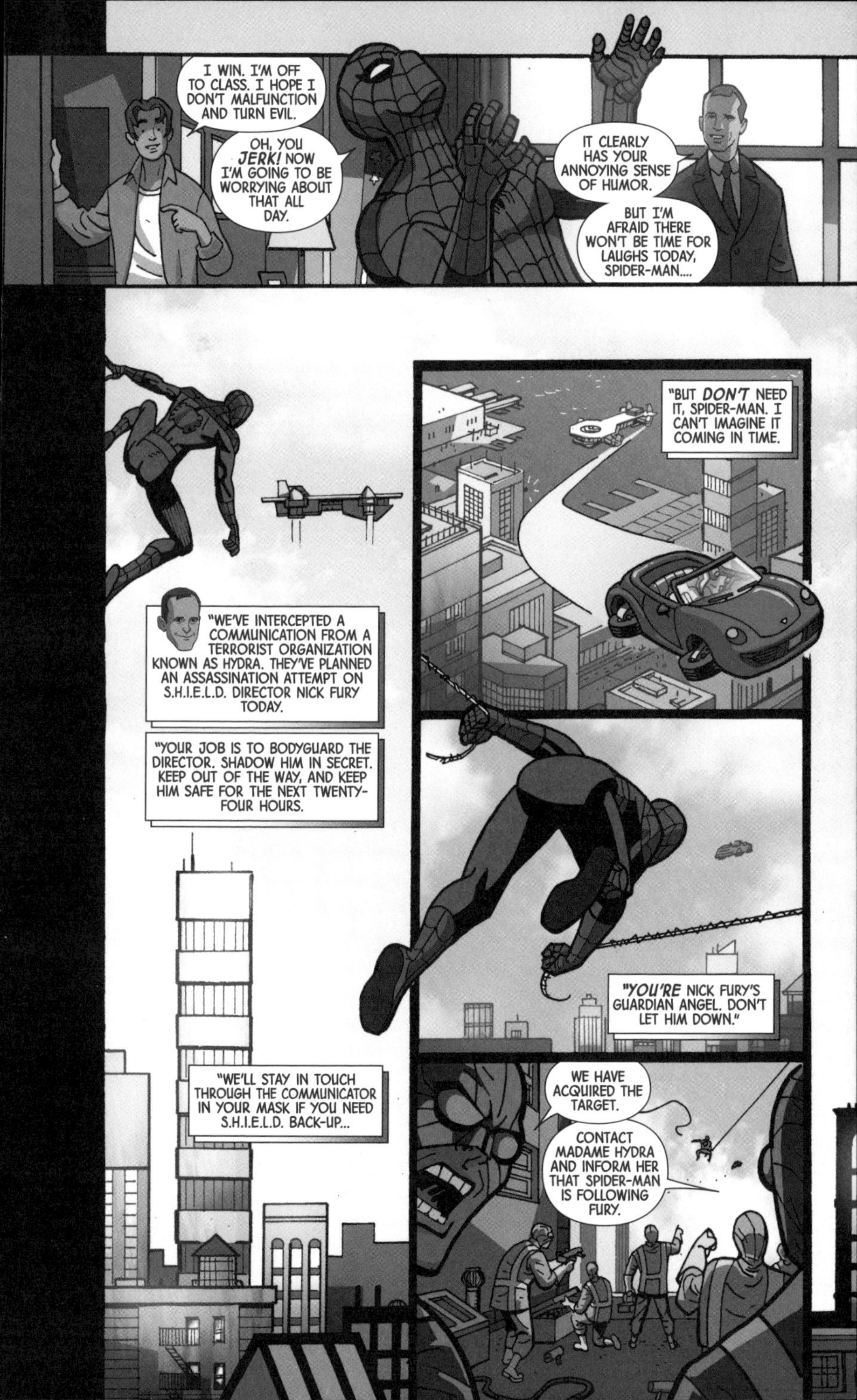

I WIN. I'M OFF TO CLASS. I HOPE I DON'T MALFUNCTION AND TURN EVIL.
OH, YOU JERK! NOW I'M GOING TO BE WORRYING ABOUT THAT ALL DAY.
IT CLEARLY HAS YOUR ANNOYING SENSE OF HUMOR.
BUT I'M AFRAID THERE WON'T BE TIME FOR LAUGHS TODAY, SPIDER-MAN....
"WE'VE INTERCEPTED A COMMUNICATION FROM A TERRORIST ORGANIZATION KNOWN AS HYDRA. THEY'VE PLANNED AN ASSASSINATION ATTEMPT ON S.H.I.E.L.D. DIRECTOR NICK FURY TODAY.
"YOUR JOB IS TO BODYGUARD THE DIRECTOR. SHADOW HIM IN SECRET. KEEP OUT OF THE WAY, AND KEEP HIM SAFE FOR THE NEXT TWENTY-FOUR HOURS.
"WE'LL STAY IN TOUCH THROUGH THE COMMUNICATOR IN YOUR MASK IF YOU NEED S.H.I.E.L.D. BACK-UP...
"BUT DON'T NEED IT, SPIDER-MAN. I CAN'T IMAGINE IT COMING IN TIME.
"YOU'RE NICK FURY'S GUARDIAN ANGEL. DON'T LET HIM DOWN."
WE HAVE ACQUIRED THE TARGET.
CONTACT MADAME HYDRA AND INFORM HER THAT SPIDER-MAN IS FOLLOWING FURY.

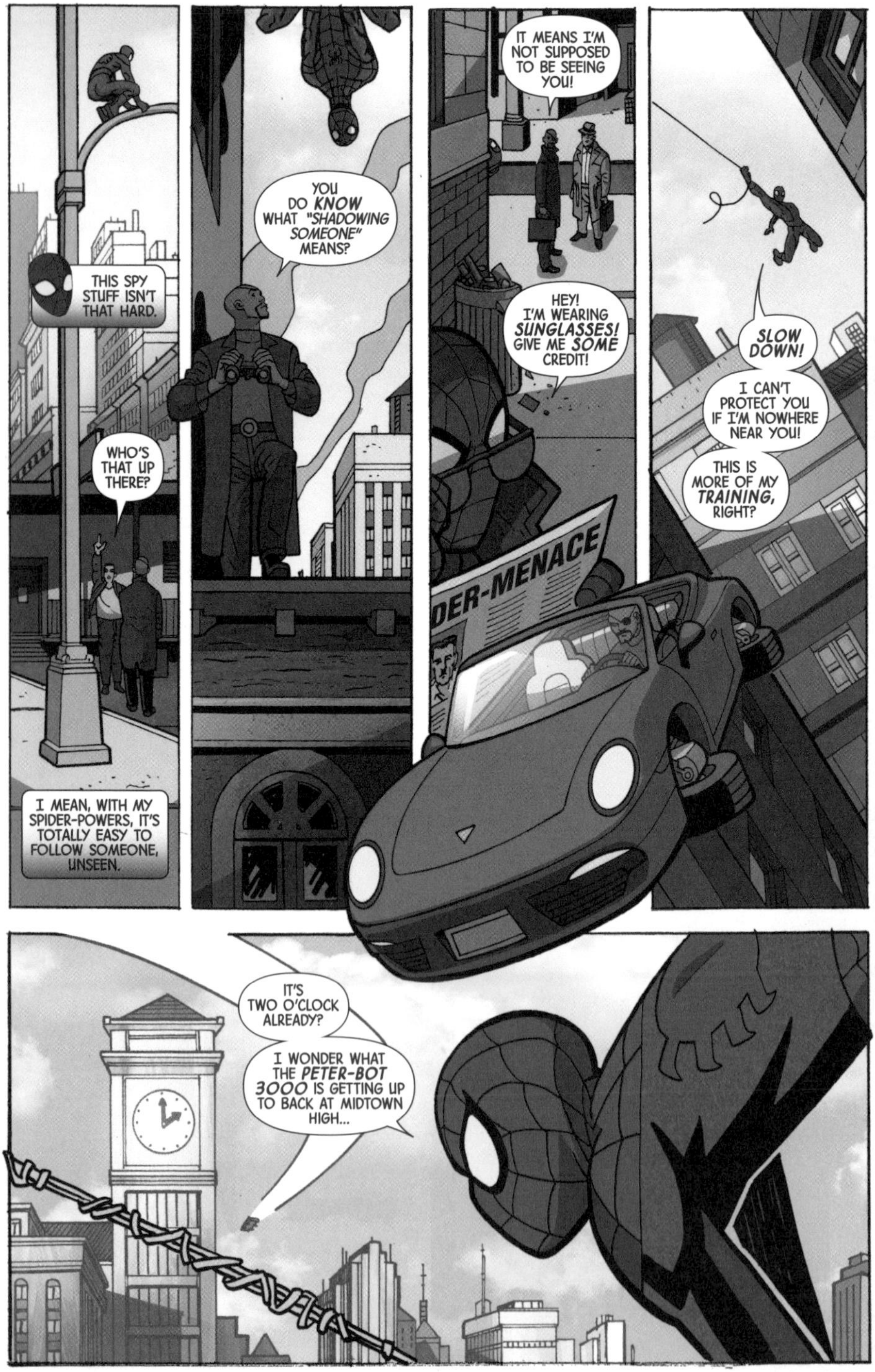

THIS SPY STUFF ISN'T THAT HARD.
WHO'S THAT UP THERE?
I MEAN, WITH MY SPIDER-POWERS, IT'S TOTALLY EASY TO FOLLOW SOMEONE, UNSEEN.
YOU DO KNOW WHAT "SHADOWING SOMEONE" MEANS?
IT MEANS I'M NOT SUPPOSED TO BE SEEING YOU!
HEY! I'M WEARING SUNGLASSES! GIVE ME SOME CREDIT!
DER-MENACE
SLOW DOWN!
I CAN'T PROTECT YOU IF I'M NOWHERE NEAR YOU!
THIS IS MORE OF MY TRAINING, RIGHT?
IT'S TWO O'CLOCK ALREADY?
I WONDER WHAT THE PETER-BOT 3000 IS GETTING UP TO BACK AT MIDTOWN HIGH...

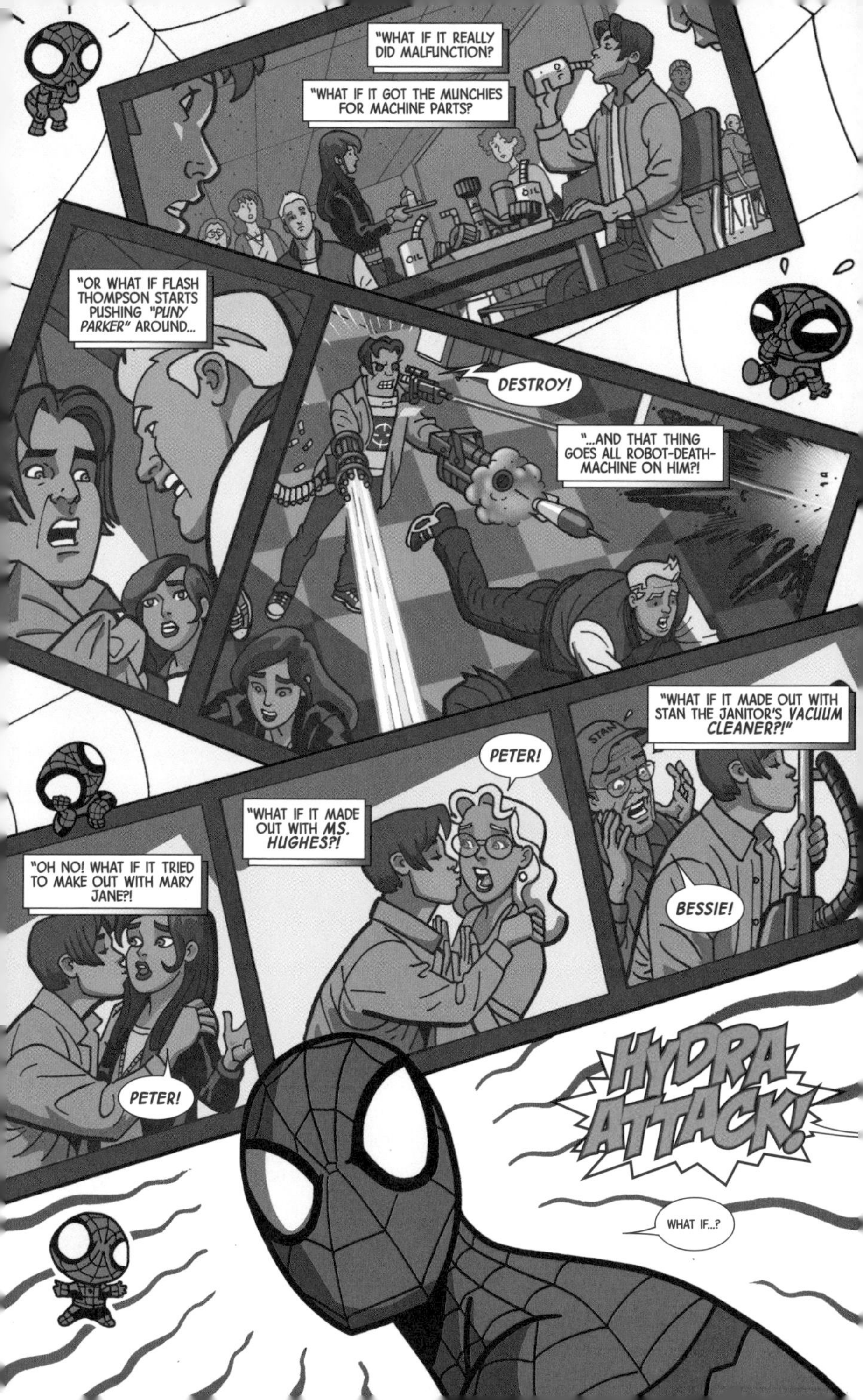
"WHAT IF IT REALLY DID MALFUNCTION?
"WHAT IF IT GOT THE MUNCHIES FOR MACHINE PARTS?
OIL
"OR WHAT IF FLASH THOMPSON STARTS PUSHING "PUNY PARKER" AROUND...
DESTROY!
"...AND THAT THING GOES ALL ROBOT-DEATH-MACHINE ON HIM?!
"WHAT IF IT MADE OUT WITH STAN THE JANITOR'S VACUUM CLEANER?!"
STAN
PETER!
"WHAT IF IT MADE OUT WITH MS. HUGHES?!
BESSIE!
"OH NO! WHAT IF IT TRIED TO MAKE OUT WITH MARY JANE?!
PETER!
HYDRA ATTACK!
WHAT IF...?

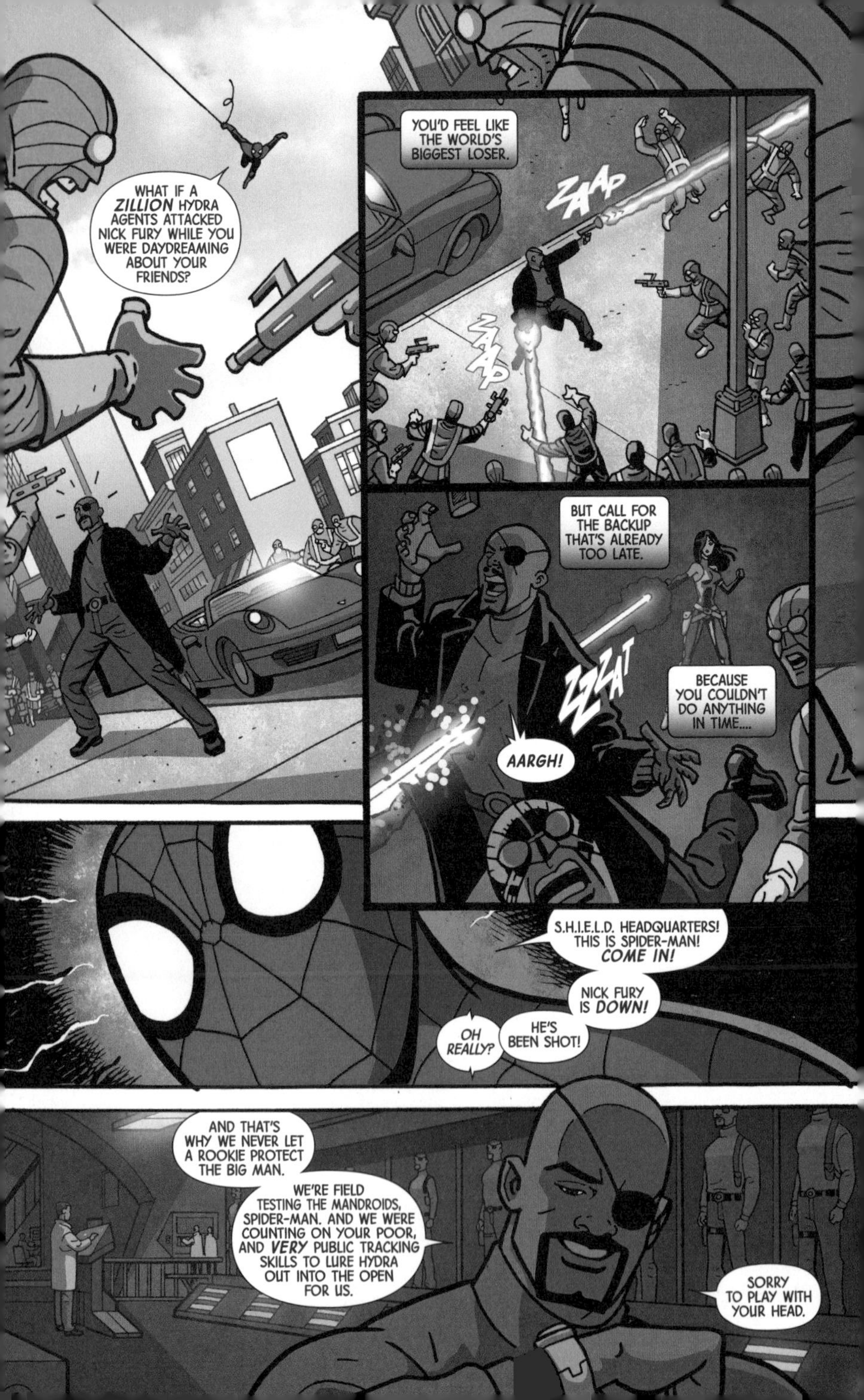
WHAT IF A ZILLION HYDRA AGENTS ATTACKED NICK FURY WHILE YOU WERE DAYDREAMING ABOUT YOUR FRIENDS?
YOU'D FEEL LIKE THE WORLD'S BIGGEST LOSER.
ZAAP
ZAAP
BUT CALL FOR THE BACKUP THAT'S ALREADY TOO LATE.
ZZZAT
BECAUSE YOU COULDN'T DO ANYTHING IN TIME....
AARGH!
S.H.I.E.L.D. HEADQUARTERS! THIS IS SPIDER-MAN! COME IN!
NICK FURY IS DOWN!
HE'S BEEN SHOT!
OH REALLY?
AND THAT'S WHY WE NEVER LET A ROOKIE PROTECT THE BIG MAN.
WE'RE FIELD TESTING THE MANDROIDS, SPIDER-MAN. AND WE WERE COUNTING ON YOUR POOR, AND VERY PUBLIC TRACKING SKILLS TO LURE HYDRA OUT INTO THE OPEN FOR US.
SORRY TO PLAY WITH YOUR HEAD.

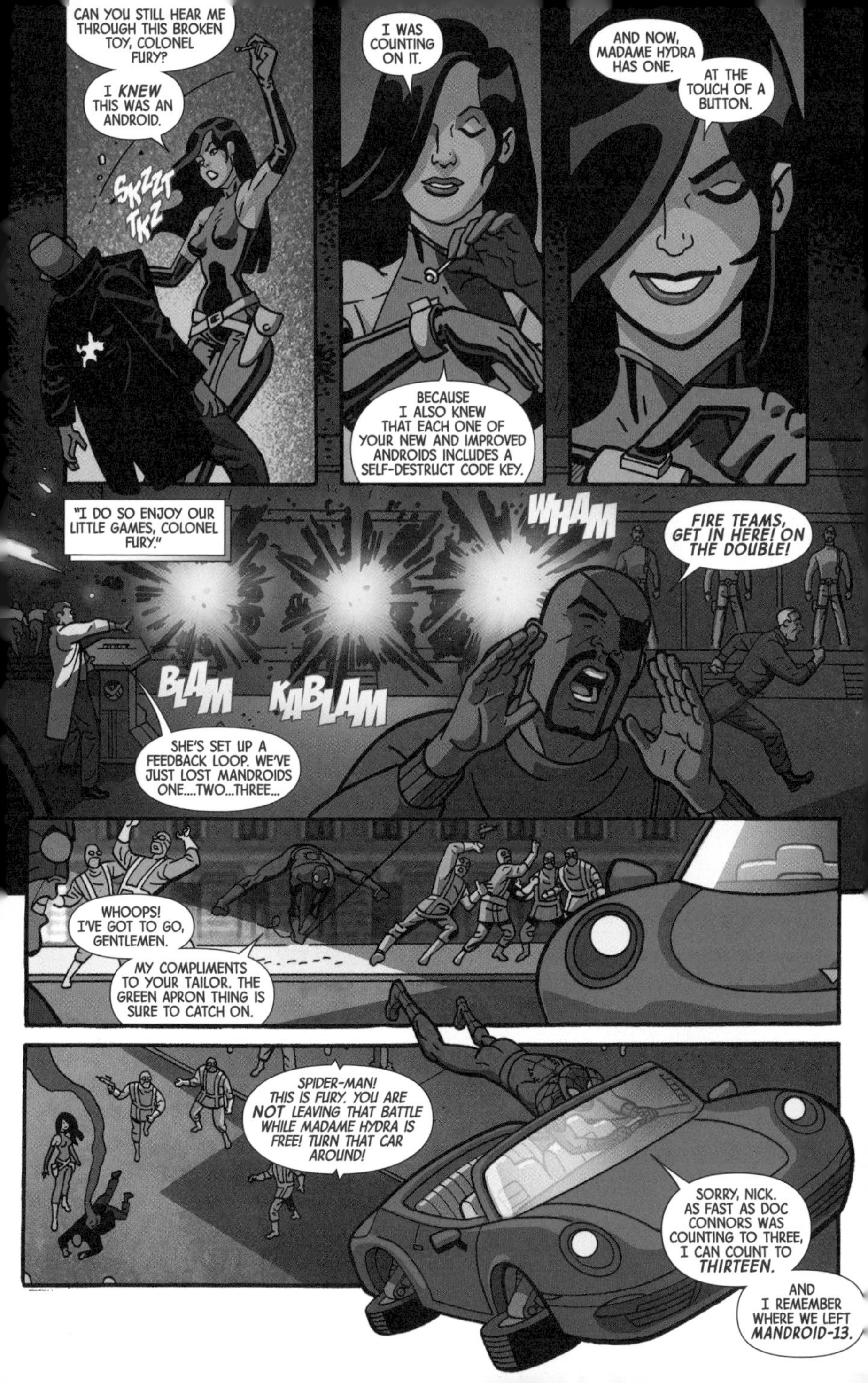
CAN YOU STILL HEAR ME THROUGH THIS BROKEN TOY, COLONEL FURY?
I KNEW THIS WAS AN ANDROID.
SKZZZT TKZ
I WAS COUNTING ON IT.
BECAUSE I ALSO KNEW THAT EACH ONE OF YOUR NEW AND IMPROVED ANDROIDS INCLUDES A SELF-DESTRUCT CODE KEY.
AND NOW, MADAME HYDRA HAS ONE.
AT THE TOUCH OF A BUTTON.
"I DO SO ENJOY OUR LITTLE GAMES, COLONEL FURY."
WHAM
FIRE TEAMS, GET IN HERE! ON THE DOUBLE!
BLAM
KABLAM
SHE'S SET UP A FEEDBACK LOOP. WE'VE JUST LOST MANDROIDS ONE....TWO...THREE...
WHOOPS! I'VE GOT TO GO, GENTLEMEN.
MY COMPLIMENTS TO YOUR TAILOR. THE GREEN APRON THING IS SURE TO CATCH ON.
SPIDER-MAN! THIS IS FURY. YOU ARE NOT LEAVING THAT BATTLE WHILE MADAME HYDRA IS FREE! TURN THAT CAR AROUND!
SORRY, NICK. AS FAST AS DOC CONNORS WAS COUNTING TO THREE, I CAN COUNT TO THIRTEEN.
AND I REMEMBER WHERE WE LEFT MANDROID-13.

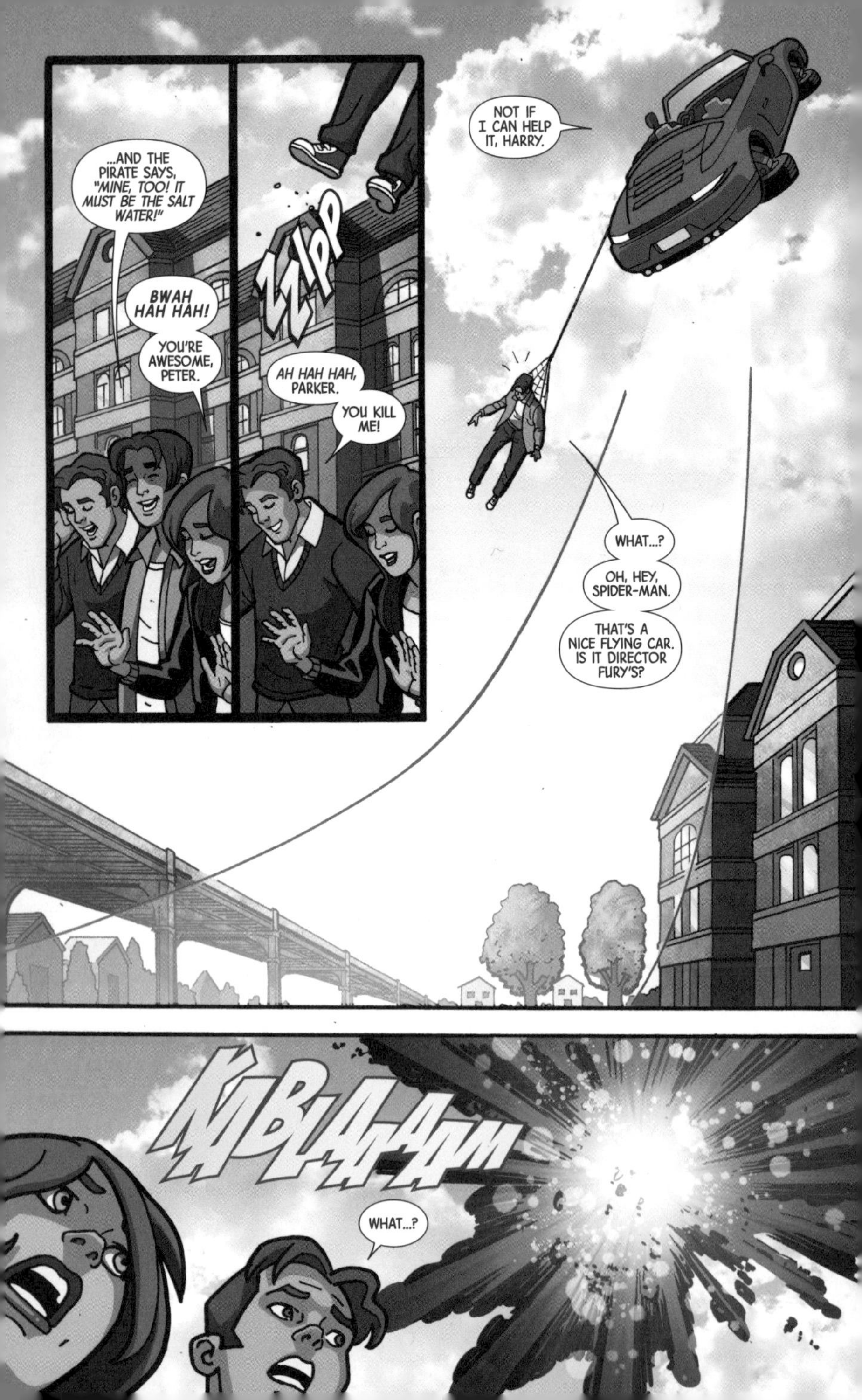
...AND THE PIRATE SAYS, "MINE, TOO! IT MUST BE THE SALT WATER!"
BWAH HAH HAH!
YOU'RE AWESOME, PETER.
ZZIPP
AH HAH HAH, PARKER.
YOU KILL ME!
NOT IF I CAN HELP IT, HARRY.
WHAT...?
OH, HEY, SPIDER-MAN.
THAT'S A NICE FLYING CAR. IS IT DIRECTOR FURY'S?
KABLAAAM
WHAT...?

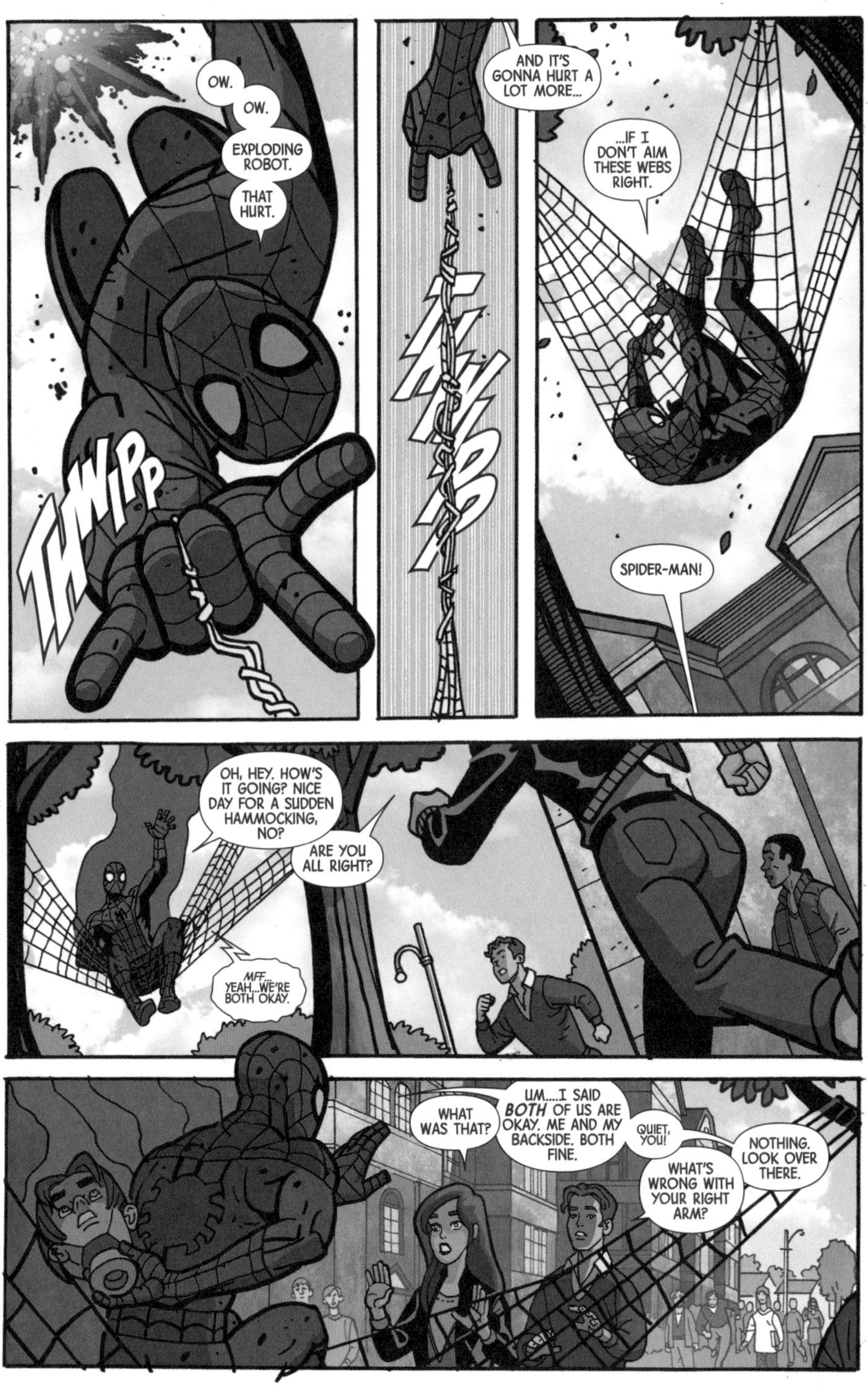
OW.
OW.
EXPLODING ROBOT.
THAT HURT.
THWIPP
AND IT'S GONNA HURT A LOT MORE...
...IF I DON'T AIM THESE WEBS RIGHT.
SPIDER-MAN!
OH, HEY. HOW'S IT GOING? NICE DAY FOR A SUDDEN HAMMOCKING, NO?
ARE YOU ALL RIGHT?
MFF... YEAH...WE'RE BOTH OKAY.
WHAT WAS THAT?
UM....I SAID BOTH OF US ARE OKAY. ME AND MY BACKSIDE. BOTH FINE.
QUIET, YOU!
NOTHING. LOOK OVER THERE.
WHAT'S WRONG WITH YOUR RIGHT ARM?

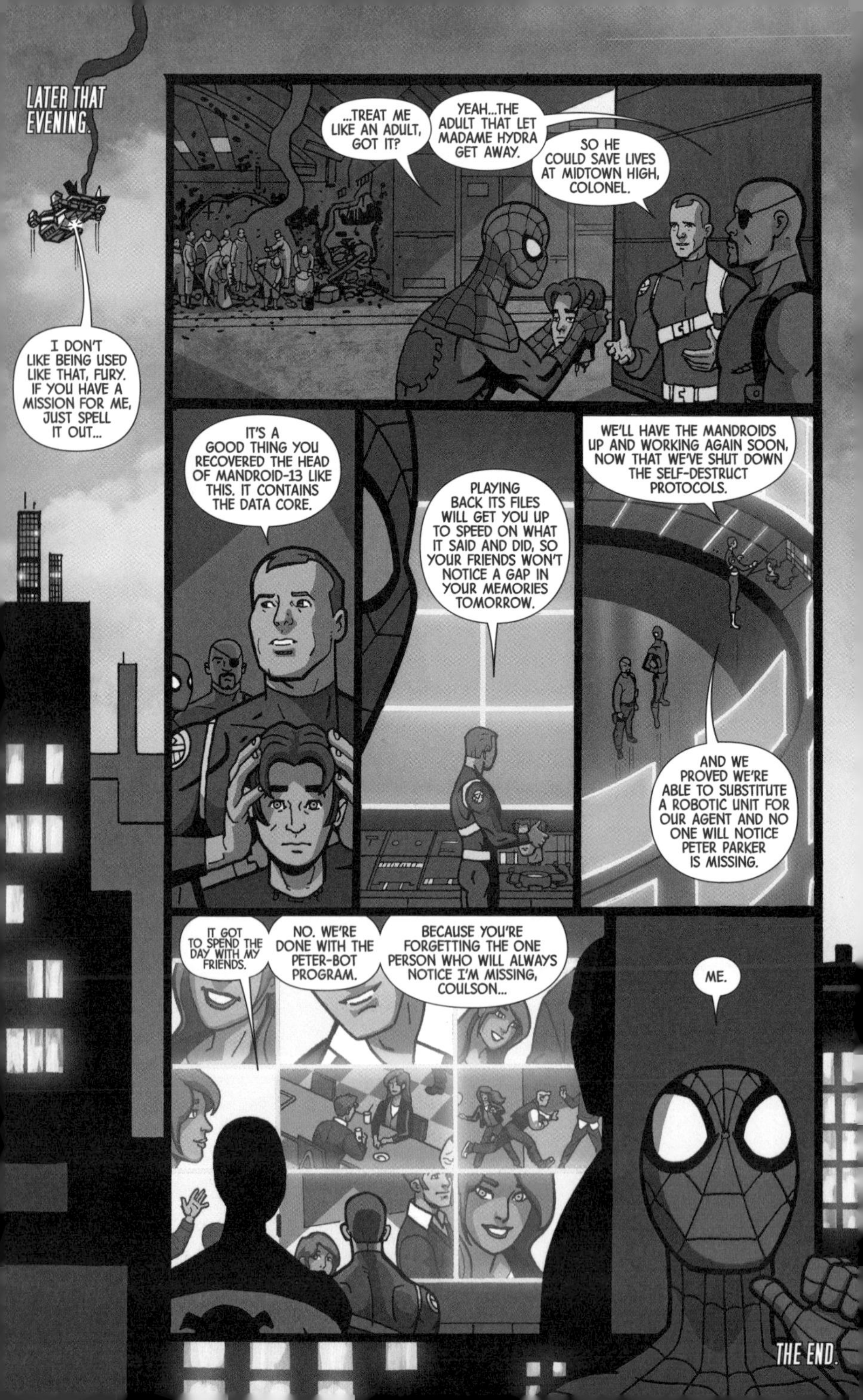
LATER THAT EVENING.
I DON'T LIKE BEING USED LIKE THAT, FURY. IF YOU HAVE A MISSION FOR ME, JUST SPELL IT OUT...
...TREAT ME LIKE AN ADULT, GOT IT?
YEAH...THE ADULT THAT LET MADAME HYDRA GET AWAY.
SO HE COULD SAVE LIVES AT MIDTOWN HIGH, COLONEL.
IT'S A GOOD THING YOU RECOVERED THE HEAD OF MANDROID-13 LIKE THIS. IT CONTAINS THE DATA CORE.
PLAYING BACK ITS FILES WILL GET YOU UP TO SPEED ON WHAT IT SAID AND DID, SO YOUR FRIENDS WON'T NOTICE A GAP IN YOUR MEMORIES TOMORROW.
WE'LL HAVE THE MANDROIDS UP AND WORKING AGAIN SOON, NOW THAT WE'VE SHUT DOWN THE SELF-DESTRUCT PROTOCOLS.
AND WE PROVED WE'RE ABLE TO SUBSTITUTE A ROBOTIC UNIT FOR OUR AGENT AND NO ONE WILL NOTICE PETER PARKER IS MISSING.
IT GOT TO SPEND THE DAY WITH MY FRIENDS.
NO. WE'RE DONE WITH THE PETER-BOT PROGRAM.
BECAUSE YOU'RE FORGETTING THE ONE PERSON WHO WILL ALWAYS NOTICE I'M MISSING, COULSON...
ME.
THE END.

2

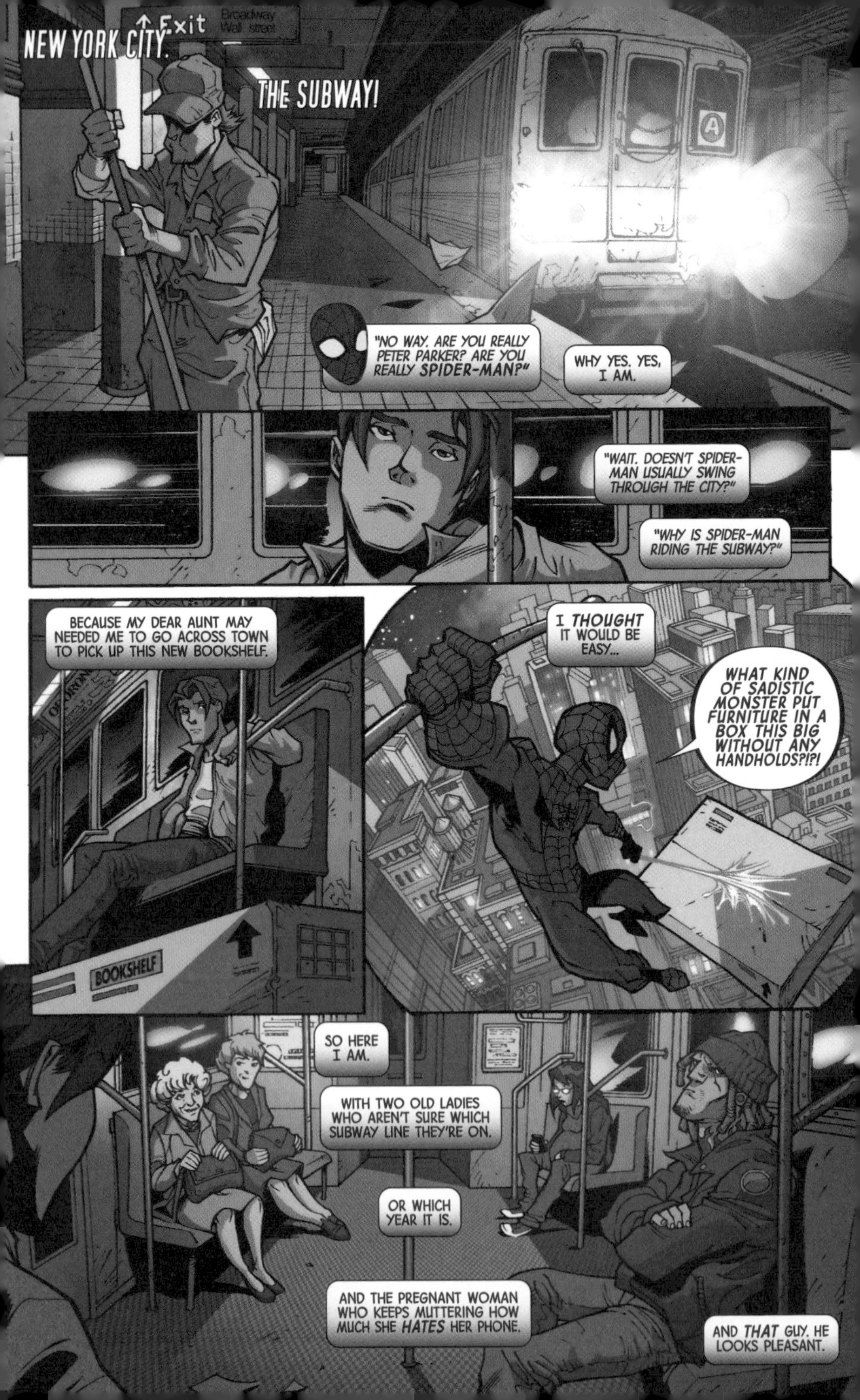

NEW YORK CITY.
↑Exit
Broadway
Wall street
THE SUBWAY!
A
"NO WAY. ARE YOU REALLY PETER PARKER? ARE YOU REALLY SPIDER-MAN?"
WHY YES. YES, I AM.
"WAIT. DOESN'T SPIDER-MAN USUALLY SWING THROUGH THE CITY?"
"WHY IS SPIDER-MAN RIDING THE SUBWAY?"
BECAUSE MY DEAR AUNT MAY NEEDED ME TO GO ACROSS TOWN TO PICK UP THIS NEW BOOKSHELF.
BOOKSHELF
I THOUGHT IT WOULD BE EASY...
WHAT KIND OF SADISTIC MONSTER PUT FURNITURE IN A BOX THIS BIG WITHOUT ANY HANDHOLDS?!?!
SO HERE I AM.
WITH TWO OLD LADIES WHO AREN'T SURE WHICH SUBWAY LINE THEY'RE ON.
OR WHICH YEAR IT IS.
AND THE PREGNANT WOMAN WHO KEEPS MUTTERING HOW MUCH SHE HATES HER PHONE.
AND THAT GUY. HE LOOKS PLEASANT.

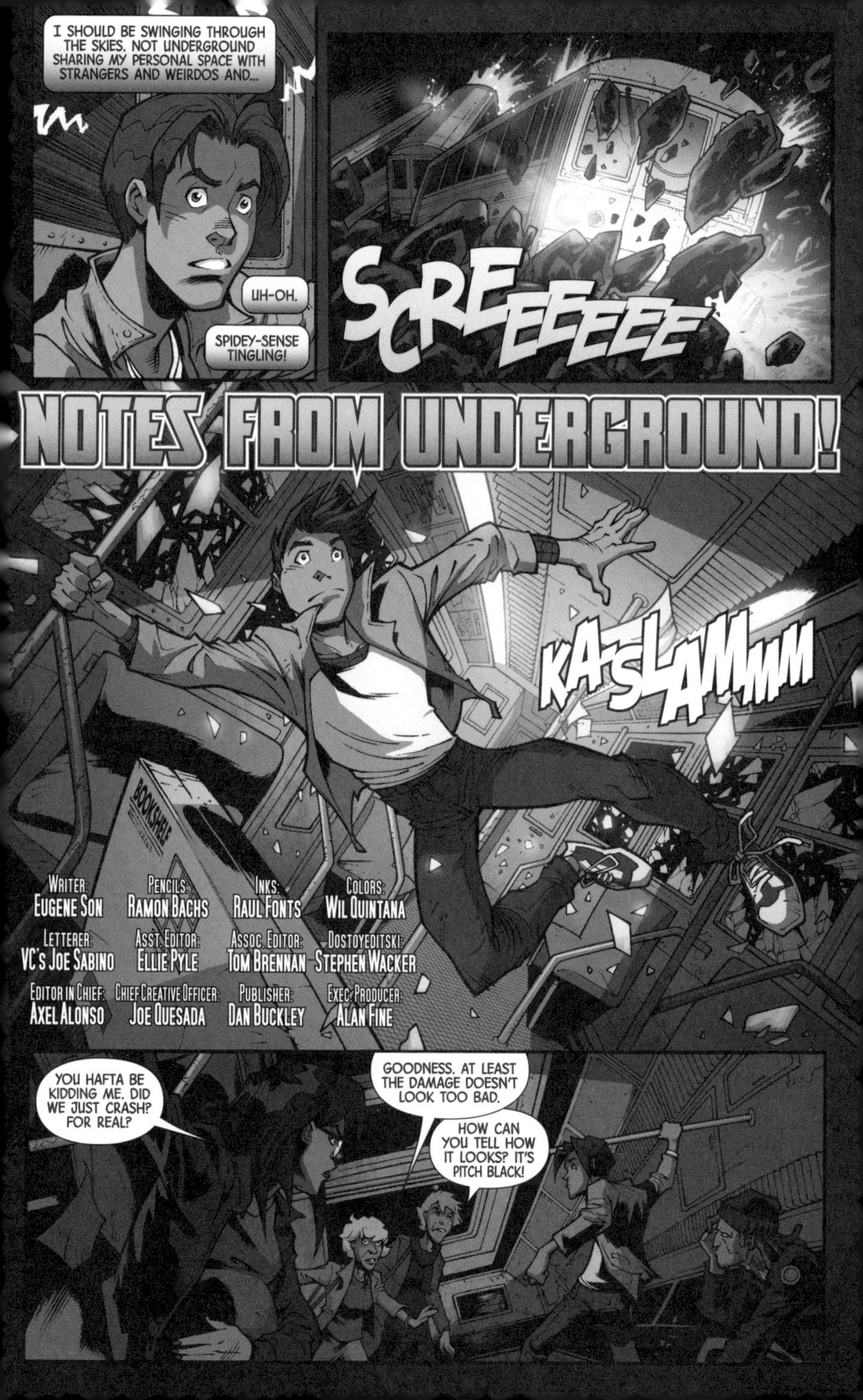
I SHOULD BE SWINGING THROUGH THE SKIES. NOT UNDERGROUND SHARING MY PERSONAL SPACE WITH STRANGERS AND WEIRDOS AND...
UH-OH.
SPIDEY-SENSE TINGLING!
SCREEEEEEE
NOTES FROM UNDERGROUND!
KA-SLAMMMM
WRITER: EUGENE SON
PENCILS: RAMON BACHS
INKS: RAUL FONTS
COLORS: WIL QUINTANA
LETTERER: VC's JOE SABINO
ASST. EDITOR: ELLIE PYLE
ASSOC. EDITOR: TOM BRENNAN
DOSTOYEDITSKI: STEPHEN WACKER
EDITOR IN CHIEF: AXEL ALONSO
CHIEF CREATIVE OFFICER: JOE QUESADA
PUBLISHER: DAN BUCKLEY
EXEC. PRODUCER: ALAN FINE
YOU HAFTA BE KIDDING ME. DID WE JUST CRASH? FOR REAL?
GOODNESS. AT LEAST THE DAMAGE DOESN'T LOOK TOO BAD.
HOW CAN YOU TELL HOW IT LOOKS? IT'S PITCH BLACK!

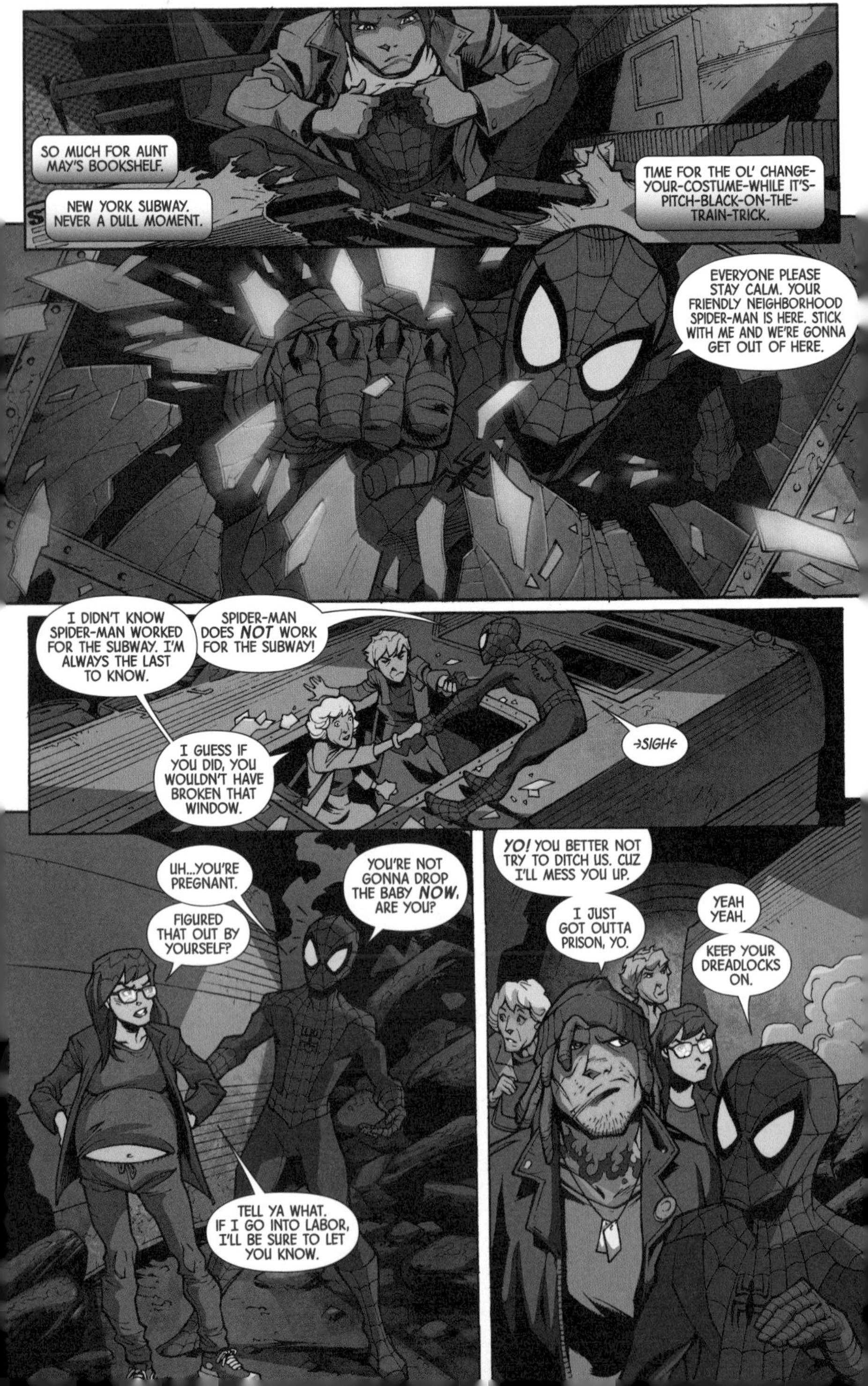
SO MUCH FOR AUNT MAY'S BOOKSHELF.
NEW YORK SUBWAY. NEVER A DULL MOMENT.
TIME FOR THE OL' CHANGE-YOUR-COSTUME-WHILE IT'S-PITCH-BLACK-ON-THE-TRAIN-TRICK.
EVERYONE PLEASE STAY CALM. YOUR FRIENDLY NEIGHBORHOOD SPIDER-MAN IS HERE. STICK WITH ME AND WE'RE GONNA GET OUT OF HERE.
I DIDN'T KNOW SPIDER-MAN WORKED FOR THE SUBWAY. I'M ALWAYS THE LAST TO KNOW.
SPIDER-MAN DOES NOT WORK FOR THE SUBWAY!
I GUESS IF YOU DID, YOU WOULDN'T HAVE BROKEN THAT WINDOW.
SIGH
UH...YOU'RE PREGNANT.
FIGURED THAT OUT BY YOURSELF?
YOU'RE NOT GONNA DROP THE BABY NOW, ARE YOU?
TELL YA WHAT. IF I GO INTO LABOR, I'LL BE SURE TO LET YOU KNOW.
YO! YOU BETTER NOT TRY TO DITCH US. CUZ I'LL MESS YOU UP.
I JUST GOT OUTTA PRISON, YO.
YEAH YEAH.
KEEP YOUR DREADLOCKS ON.

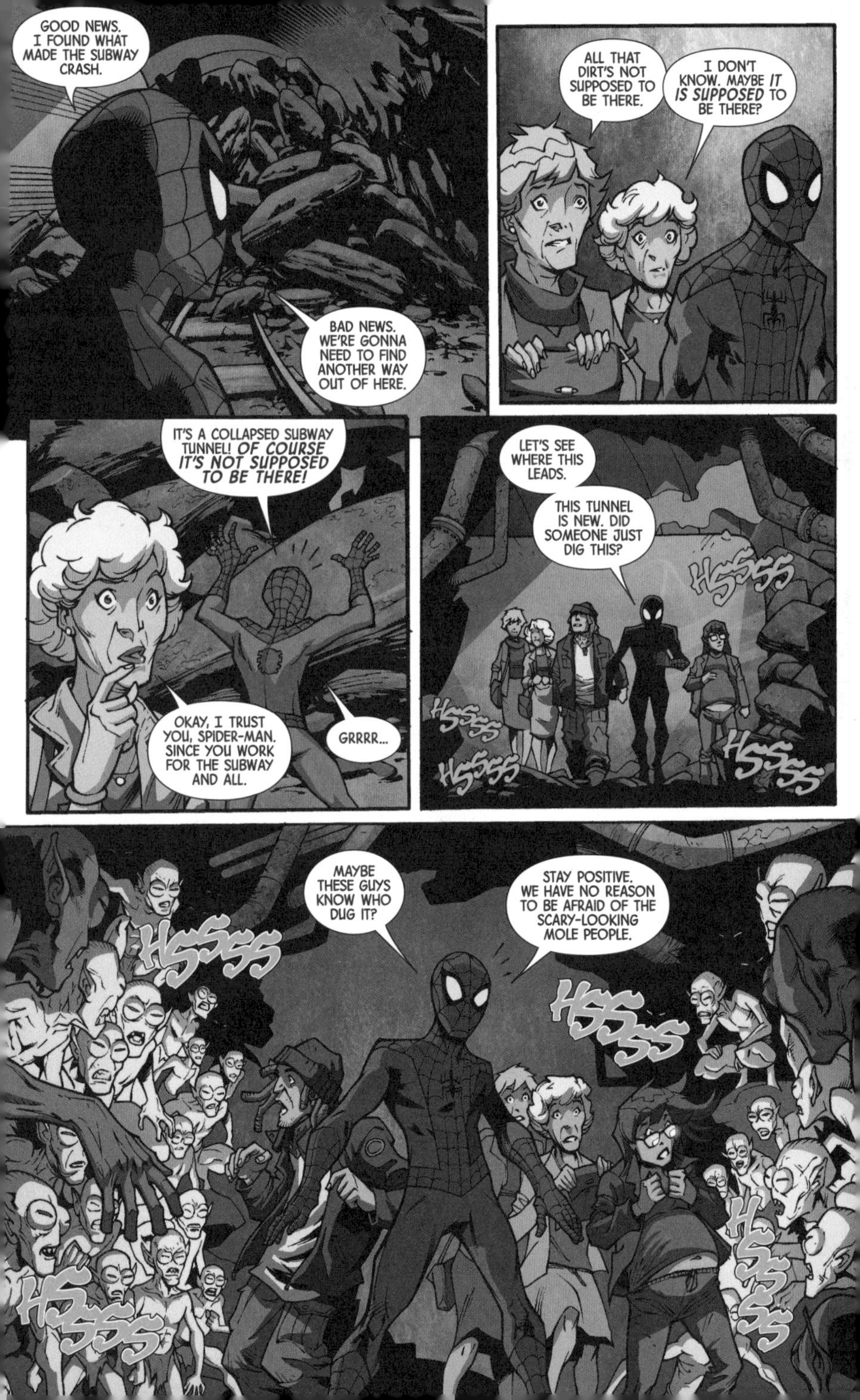
GOOD NEWS. I FOUND WHAT MADE THE SUBWAY CRASH.
BAD NEWS. WE'RE GONNA NEED TO FIND ANOTHER WAY OUT OF HERE.
ALL THAT DIRT'S NOT SUPPOSED TO BE THERE.
I DON'T KNOW. MAYBE IT IS SUPPOSED TO BE THERE?
IT'S A COLLAPSED SUBWAY TUNNEL! OF COURSE IT'S NOT SUPPOSED TO BE THERE!
OKAY, I TRUST YOU, SPIDER-MAN. SINCE YOU WORK FOR THE SUBWAY AND ALL.
GRRRR...
LET'S SEE WHERE THIS LEADS.
THIS TUNNEL IS NEW. DID SOMEONE JUST DIG THIS?
HSSSS
HSSSS
HSSSS
HSSSS
HSSSS
MAYBE THESE GUYS KNOW WHO DUG IT?
STAY POSITIVE. WE HAVE NO REASON TO BE AFRAID OF THE SCARY-LOOKING MOLE PEOPLE.
HSSSS
HSSSS
HSSSS

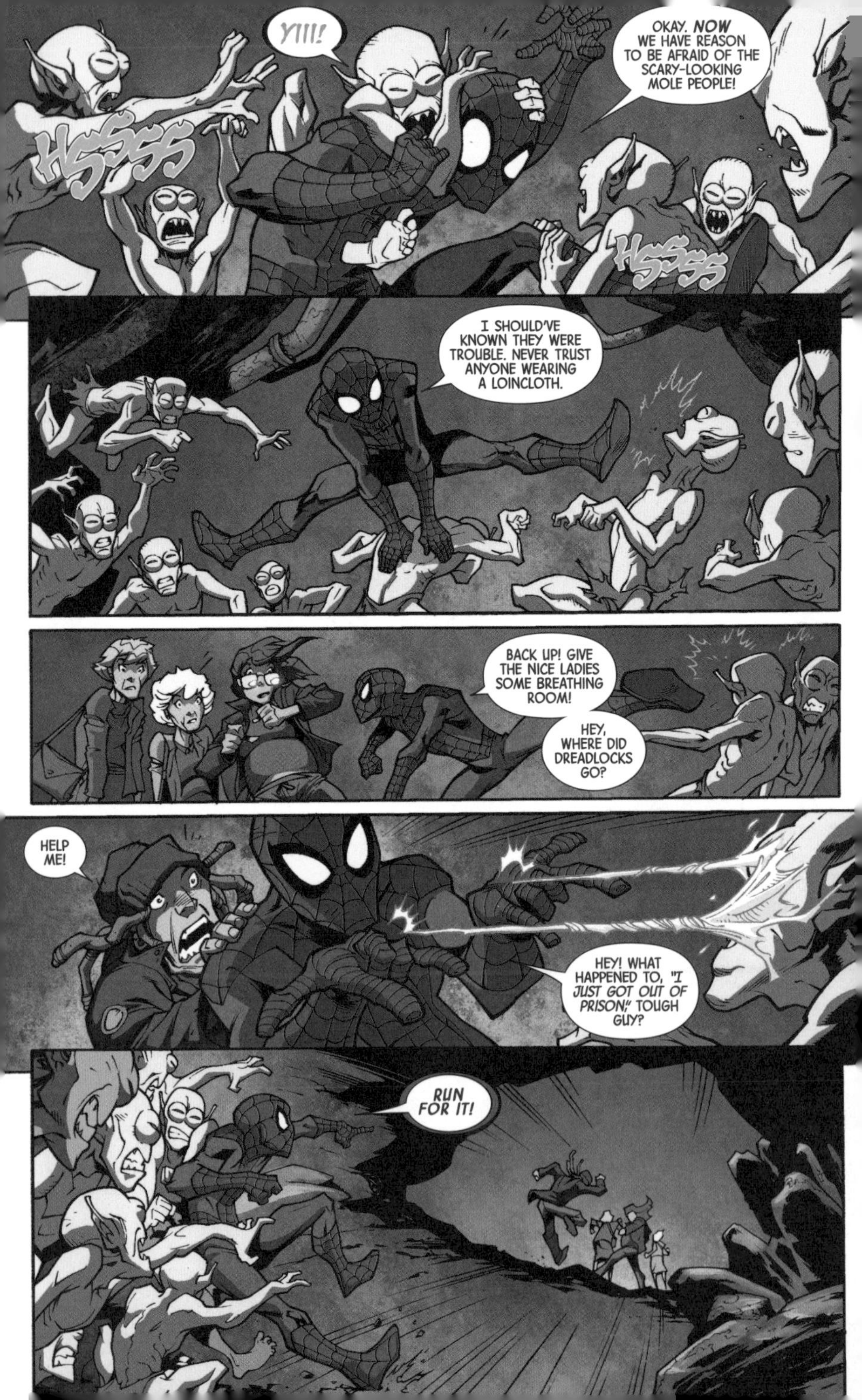
YIII!
HSSSS
OKAY. NOW WE HAVE REASON TO BE AFRAID OF THE SCARY-LOOKING MOLE PEOPLE!
HSSSS
I SHOULD'VE KNOWN THEY WERE TROUBLE. NEVER TRUST ANYONE WEARING A LOINCLOTH.
BACK UP! GIVE THE NICE LADIES SOME BREATHING ROOM!
HEY, WHERE DID DREADLOCKS GO?
HELP ME!
HEY! WHAT HAPPENED TO, "I JUST GOT OUT OF PRISON," TOUGH GUY?
RUN FOR IT!

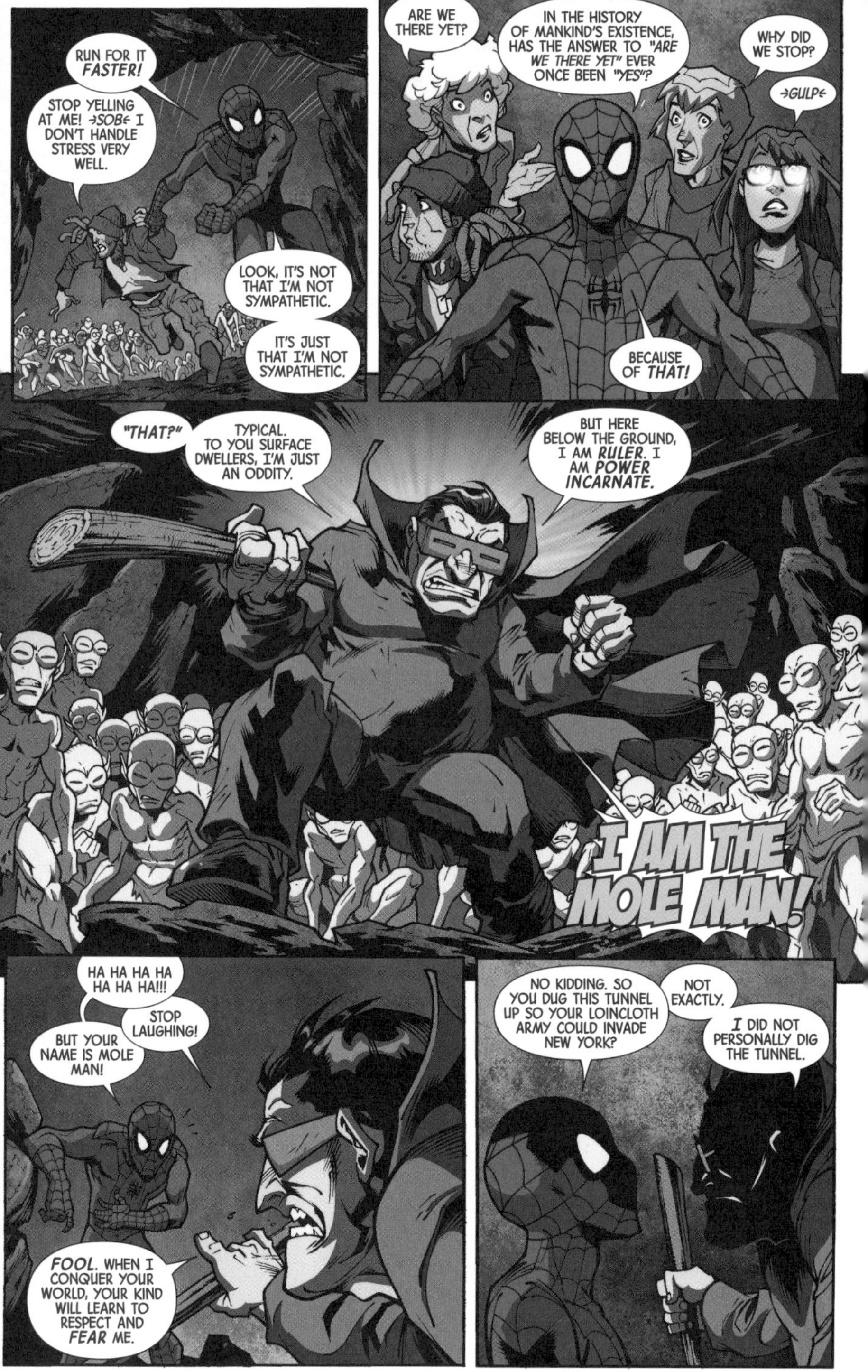
RUN FOR IT FASTER!
STOP YELLING AT ME! →SOB← I DON'T HANDLE STRESS VERY WELL.
LOOK, IT'S NOT THAT I'M NOT SYMPATHETIC.
IT'S JUST THAT I'M NOT SYMPATHETIC.
ARE WE THERE YET?
IN THE HISTORY OF MANKIND'S EXISTENCE, HAS THE ANSWER TO "ARE WE THERE YET" EVER ONCE BEEN "YES"?
WHY DID WE STOP?
→GULP←
BECAUSE OF THAT!
"THAT?"
TYPICAL. TO YOU SURFACE DWELLERS, I'M JUST AN ODDITY.
BUT HERE BELOW THE GROUND, I AM RULER. I AM POWER INCARNATE.
I AM THE MOLE MAN!
HA HA HA HA HA HA HA!!!
STOP LAUGHING!
BUT YOUR NAME IS MOLE MAN!
FOOL. WHEN I CONQUER YOUR WORLD, YOUR KIND WILL LEARN TO RESPECT AND FEAR ME.
NO KIDDING. SO YOU DUG THIS TUNNEL UP SO YOUR LOINCLOTH ARMY COULD INVADE NEW YORK?
NOT EXACTLY.
I DID NOT PERSONALLY DIG THE TUNNEL.

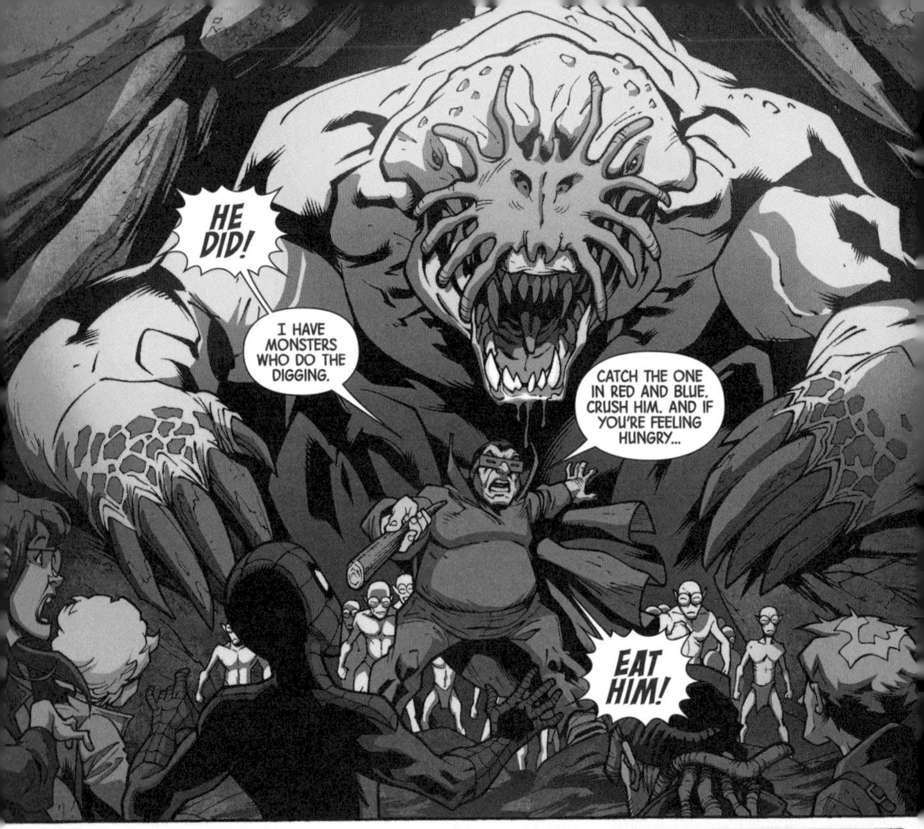
HE DID!
I HAVE MONSTERS WHO DO THE DIGGING.
CATCH THE ONE IN RED AND BLUE. CRUSH HIM. AND IF YOU'RE FEELING HUNGRY...
EAT HIM!

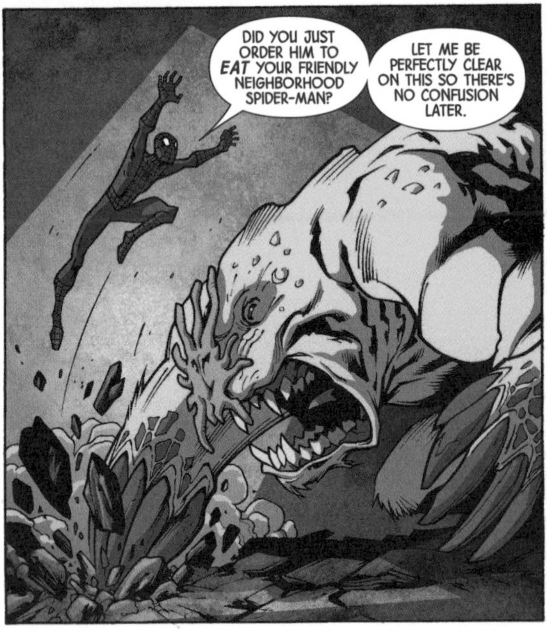
DID YOU JUST ORDER HIM TO EAT YOUR FRIENDLY NEIGHBORHOOD SPIDER-MAN?
LET ME BE PERFECTLY CLEAR ON THIS SO THERE'S NO CONFUSION LATER.

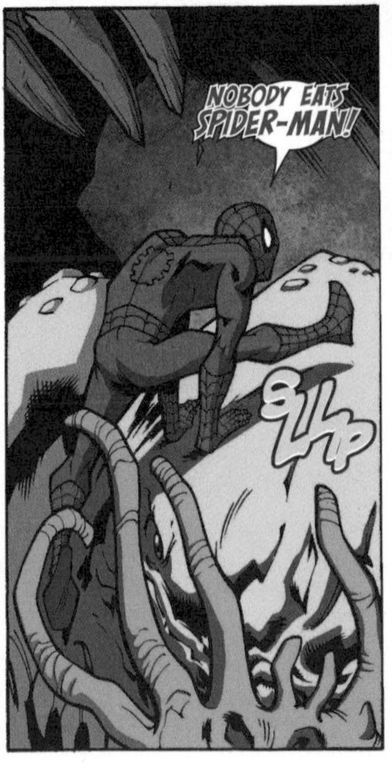
NOBODY EATS SPIDER-MAN!
SLAP

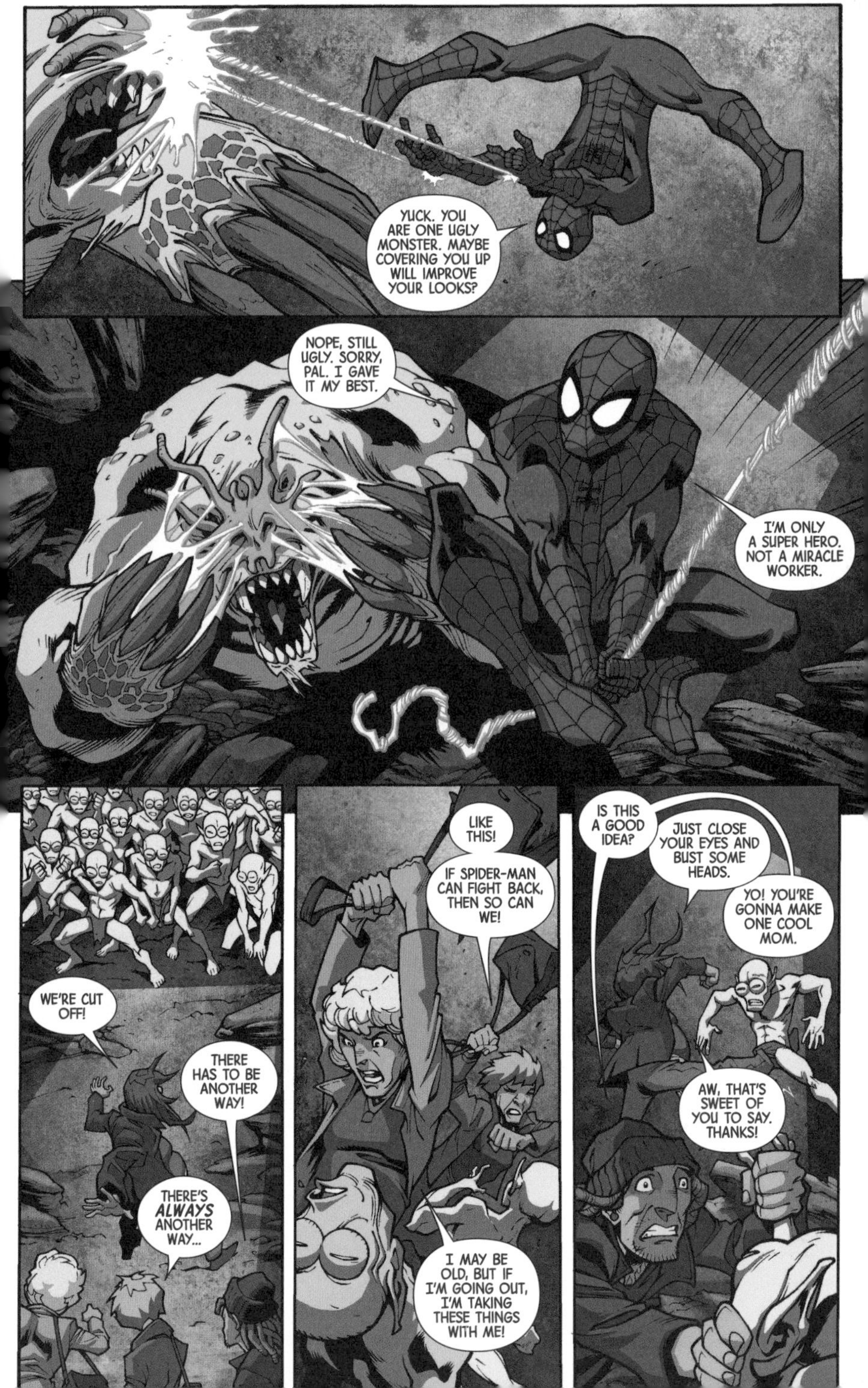
YUCK. YOU ARE ONE UGLY MONSTER. MAYBE COVERING YOU UP WILL IMPROVE YOUR LOOKS?
NOPE, STILL UGLY. SORRY, PAL. I GAVE IT MY BEST.
I'M ONLY A SUPER HERO. NOT A MIRACLE WORKER.
WE'RE CUT OFF!
THERE HAS TO BE ANOTHER WAY!
THERE'S *ALWAYS* ANOTHER WAY...
LIKE THIS!
IF SPIDER-MAN CAN FIGHT BACK, THEN SO CAN WE!
I MAY BE OLD, BUT IF I'M GOING OUT, I'M TAKING THESE THINGS WITH ME!
IS THIS A GOOD IDEA?
JUST CLOSE YOUR EYES AND BUST SOME HEADS.
YO! YOU'RE GONNA MAKE ONE COOL MOM.
AW, THAT'S SWEET OF YOU TO SAY. THANKS!

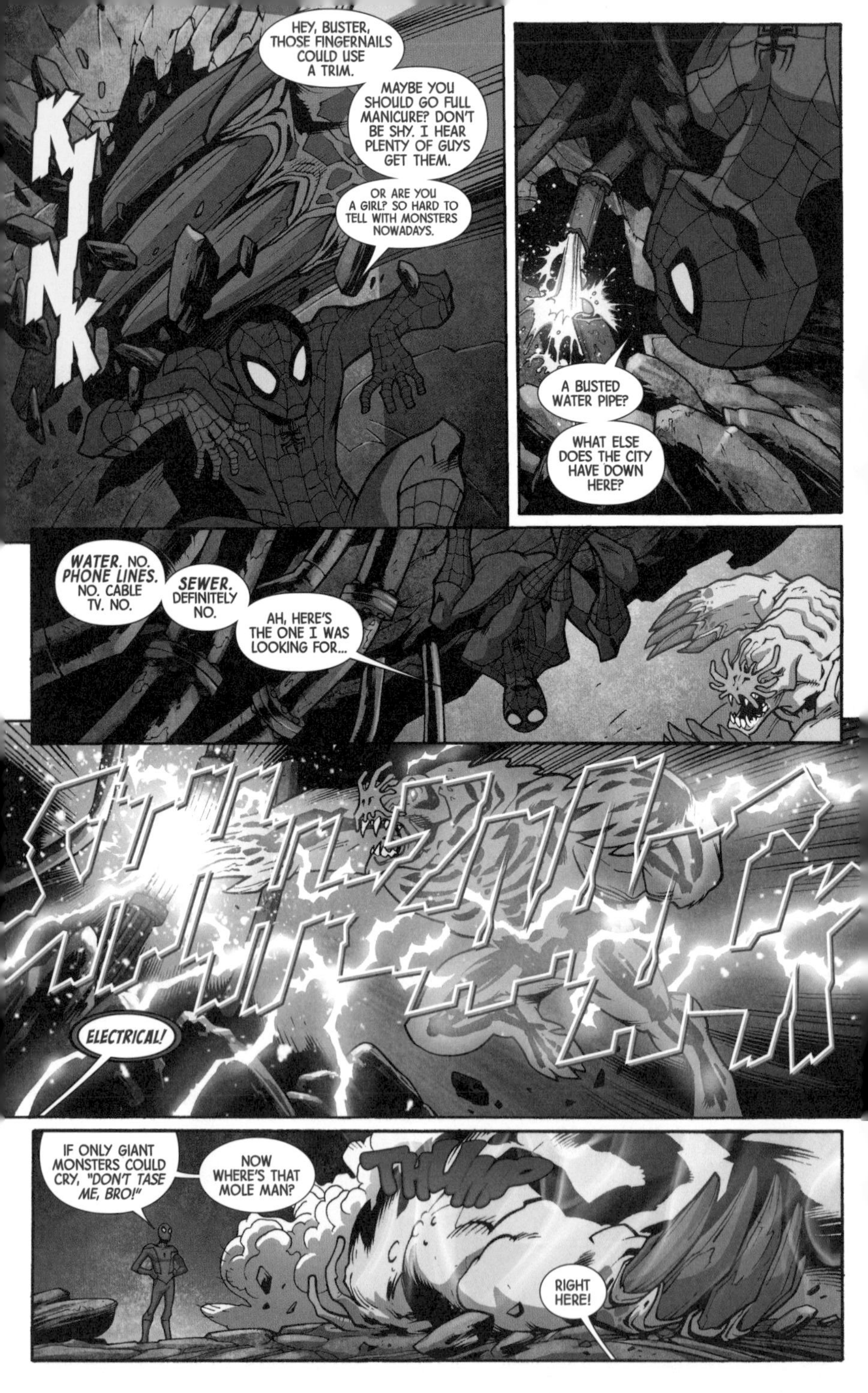
HEY, BUSTER, THOSE FINGERNAILS COULD USE A TRIM.
MAYBE YOU SHOULD GO FULL MANICURE? DON'T BE SHY. I HEAR PLENTY OF GUYS GET THEM.
OR ARE YOU A GIRL? SO HARD TO TELL WITH MONSTERS NOWADAYS.
A BUSTED WATER PIPE?
WHAT ELSE DOES THE CITY HAVE DOWN HERE?
WATER. NO. PHONE LINES. NO. CABLE TV. NO.
SEWER. DEFINITELY NO.
AH, HERE'S THE ONE I WAS LOOKING FOR...
ELECTRICAL!
IF ONLY GIANT MONSTERS COULD CRY, "DON'T TASE ME, BRO!"
NOW WHERE'S THAT MOLE MAN?
THUMP
RIGHT HERE!

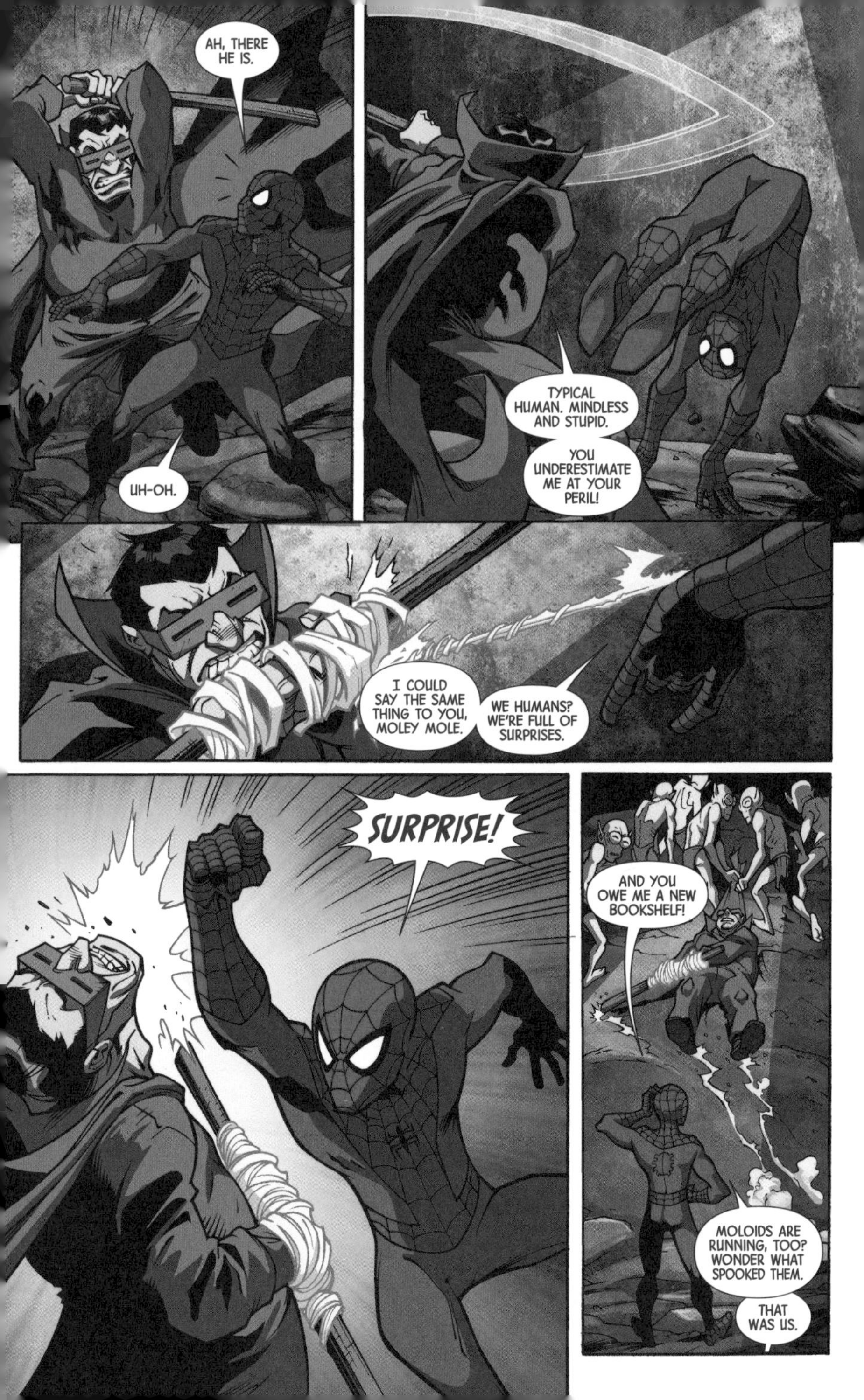
AH, THERE HE IS.
UH-OH.
TYPICAL HUMAN. MINDLESS AND STUPID.
YOU UNDERESTIMATE ME AT YOUR PERIL!
I COULD SAY THE SAME THING TO YOU, MOLEY MOLE.
WE HUMANS? WE'RE FULL OF SURPRISES.
SURPRISE!
AND YOU OWE ME A NEW BOOKSHELF!
MOLOIDS ARE RUNNING, TOO? WONDER WHAT SPOOKED THEM.
THAT WAS US.

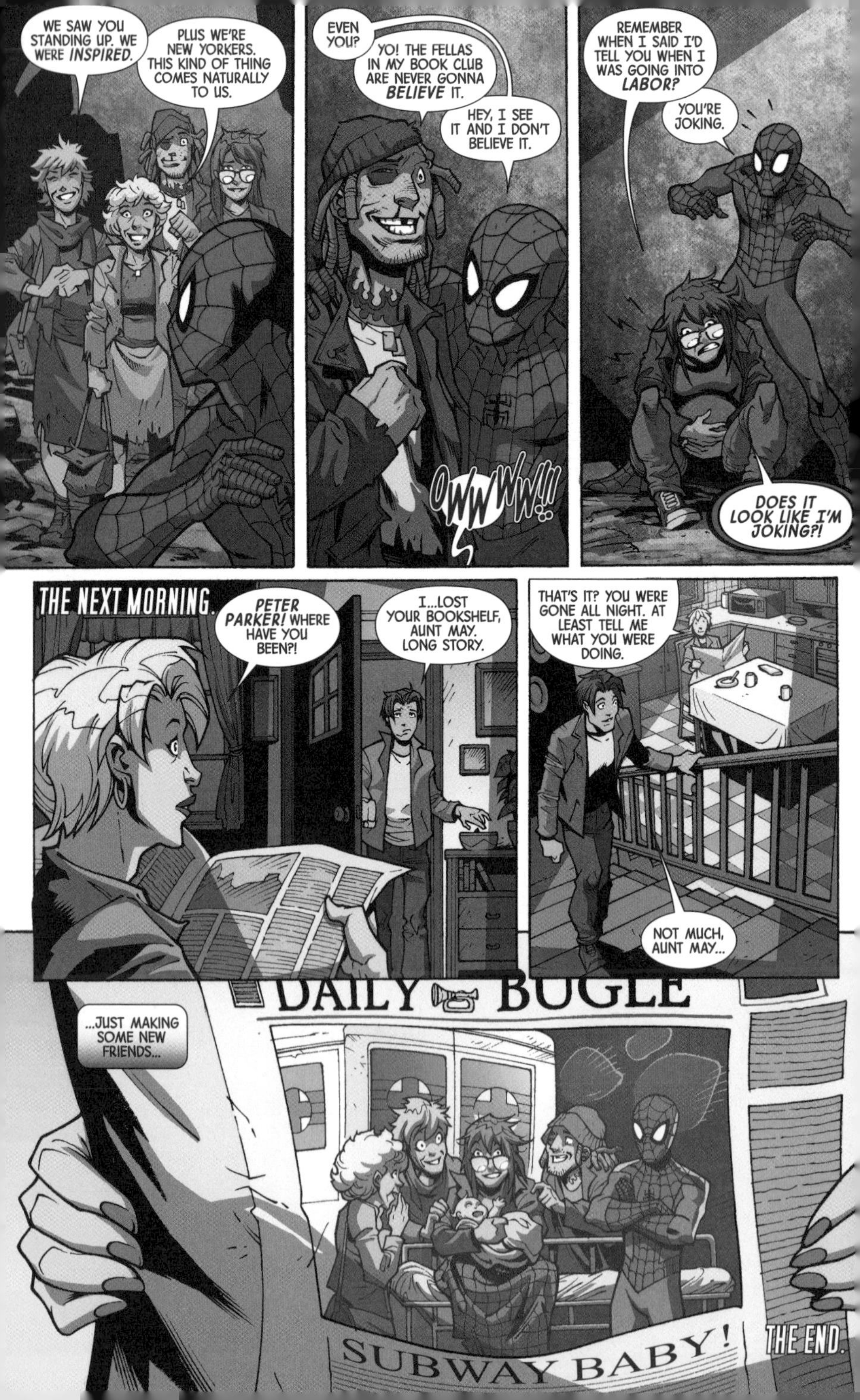

WE SAW YOU STANDING UP. WE WERE INSPIRED.
PLUS WE'RE NEW YORKERS. THIS KIND OF THING COMES NATURALLY TO US.
EVEN YOU?
YO! THE FELLAS IN MY BOOK CLUB ARE NEVER GONNA BELIEVE IT.
HEY, I SEE IT AND I DON'T BELIEVE IT.
OWWWW!!!
REMEMBER WHEN I SAID I'D TELL YOU WHEN I WAS GOING INTO LABOR?
YOU'RE JOKING.
DOES IT LOOK LIKE I'M JOKING?!
THE NEXT MORNING.
PETER PARKER! WHERE HAVE YOU BEEN?!
I...LOST YOUR BOOKSHELF, AUNT MAY. LONG STORY.
THAT'S IT? YOU WERE GONE ALL NIGHT. AT LEAST TELL ME WHAT YOU WERE DOING.
NOT MUCH, AUNT MAY...
...JUST MAKING SOME NEW FRIENDS...
DAILY BUGLE
SUBWAY BABY!
THE END.

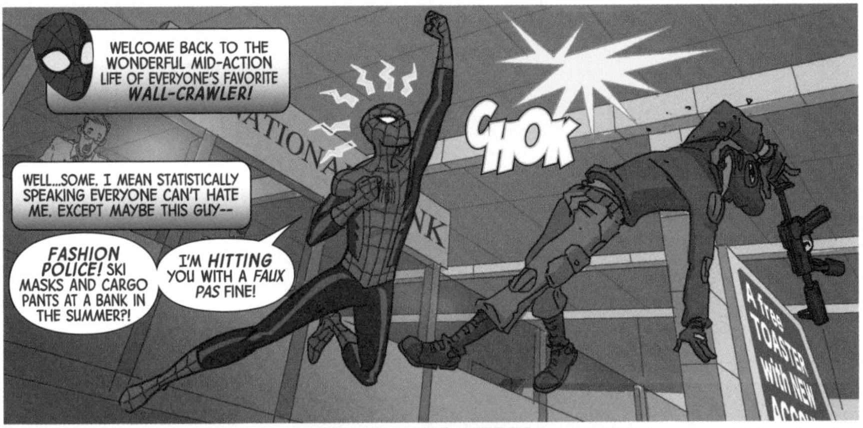
WELCOME BACK TO THE WONDERFUL MID-ACTION LIFE OF EVERYONE'S FAVORITE WALL-CRAWLER!
CHOK
WELL...SOME. I MEAN STATISTICALLY SPEAKING EVERYONE CAN'T HATE ME. EXCEPT MAYBE THIS GUY--
FASHION POLICE! SKI MASKS AND CARGO PANTS AT A BANK IN THE SUMMER?!
I'M HITTING YOU WITH A FAUX PAS FINE!
A free TOASTER with NEW

"LOOK MA, NO WEBS!"

JACOB SEMAHN - writer NUNO PLATI - artist

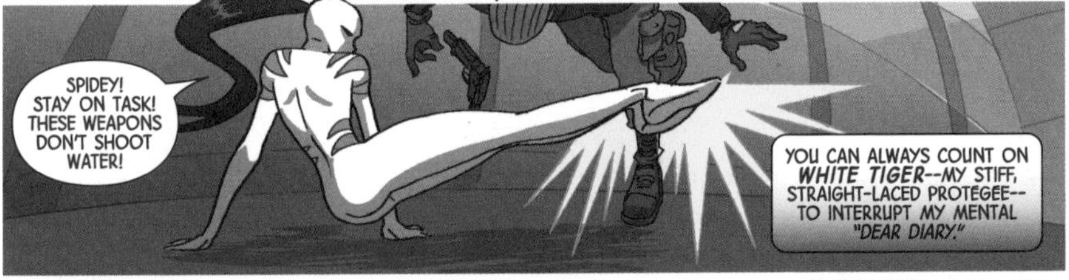
SPIDEY! STAY ON TASK! THESE WEAPONS DON'T SHOOT WATER!
YOU CAN ALWAYS COUNT ON WHITE TIGER--MY STIFF, STRAIGHT-LACED PROTEGEE--TO INTERRUPT MY MENTAL "DEAR DIARY."

VC's JOE SABINO - letterer ELLIE PYLE - asst. editor TOM BRENNAN - assoc. editor

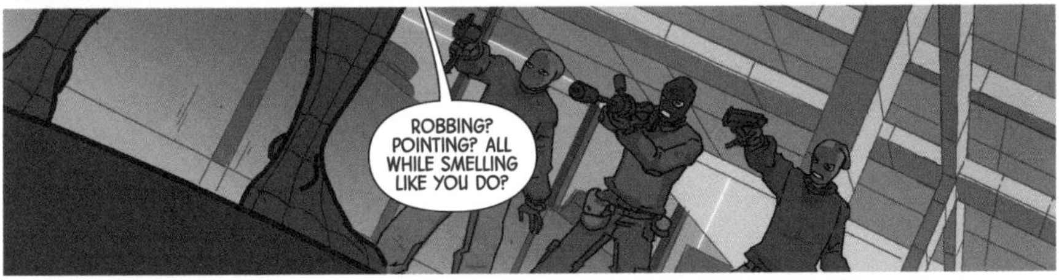
ROBBING? POINTING? ALL WHILE SMELLING LIKE YOU DO?

STEPHEN WACKER - senior editor AXEL ALONSO - editor in chief

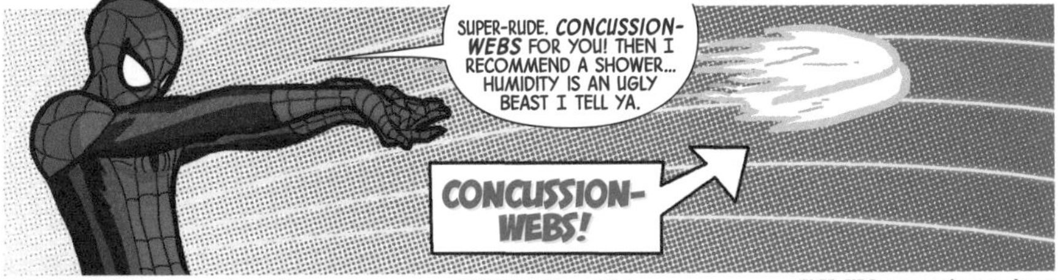
SUPER-RUDE. CONCUSSION-WEBS FOR YOU! THEN I RECOMMEND A SHOWER... HUMIDITY IS AN UGLY BEAST I TELL YA.
CONCUSSION-WEBS!

JOE QUESADA - chief creative officer DAN BUCKLEY - publisher ALAN FINE - executive producer

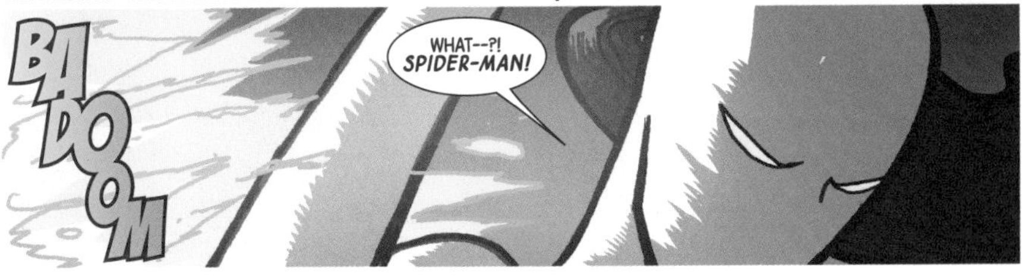
BADOOM
WHAT--?! SPIDER-MAN!

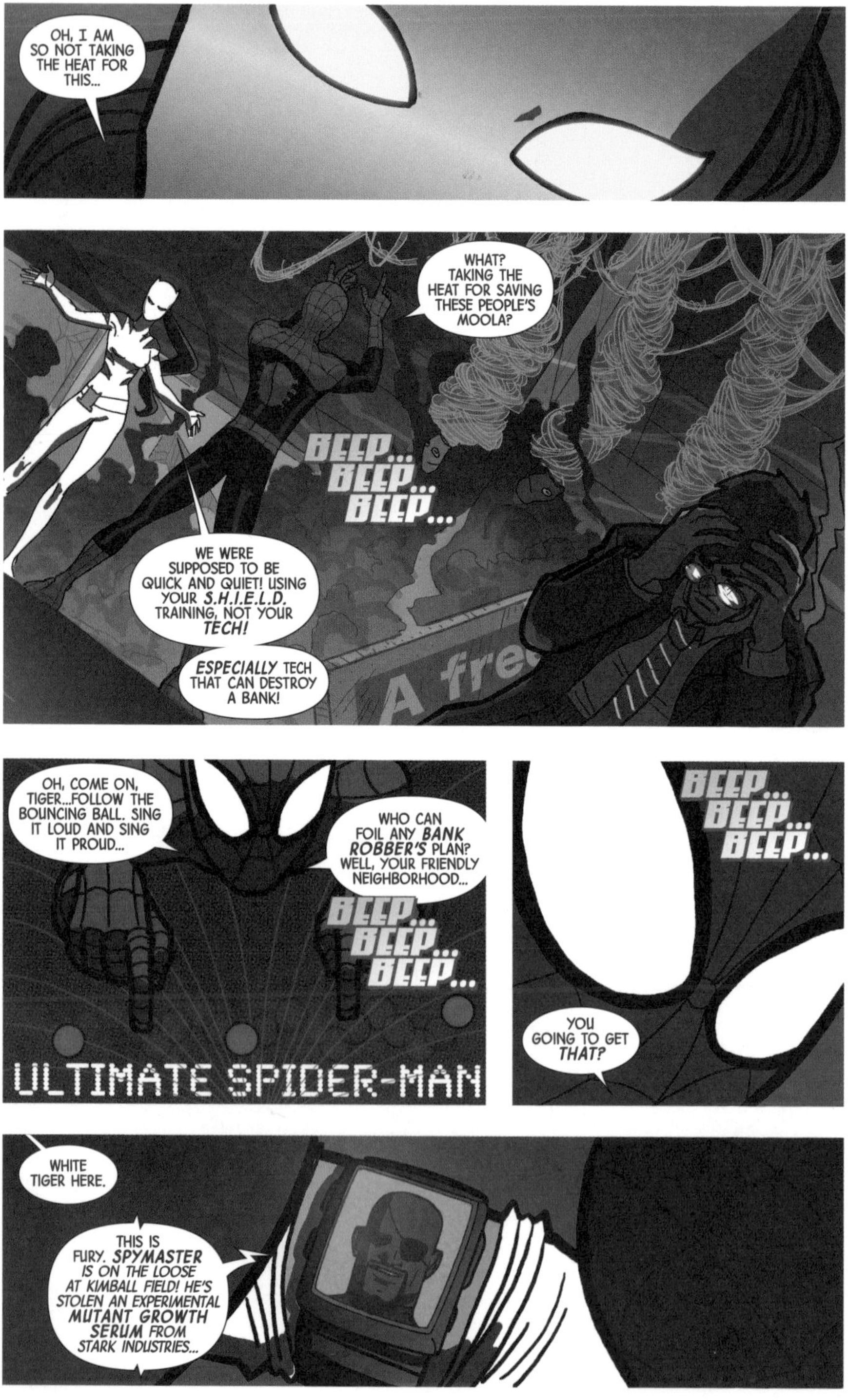

OH, I AM SO NOT TAKING THE HEAT FOR THIS...
WHAT? TAKING THE HEAT FOR SAVING THESE PEOPLE'S MOOLA?
BEEP... BEEP... BEEP...
WE WERE SUPPOSED TO BE QUICK AND QUIET! USING YOUR S.H.I.E.L.D. TRAINING, NOT YOUR TECH!
ESPECIALLY TECH THAT CAN DESTROY A BANK!
A fre
OH, COME ON, TIGER...FOLLOW THE BOUNCING BALL. SING IT LOUD AND SING IT PROUD...
WHO CAN FOIL ANY BANK ROBBER'S PLAN? WELL, YOUR FRIENDLY NEIGHBORHOOD...
BEEP... BEEP... BEEP...
ULTIMATE SPIDER-MAN
BEEP... BEEP... BEEP...
YOU GOING TO GET THAT?
WHITE TIGER HERE.
THIS IS FURY. SPYMASTER IS ON THE LOOSE AT KIMBALL FIELD! HE'S STOLEN AN EXPERIMENTAL MUTANT GROWTH SERUM FROM STARK INDUSTRIES...

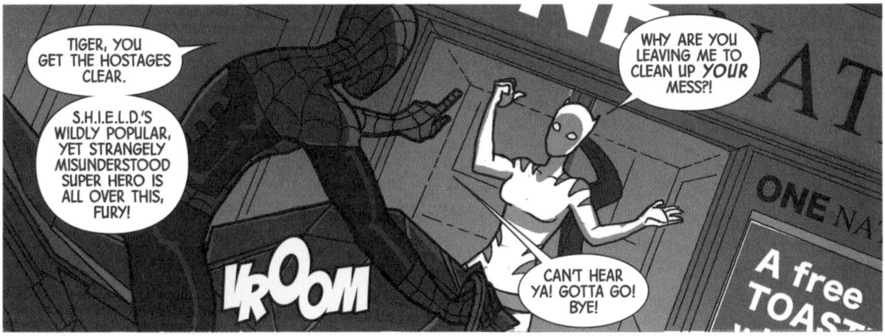
TIGER, YOU GET THE HOSTAGES CLEAR.
S.H.I.E.L.D.'S WILDLY POPULAR, YET STRANGELY MISUNDERSTOOD SUPER HERO IS ALL OVER THIS, FURY!
WHY ARE YOU LEAVING ME TO CLEAN UP YOUR MESS?!
ONE NA
A free TOAST
VROOM
CAN'T HEAR YA! GOTTA GO! BYE!

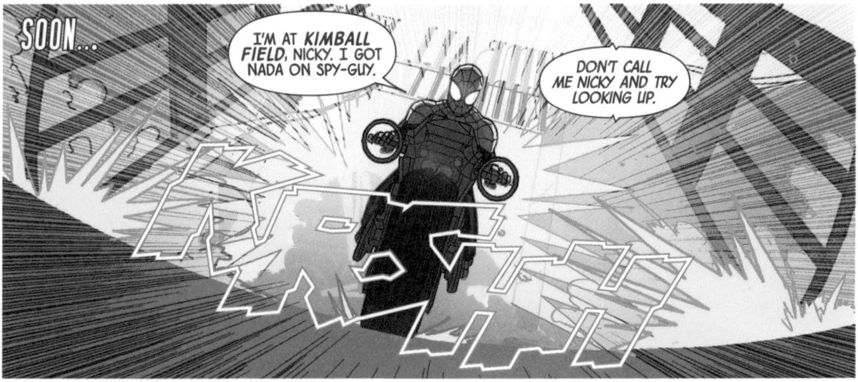
SOON...
I'M AT KIMBALL FIELD, NICKY. I GOT NADA ON SPY-GUY.
DON'T CALL ME NICKY AND TRY LOOKING UP.

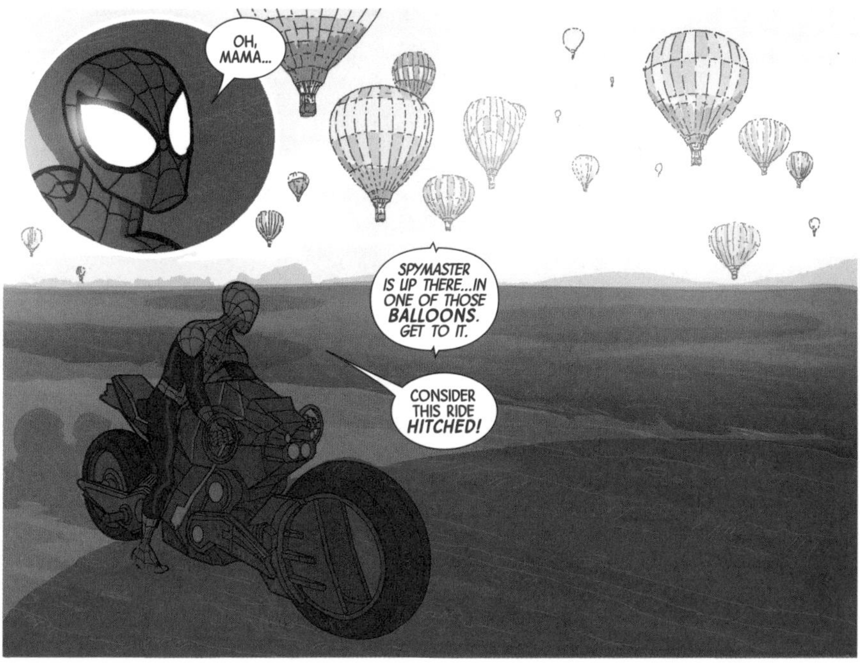
OH, MAMA...
SPYMASTER IS UP THERE...IN ONE OF THOSE BALLOONS. GET TO IT.
CONSIDER THIS RIDE HITCHED!

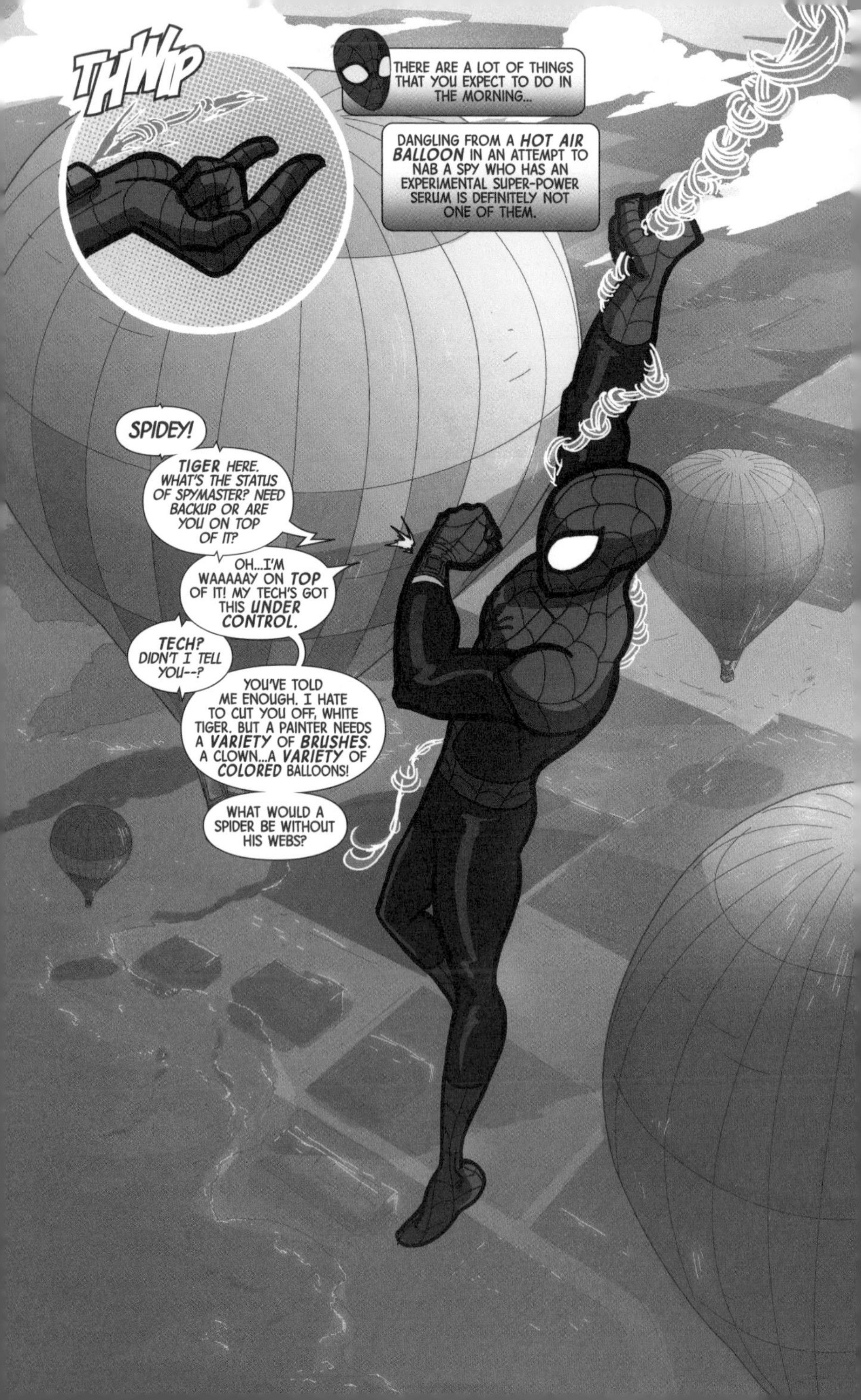
THWIP
THERE ARE A LOT OF THINGS THAT YOU EXPECT TO DO IN THE MORNING...
DANGLING FROM A HOT AIR BALLOON IN AN ATTEMPT TO NAB A SPY WHO HAS AN EXPERIMENTAL SUPER-POWER SERUM IS DEFINITELY NOT ONE OF THEM.
SPIDEY!
TIGER HERE. WHAT'S THE STATUS OF SPYMASTER? NEED BACKUP OR ARE YOU ON TOP OF IT?
OH...I'M WAAAAAY ON TOP OF IT! MY TECH'S GOT THIS UNDER CONTROL.
TECH? DIDN'T I TELL YOU--?
YOU'VE TOLD ME ENOUGH. I HATE TO CUT YOU OFF, WHITE TIGER. BUT A PAINTER NEEDS A VARIETY OF BRUSHES. A CLOWN...A VARIETY OF COLORED BALLOONS!
WHAT WOULD A SPIDER BE WITHOUT HIS WEBS?

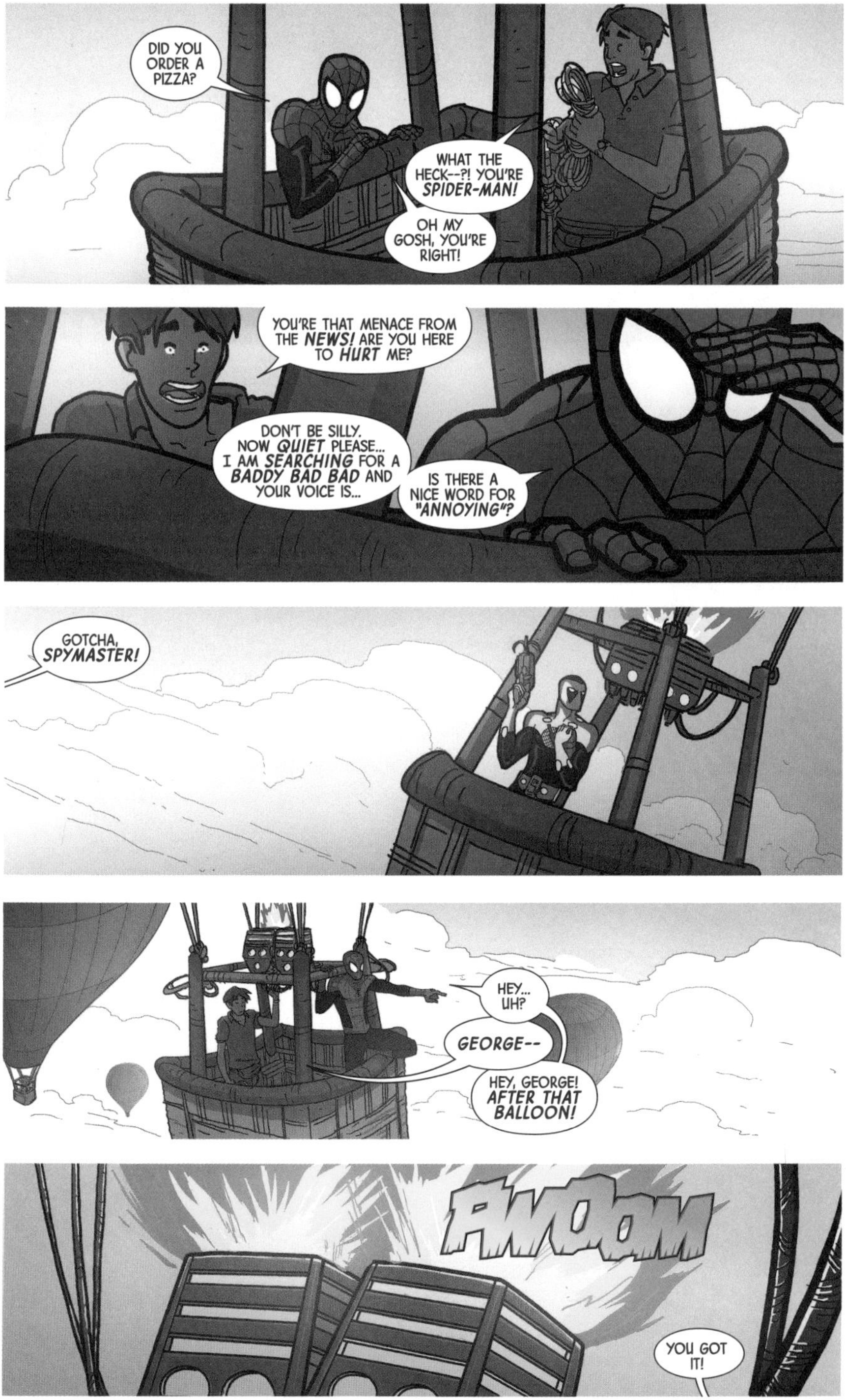
DID YOU ORDER A PIZZA?
WHAT THE HECK--?! YOU'RE SPIDER-MAN!
OH MY GOSH, YOU'RE RIGHT!
YOU'RE THAT MENACE FROM THE NEWS! ARE YOU HERE TO HURT ME?
DON'T BE SILLY. NOW QUIET PLEASE... I AM SEARCHING FOR A BADDY BAD BAD AND YOUR VOICE IS...
IS THERE A NICE WORD FOR "ANNOYING"?
GOTCHA, SPYMASTER!
HEY... UH?
GEORGE--
HEY, GEORGE! AFTER THAT BALLOON!
FWOOM
YOU GOT IT!

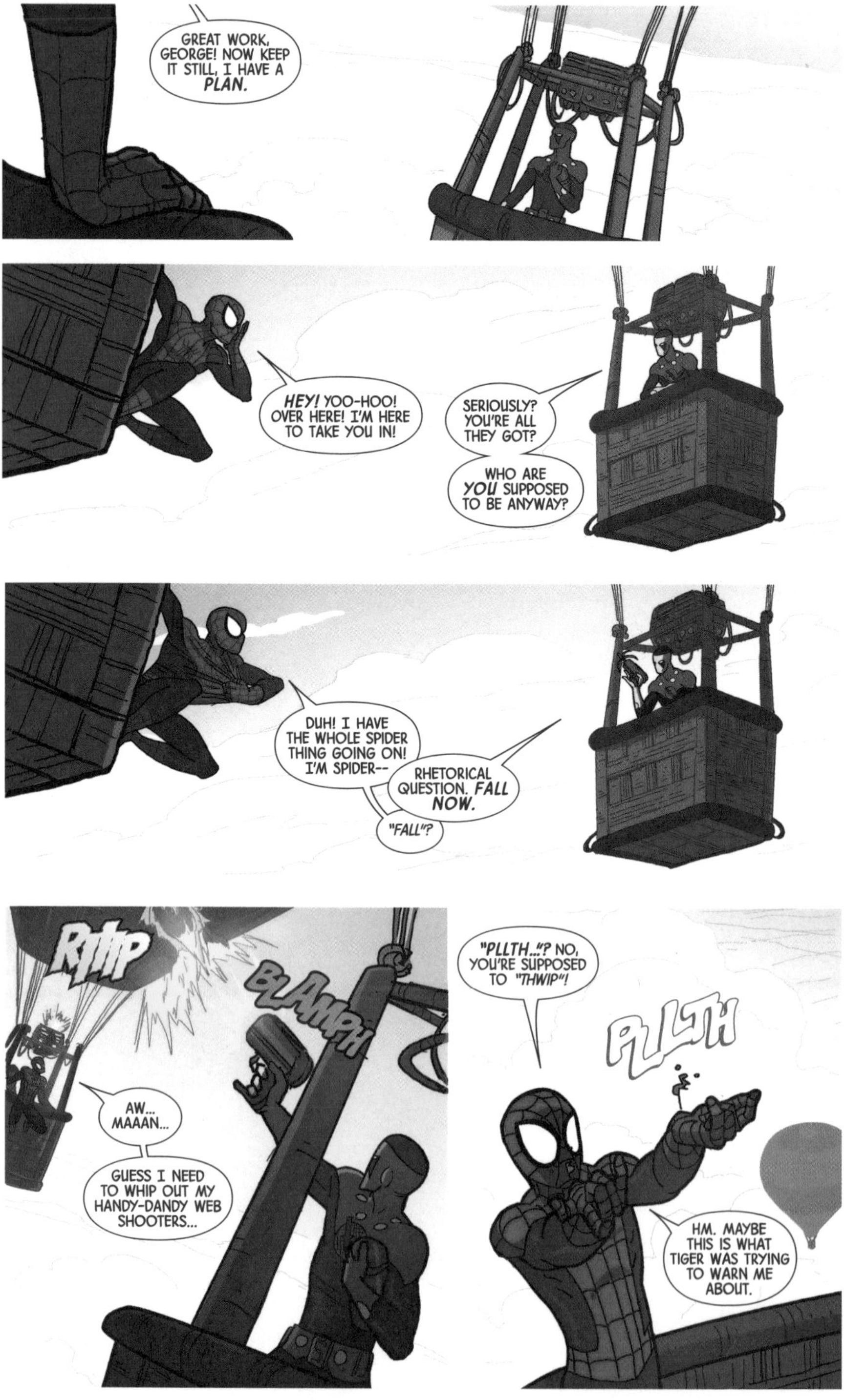
GREAT WORK, GEORGE! NOW KEEP IT STILL, I HAVE A PLAN.
HEY! YOO-HOO! OVER HERE! I'M HERE TO TAKE YOU IN!
SERIOUSLY? YOU'RE ALL THEY GOT?
WHO ARE YOU SUPPOSED TO BE ANYWAY?
DUH! I HAVE THE WHOLE SPIDER THING GOING ON! I'M SPIDER--
RHETORICAL QUESTION. FALL NOW.
"FALL"?
RIIIP
BLAMPH
AW... MAAAN...
GUESS I NEED TO WHIP OUT MY HANDY-DANDY WEB SHOOTERS...
"PLLTH..."? NO, YOU'RE SUPPOSED TO "THWIP"!
PLLTH
HM. MAYBE THIS IS WHAT TIGER WAS TRYING TO WARN ME ABOUT.

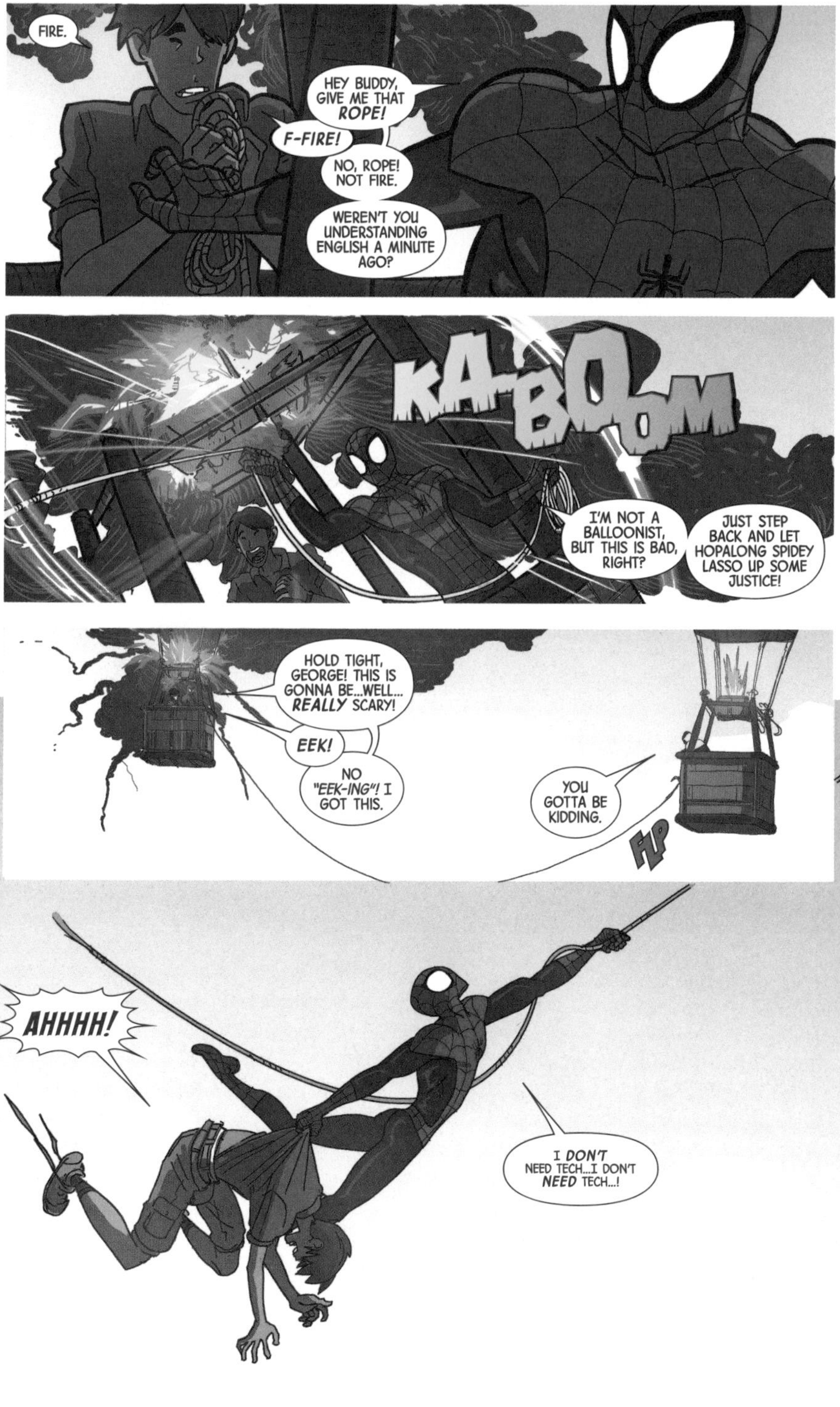
FIRE.
HEY BUDDY, GIVE ME THAT ROPE!
F-FIRE!
NO, ROPE! NOT FIRE.
WEREN'T YOU UNDERSTANDING ENGLISH A MINUTE AGO?
KA-BOOM
I'M NOT A BALLOONIST, BUT THIS IS BAD, RIGHT?
JUST STEP BACK AND LET HOPALONG SPIDEY LASSO UP SOME JUSTICE!
HOLD TIGHT, GEORGE! THIS IS GONNA BE...WELL... REALLY SCARY!
EEK!
NO "EEK-ING"! I GOT THIS.
YOU GOTTA BE KIDDING.
FLP
AHHHH!
I DON'T NEED TECH...I DON'T NEED TECH...!

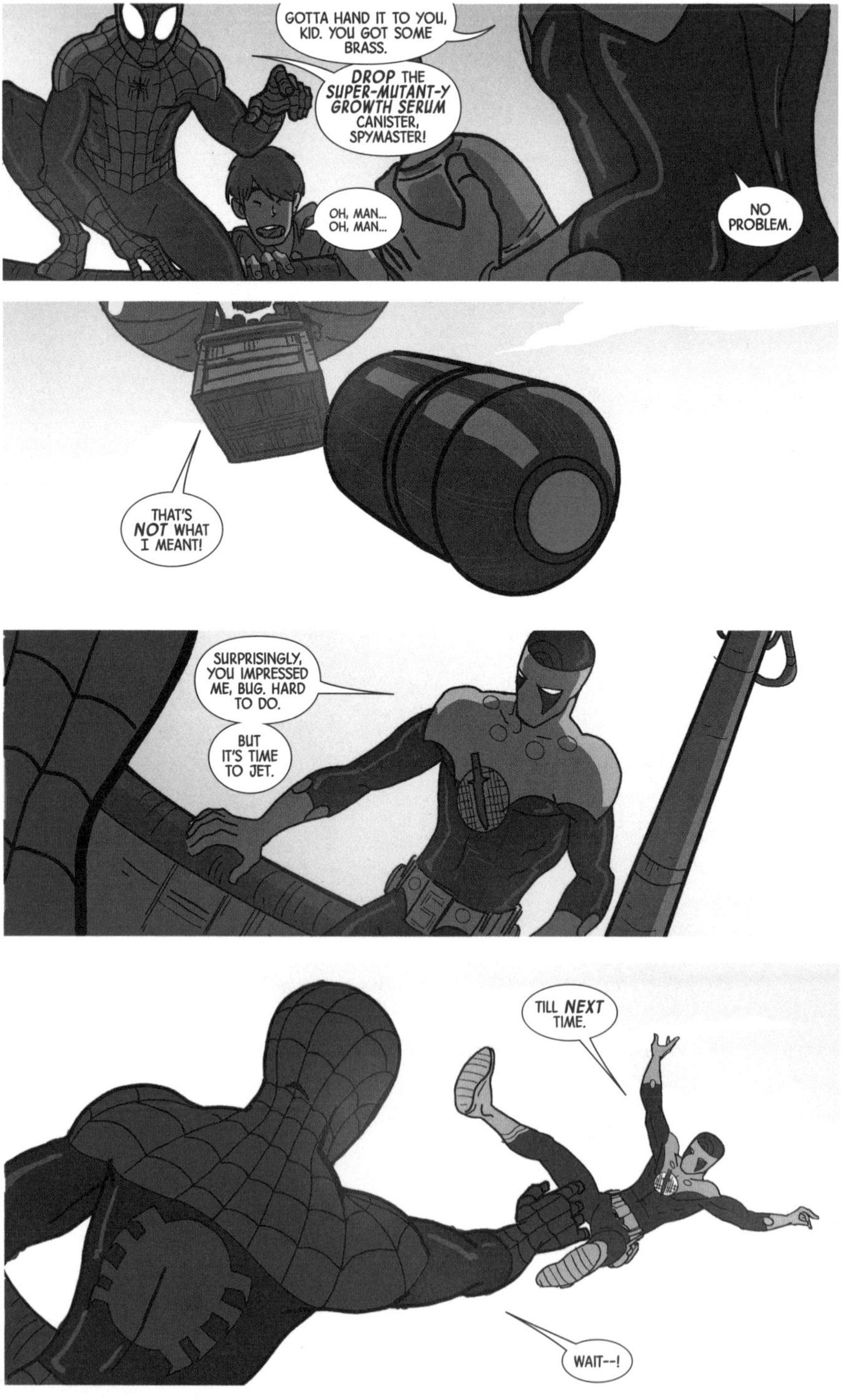
GOTTA HAND IT TO YOU, KID. YOU GOT SOME BRASS.
DROP THE SUPER-MUTANT-Y GROWTH SERUM CANISTER, SPYMASTER!
OH, MAN... OH, MAN...
NO PROBLEM.
THAT'S NOT WHAT I MEANT!
SURPRISINGLY, YOU IMPRESSED ME, BUG. HARD TO DO.
BUT IT'S TIME TO JET.
TILL NEXT TIME.
WAIT--!

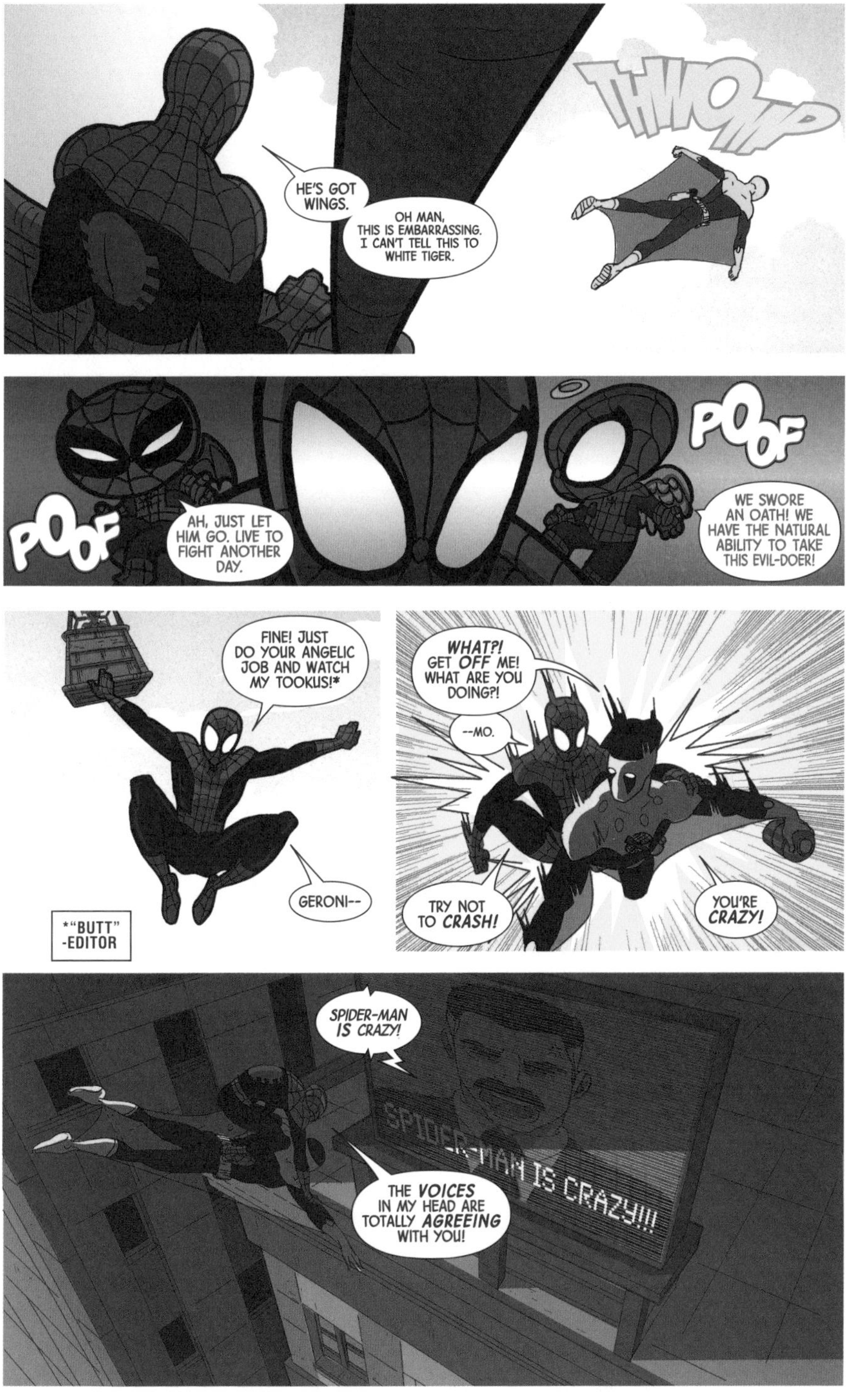
THWOMP
HE'S GOT WINGS.
OH MAN, THIS IS EMBARRASSING. I CAN'T TELL THIS TO WHITE TIGER.
POOF
AH, JUST LET HIM GO. LIVE TO FIGHT ANOTHER DAY.
POOF
WE SWORE AN OATH! WE HAVE THE NATURAL ABILITY TO TAKE THIS EVIL-DOER!
FINE! JUST DO YOUR ANGELIC JOB AND WATCH MY TOOKUS!*
GERONI--
*"BUTT" -EDITOR
WHAT?! GET OFF ME! WHAT ARE YOU DOING?!
--MO.
TRY NOT TO CRASH!
YOU'RE CRAZY!
SPIDER-MAN IS CRAZY!
SPIDER-MAN IS CRAZY!!!
THE VOICES IN MY HEAD ARE TOTALLY AGREEING WITH YOU!

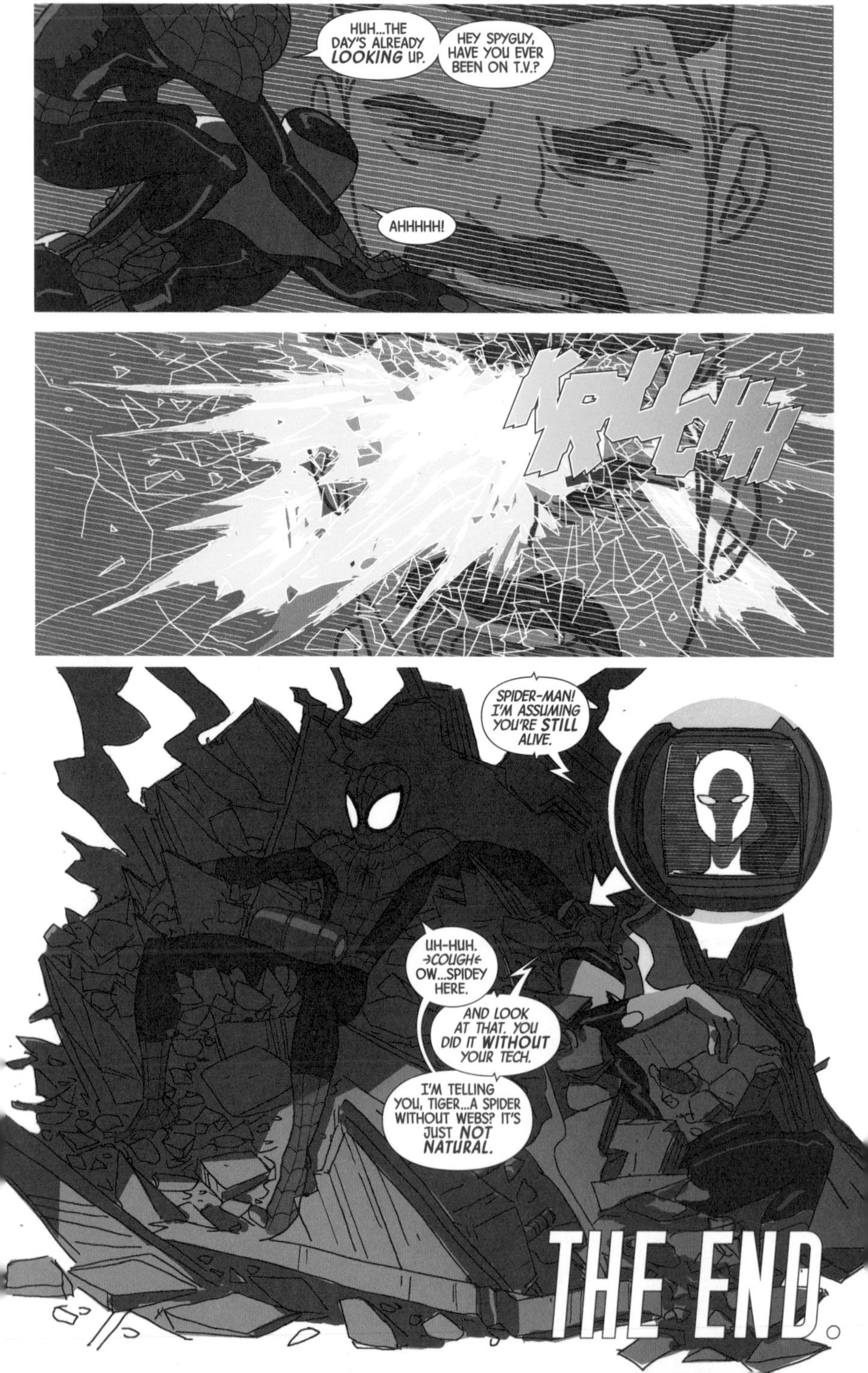
HUH...THE DAY'S ALREADY LOOKING UP.
HEY SPYGUY, HAVE YOU EVER BEEN ON T.V.?
AHHHHH!
KRUNCH
SPIDER-MAN! I'M ASSUMING YOU'RE STILL ALIVE.
UH-HUH. →COUGH← OW...SPIDEY HERE.
AND LOOK AT THAT. YOU DID IT WITHOUT YOUR TECH.
I'M TELLING YOU, TIGER...A SPIDER WITHOUT WEBS? IT'S JUST NOT NATURAL.
THE END.

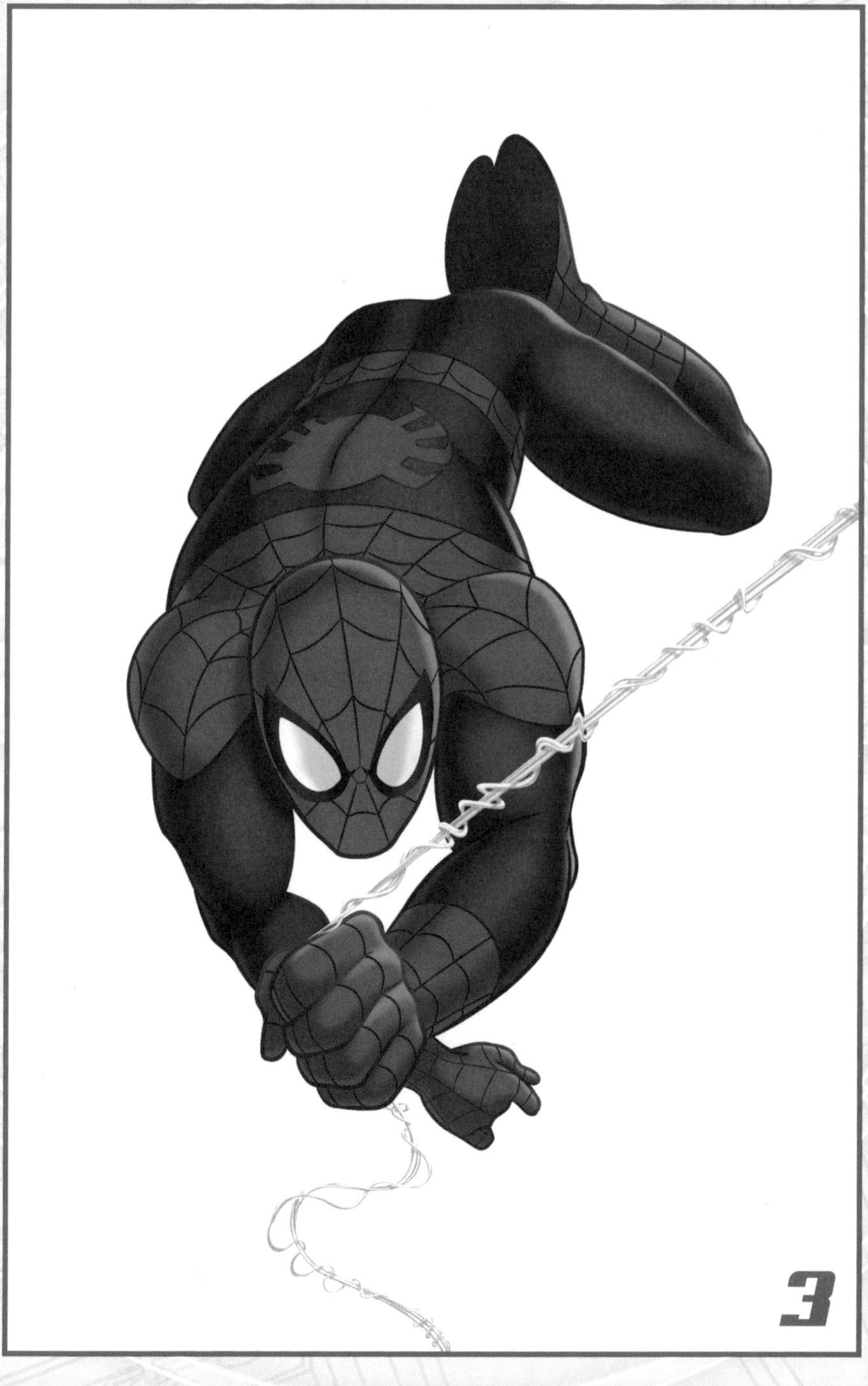

3

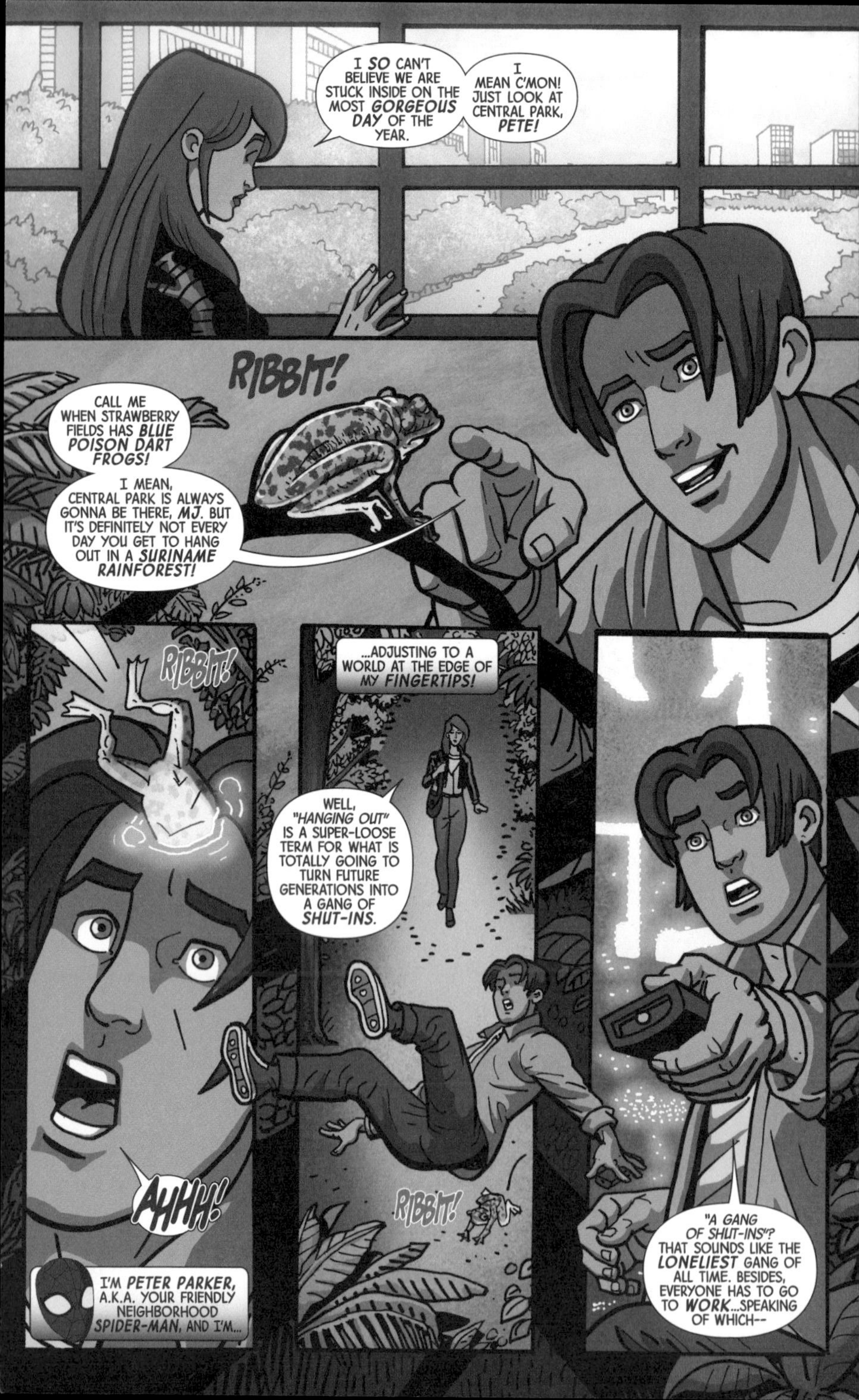
I SO CAN'T BELIEVE WE ARE STUCK INSIDE ON THE MOST GORGEOUS DAY OF THE YEAR.
I MEAN C'MON! JUST LOOK AT CENTRAL PARK, PETE!
RIBBIT!
CALL ME WHEN STRAWBERRY FIELDS HAS BLUE POISON DART FROGS!
I MEAN, CENTRAL PARK IS ALWAYS GONNA BE THERE, MJ. BUT IT'S DEFINITELY NOT EVERY DAY YOU GET TO HANG OUT IN A SURINAME RAINFOREST!
RIBBIT!
AHHH!
I'M PETER PARKER, A.K.A. YOUR FRIENDLY NEIGHBORHOOD SPIDER-MAN, AND I'M...
...ADJUSTING TO A WORLD AT THE EDGE OF MY FINGERTIPS!
WELL, "HANGING OUT" IS A SUPER-LOOSE TERM FOR WHAT IS TOTALLY GOING TO TURN FUTURE GENERATIONS INTO A GANG OF SHUT-INS.
RIBBIT!
"A GANG OF SHUT-INS"? THAT SOUNDS LIKE THE LONELIEST GANG OF ALL TIME. BESIDES, EVERYONE HAS TO GO TO WORK...SPEAKING OF WHICH--

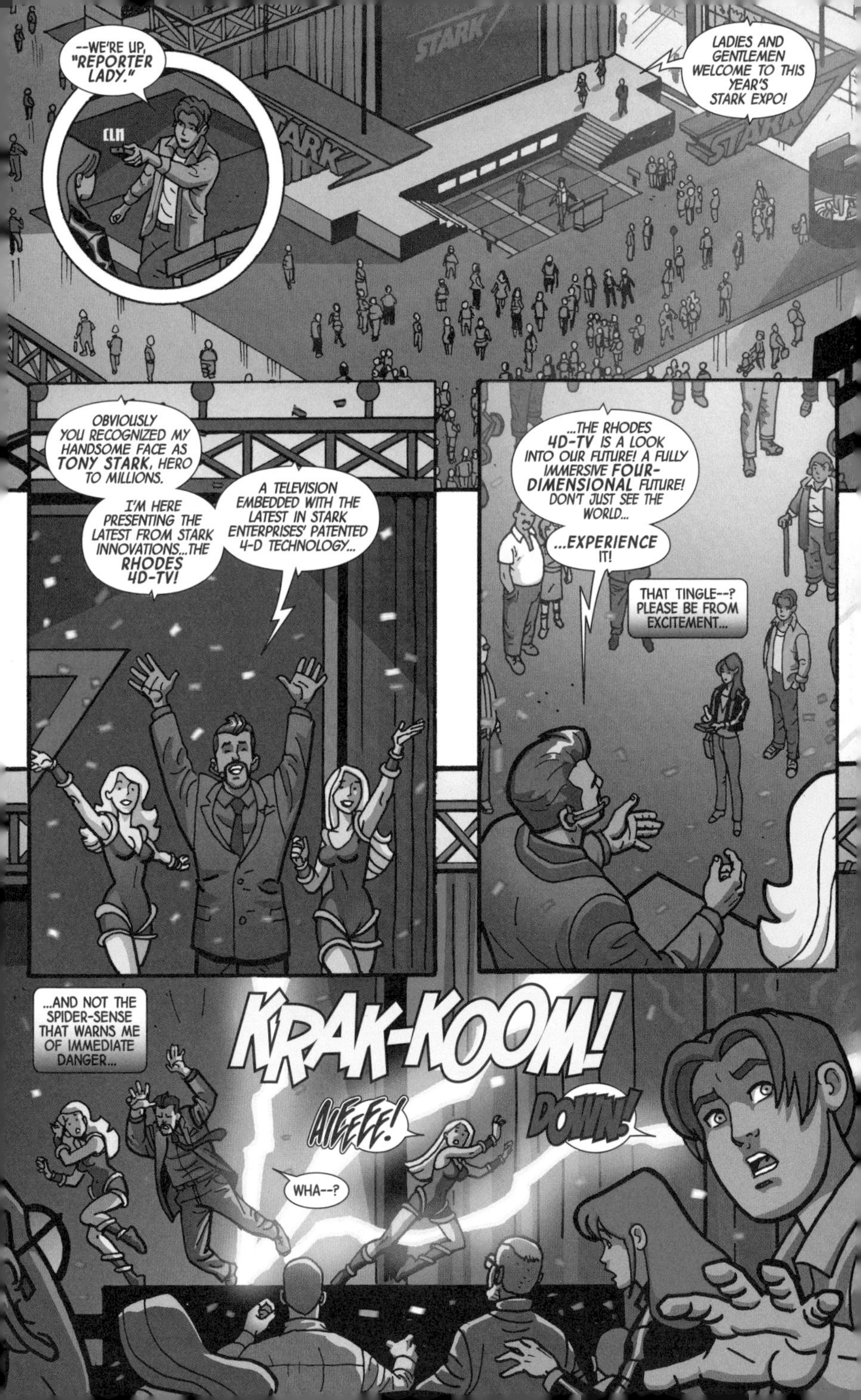
--WE'RE UP, "REPORTER LADY."
LADIES AND GENTLEMEN WELCOME TO THIS YEAR'S STARK EXPO!
OBVIOUSLY YOU RECOGNIZED MY HANDSOME FACE AS TONY STARK, HERO TO MILLIONS.
I'M HERE PRESENTING THE LATEST FROM STARK INNOVATIONS...THE RHODES 4D-TV!
A TELEVISION EMBEDDED WITH THE LATEST IN STARK ENTERPRISES' PATENTED 4-D TECHNOLOGY...
...THE RHODES 4D-TV IS A LOOK INTO OUR FUTURE! A FULLY IMMERSIVE FOUR-DIMENSIONAL FUTURE! DON'T JUST SEE THE WORLD...
...EXPERIENCE IT!
THAT TINGLE--? PLEASE BE FROM EXCITEMENT...
...AND NOT THE SPIDER-SENSE THAT WARNS ME OF IMMEDIATE DANGER...
KRAK-KOOM!
AIEEEE!
DOWN!
WHA--?

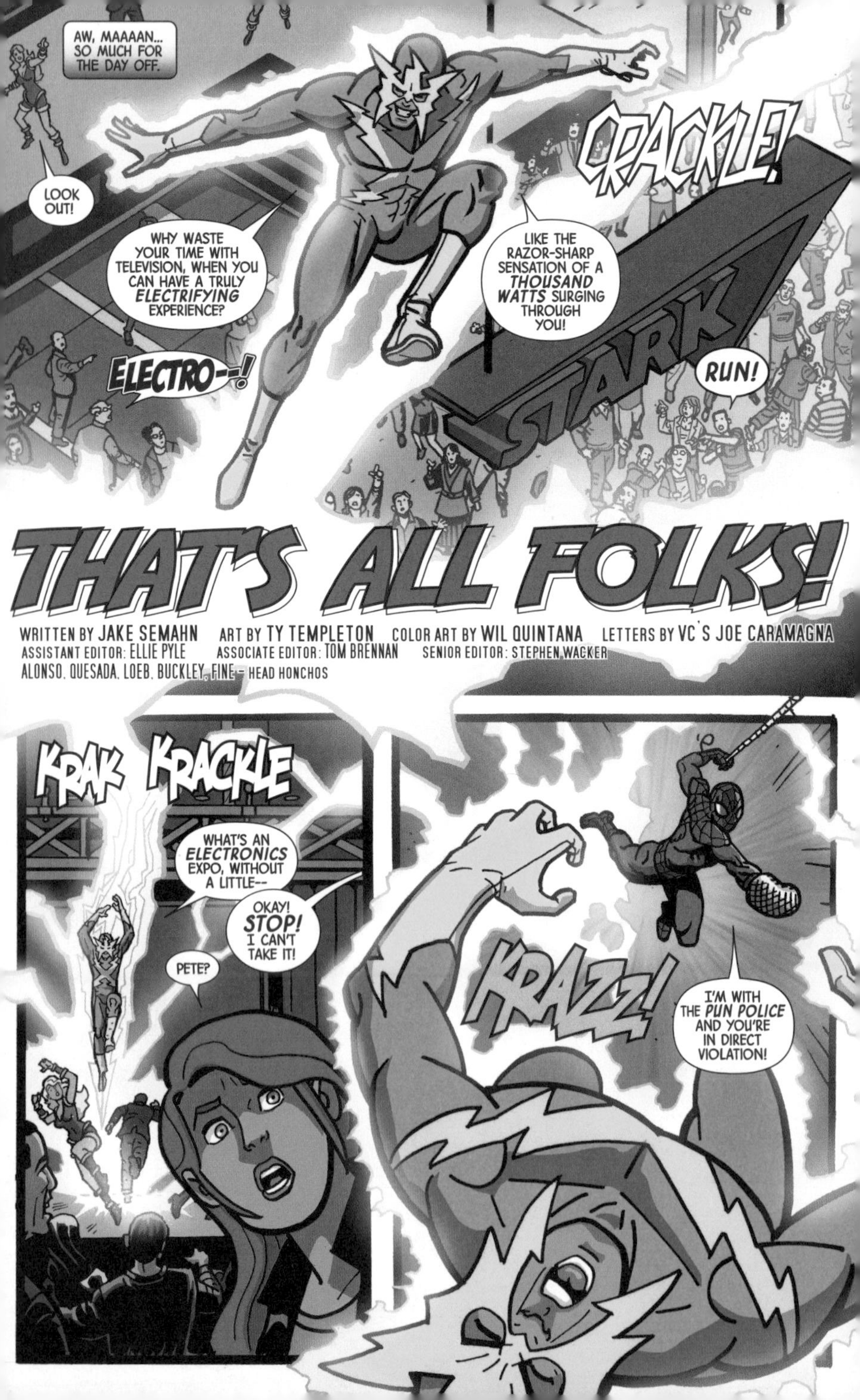
AW, MAAAAN... SO MUCH FOR THE DAY OFF.
LOOK OUT!
WHY WASTE YOUR TIME WITH TELEVISION, WHEN YOU CAN HAVE A TRULY ELECTRIFYING EXPERIENCE?
LIKE THE RAZOR-SHARP SENSATION OF A THOUSAND WATTS SURGING THROUGH YOU!
CRACKLE!
STARK
ELECTRO--!
RUN!
THAT'S ALL FOLKS!
WRITTEN BY JAKE SEMAHN ART BY TY TEMPLETON COLOR ART BY WIL QUINTANA LETTERS BY VC'S JOE CARAMAGNA
ASSISTANT EDITOR: ELLIE PYLE ASSOCIATE EDITOR: TOM BRENNAN SENIOR EDITOR: STEPHEN WACKER
ALONSO, QUESADA, LOEB, BUCKLEY, FINE – HEAD HONCHOS
KRAK KRACKLE
WHAT'S AN ELECTRONICS EXPO, WITHOUT A LITTLE--
OKAY! STOP! I CAN'T TAKE IT!
PETE?
KRAZZ!
I'M WITH THE PUN POLICE AND YOU'RE IN DIRECT VIOLATION!

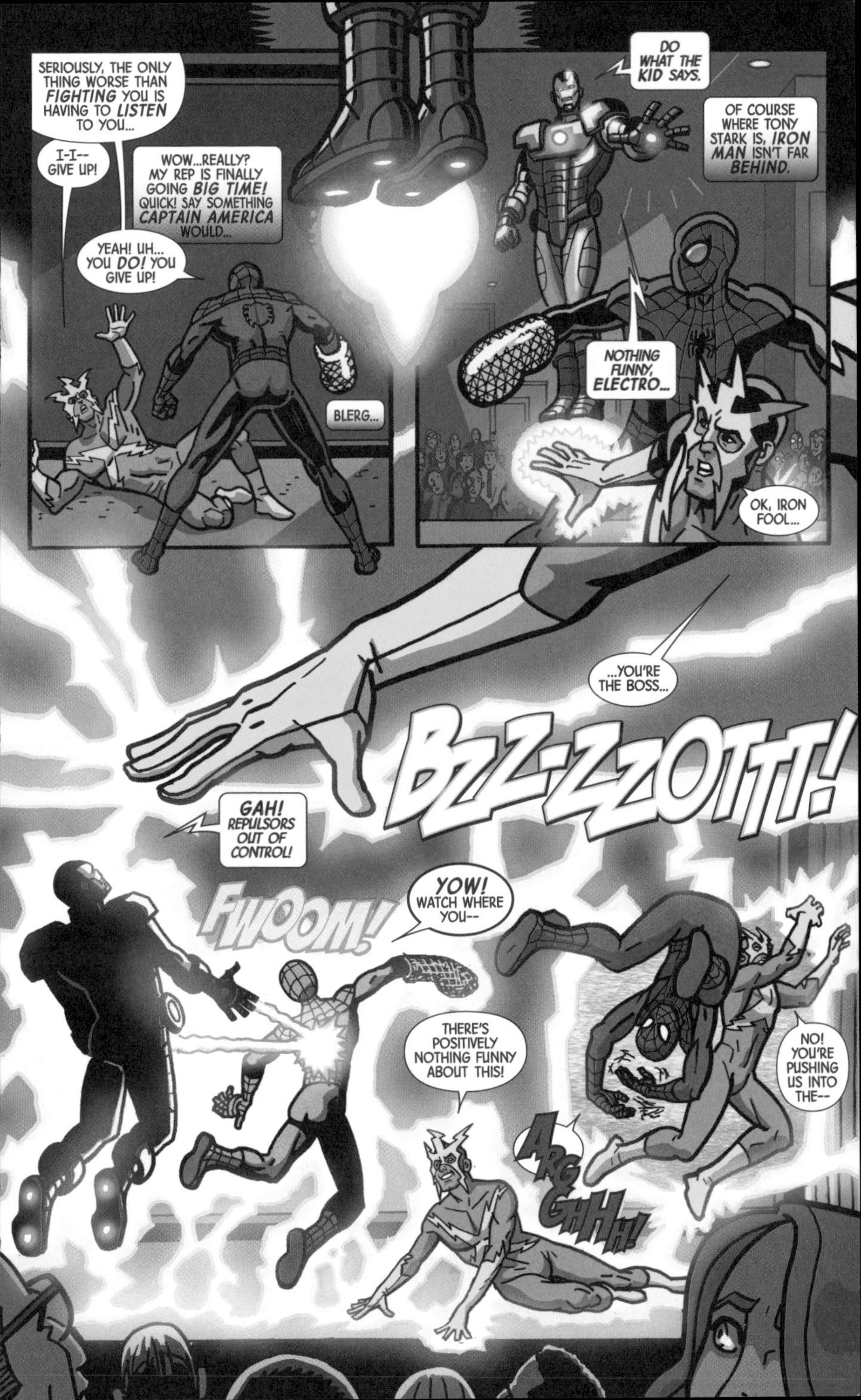
SERIOUSLY, THE ONLY THING WORSE THAN FIGHTING YOU IS HAVING TO LISTEN TO YOU...
I-I-- GIVE UP!
WOW...REALLY? MY REP IS FINALLY GOING BIG TIME! QUICK! SAY SOMETHING CAPTAIN AMERICA WOULD...
YEAH! UH... YOU DO! YOU GIVE UP!
BLERG...
DO WHAT THE KID SAYS.
OF COURSE WHERE TONY STARK IS, IRON MAN ISN'T FAR BEHIND.
NOTHING FUNNY, ELECTRO...
OK, IRON FOOL...
...YOU'RE THE BOSS...
BZZ-ZZZOTTT!
GAH! REPULSORS OUT OF CONTROL!
FWOOM!
YOW! WATCH WHERE YOU--
THERE'S POSITIVELY NOTHING FUNNY ABOUT THIS!
NO! YOU'RE PUSHING US INTO THE--
ARGGHHH!

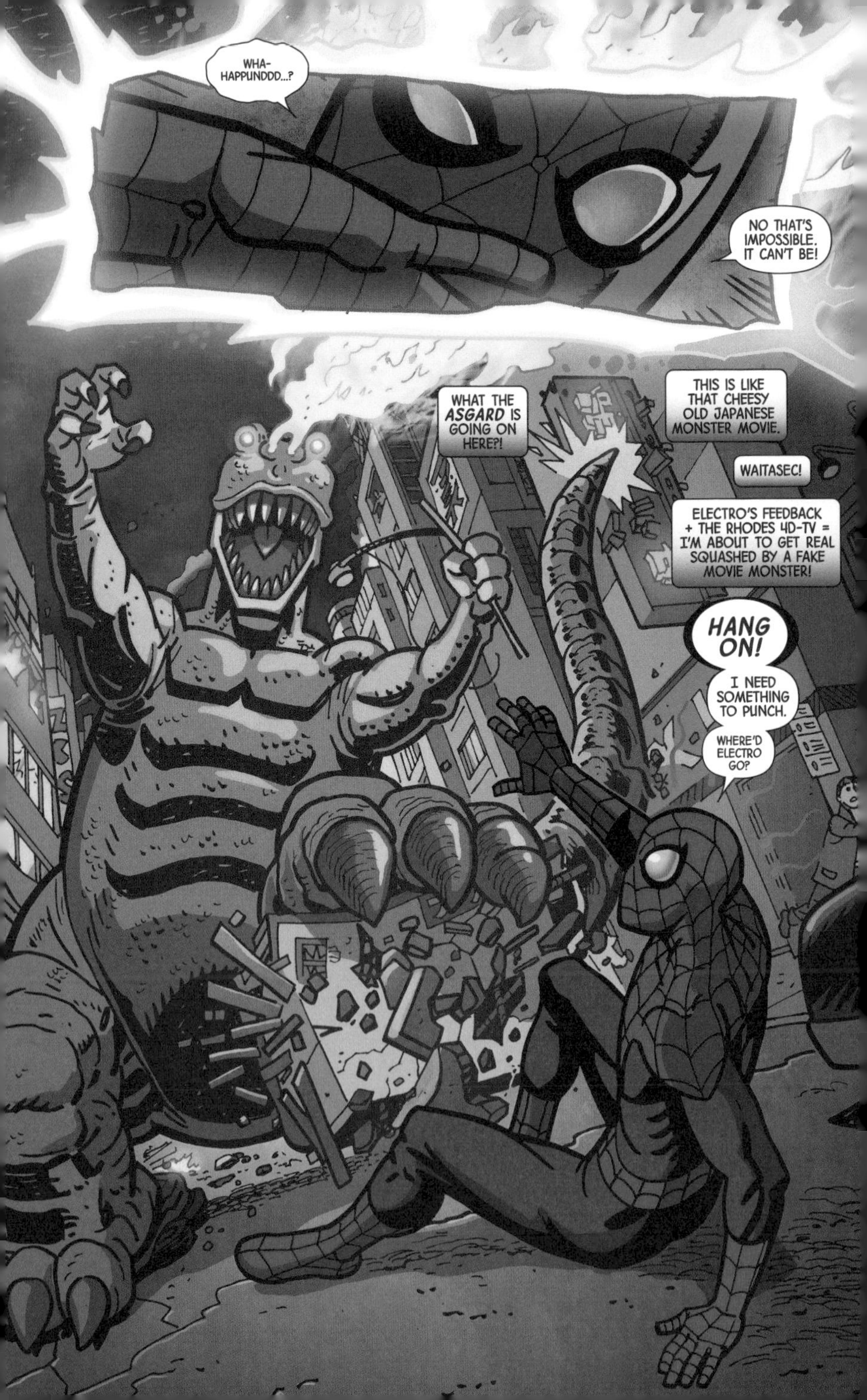
WHA-HAPPUNDDD...?
NO THAT'S IMPOSSIBLE. IT CAN'T BE!
WHAT THE ASGARD IS GOING ON HERE?!
THIS IS LIKE THAT CHEESY OLD JAPANESE MONSTER MOVIE.
WAITASEC!
ELECTRO'S FEEDBACK + THE RHODES 4D-TV = I'M ABOUT TO GET REAL SQUASHED BY A FAKE MOVIE MONSTER!
HANG ON!
I NEED SOMETHING TO PUNCH.
WHERE'D ELECTRO GO?

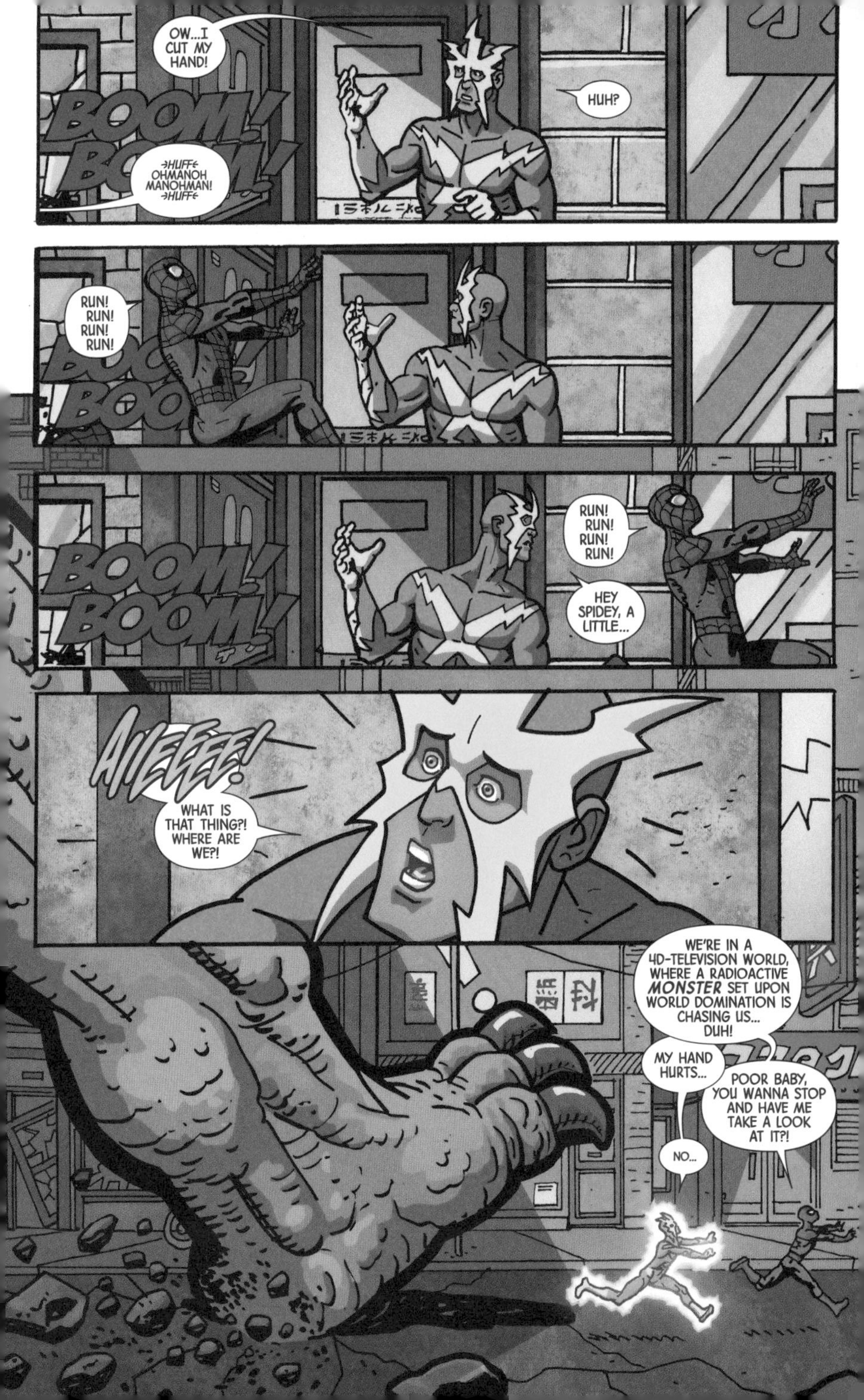
OW...I CUT MY HAND!
HUH?
BOOM! BOOM!
→HUFF← OHMANOH MANOHMAN! →HUFF←
RUN! RUN! RUN! RUN!
BOOM! BOOM!
RUN! RUN! RUN! RUN!
HEY SPIDEY, A LITTLE...
AIIEEEE!
WHAT IS THAT THING?! WHERE ARE WE?!
WE'RE IN A 4D-TELEVISION WORLD, WHERE A RADIOACTIVE *MONSTER* SET UPON WORLD DOMINATION IS CHASING US... DUH!
MY HAND HURTS...
POOR BABY, YOU WANNA STOP AND HAVE ME TAKE A LOOK AT IT?!
NO...

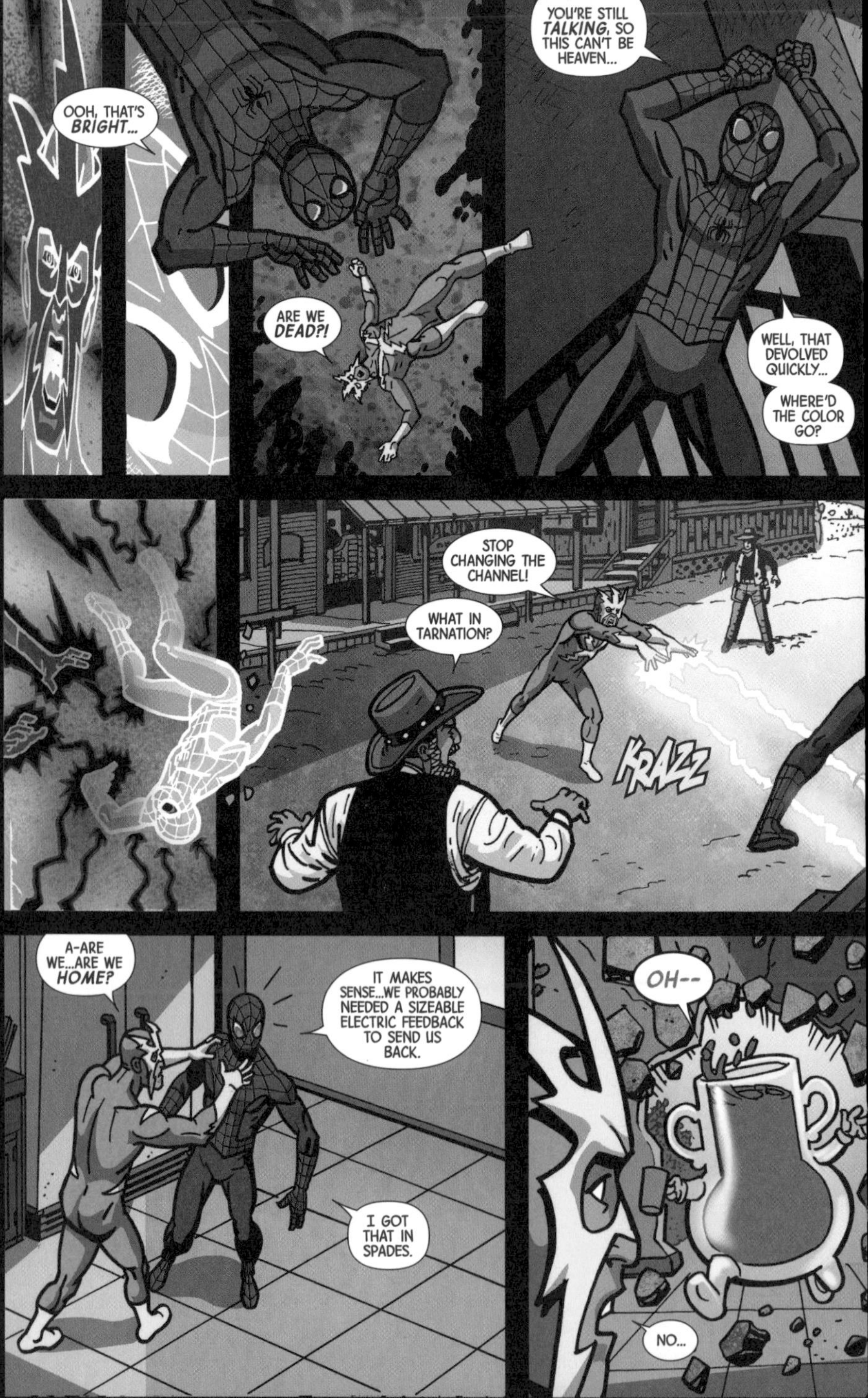
OOH, THAT'S BRIGHT...
ARE WE DEAD?!
YOU'RE STILL TALKING, SO THIS CAN'T BE HEAVEN...
WELL, THAT DEVOLVED QUICKLY...
WHERE'D THE COLOR GO?
STOP CHANGING THE CHANNEL!
WHAT IN TARNATION?
KRAZZ
A-ARE WE...ARE WE HOME?
IT MAKES SENSE...WE PROBABLY NEEDED A SIZEABLE ELECTRIC FEEDBACK TO SEND US BACK.
I GOT THAT IN SPADES.
OH--
NO...

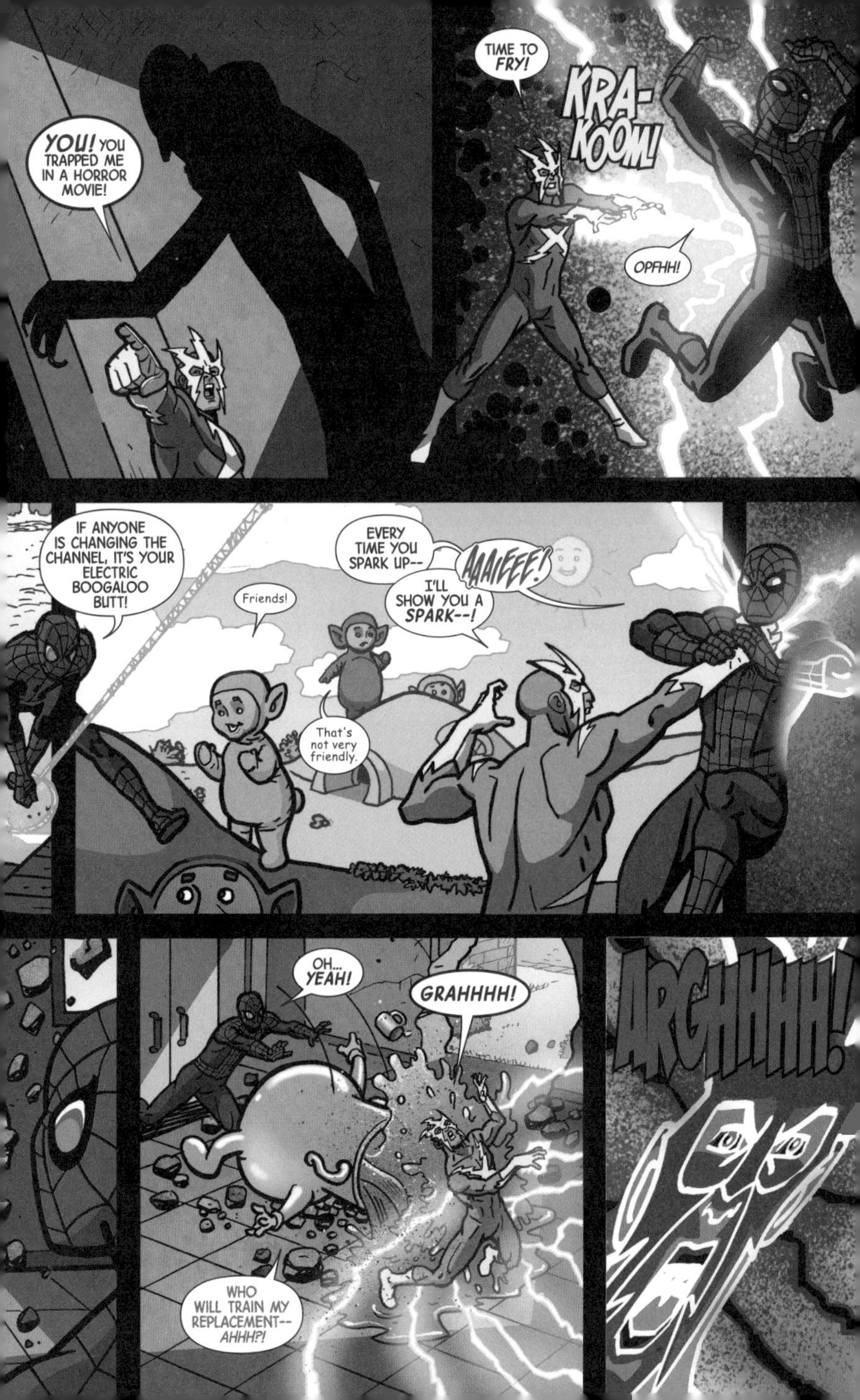
YOU! YOU TRAPPED ME IN A HORROR MOVIE!
TIME TO FRY!
KRA-KOOM!
OPFHH!
IF ANYONE IS CHANGING THE CHANNEL, IT'S YOUR ELECTRIC BOOGALOO BUTT!
Friends!
EVERY TIME YOU SPARK UP--
AAAIEEE!
I'LL SHOW YOU A SPARK--!
That's not very friendly.
OH... YEAH!
GRAHHHH!
WHO WILL TRAIN MY REPLACEMENT-- AHHH?!
ARGHHHH!

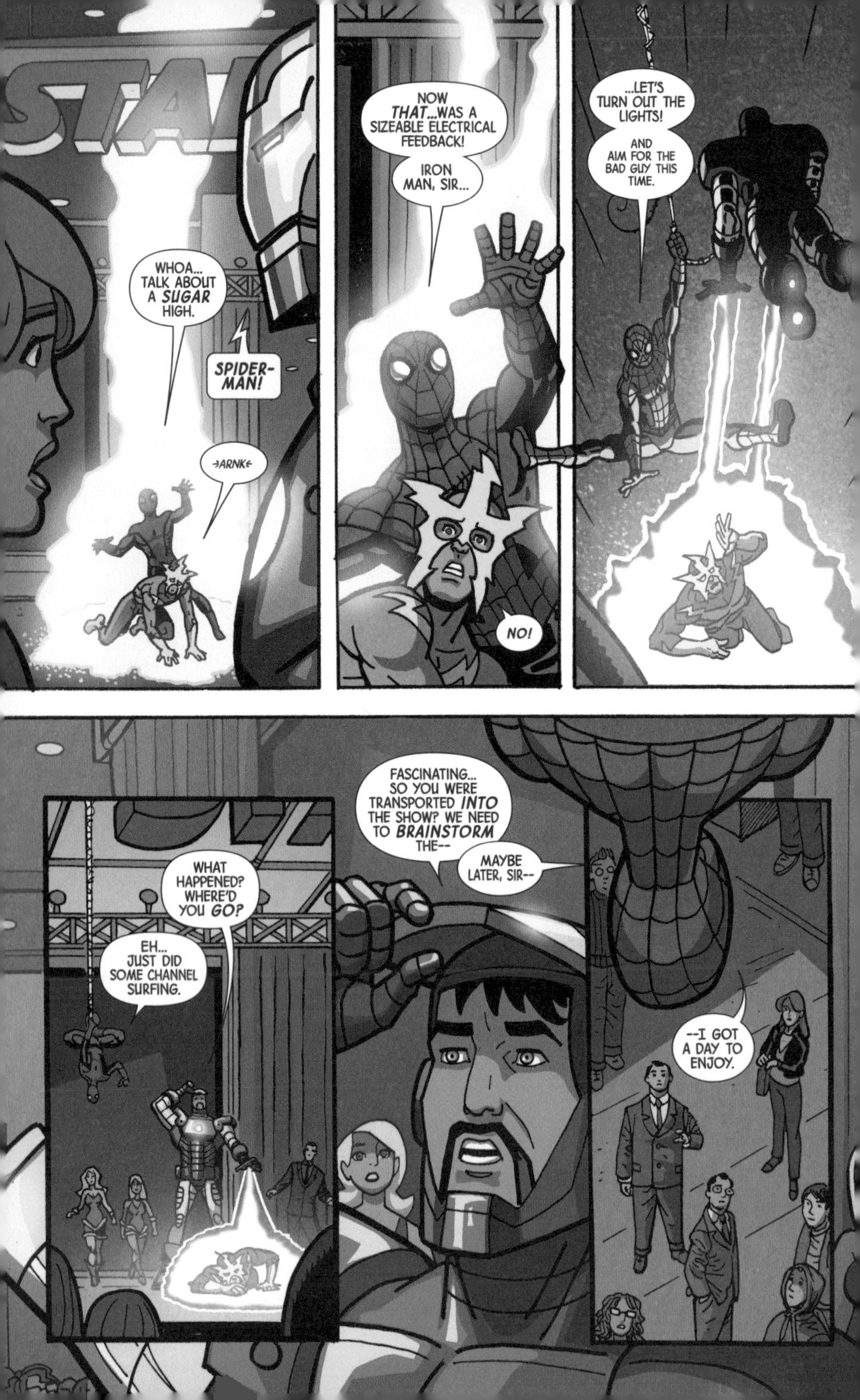
WHOA... TALK ABOUT A SUGAR HIGH.
SPIDER-MAN!
ARNK
NOW THAT...WAS A SIZEABLE ELECTRICAL FEEDBACK!
IRON MAN, SIR...
NO!
...LET'S TURN OUT THE LIGHTS!
AND AIM FOR THE BAD GUY THIS TIME.
WHAT HAPPENED? WHERE'D YOU GO?
EH... JUST DID SOME CHANNEL SURFING.
FASCINATING... SO YOU WERE TRANSPORTED INTO THE SHOW? WE NEED TO BRAINSTORM THE--
MAYBE LATER, SIR--
--I GOT A DAY TO ENJOY.

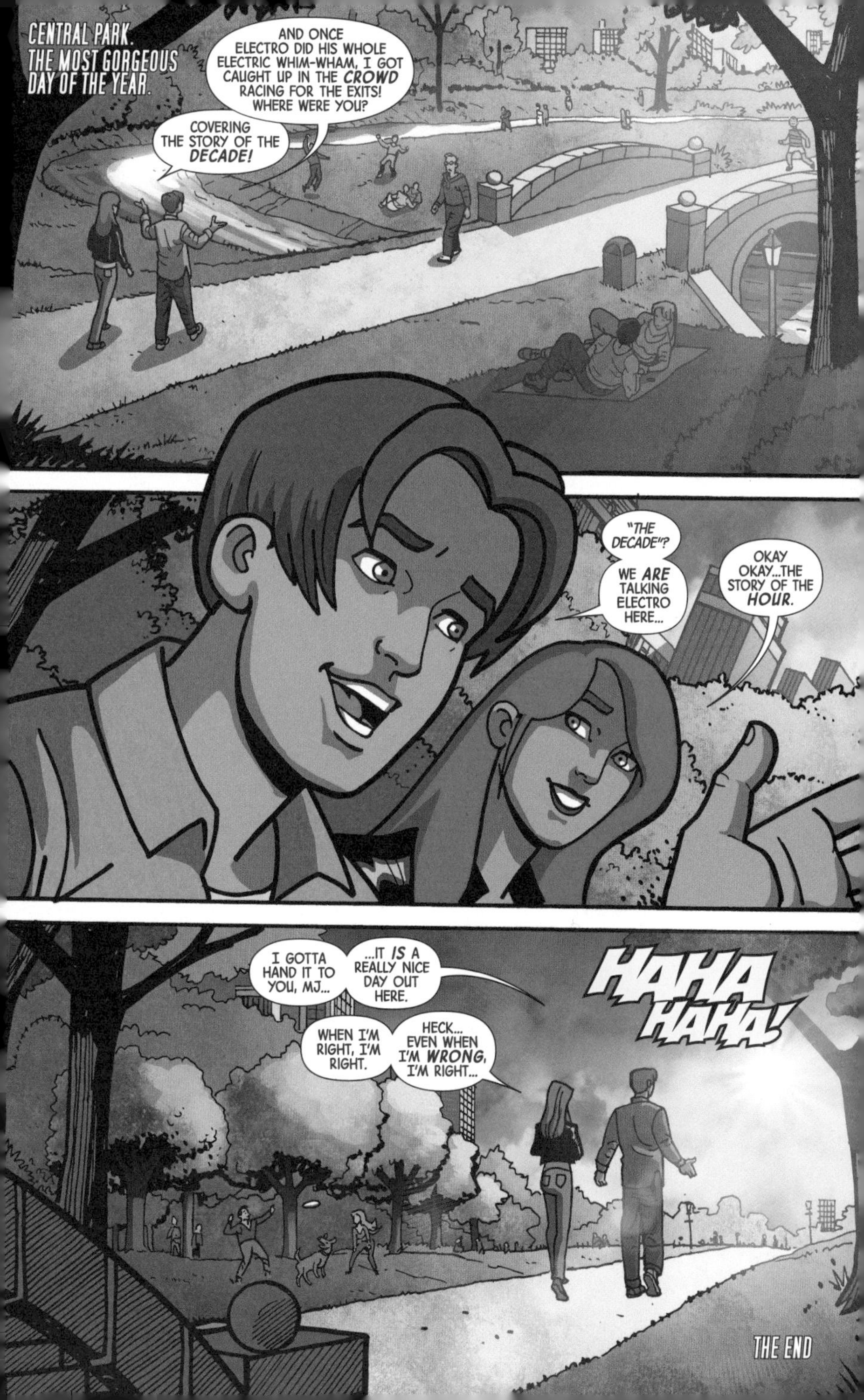
CENTRAL PARK. THE MOST GORGEOUS DAY OF THE YEAR.
AND ONCE ELECTRO DID HIS WHOLE ELECTRIC WHIM-WHAM, I GOT CAUGHT UP IN THE CROWD RACING FOR THE EXITS! WHERE WERE YOU?
COVERING THE STORY OF THE DECADE!
"THE DECADE"?
WE ARE TALKING ELECTRO HERE...
OKAY OKAY...THE STORY OF THE HOUR.
I GOTTA HAND IT TO YOU, MJ...
...IT IS A REALLY NICE DAY OUT HERE.
WHEN I'M RIGHT, I'M RIGHT.
HECK... EVEN WHEN I'M WRONG, I'M RIGHT...
HAHA HAHA!
THE END

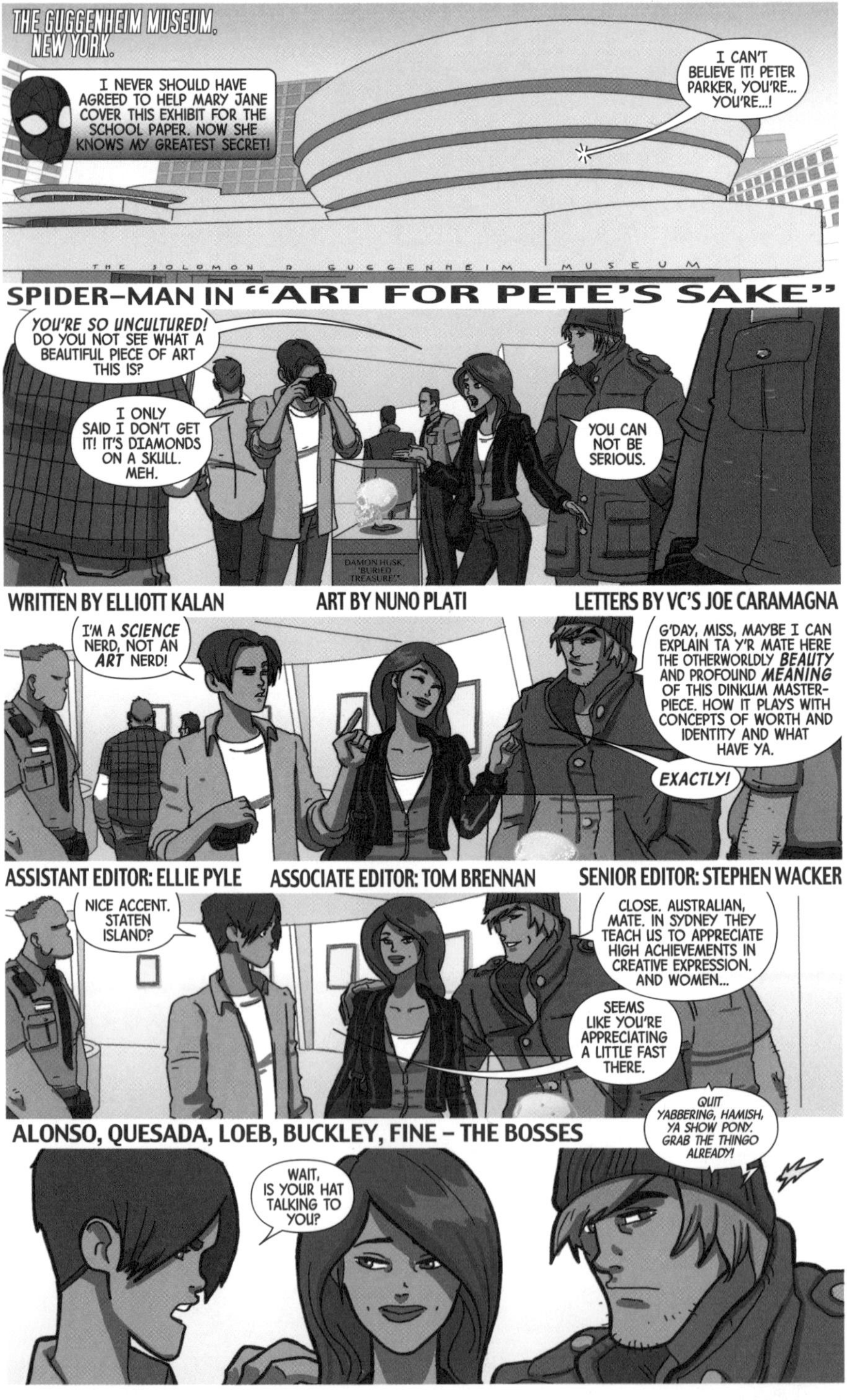
THE GUGGENHEIM MUSEUM, NEW YORK.
I NEVER SHOULD HAVE AGREED TO HELP MARY JANE COVER THIS EXHIBIT FOR THE SCHOOL PAPER. NOW SHE KNOWS MY GREATEST SECRET!
I CAN'T BELIEVE IT! PETER PARKER, YOU'RE... YOU'RE...!
THE SOLOMON R GUGGENHEIM MUSEUM
SPIDER-MAN IN "ART FOR PETE'S SAKE"
YOU'RE SO UNCULTURED! DO YOU NOT SEE WHAT A BEAUTIFUL PIECE OF ART THIS IS?
I ONLY SAID I DON'T GET IT! IT'S DIAMONDS ON A SKULL. MEH.
YOU CAN NOT BE SERIOUS.
DAMON HUSK, 'BURIED TREASURE'.
WRITTEN BY ELLIOTT KALAN
ART BY NUNO PLATI
LETTERS BY VC'S JOE CARAMAGNA
I'M A SCIENCE NERD, NOT AN ART NERD!
G'DAY, MISS, MAYBE I CAN EXPLAIN TA Y'R MATE HERE THE OTHERWORLDLY BEAUTY AND PROFOUND MEANING OF THIS DINKUM MASTER-PIECE. HOW IT PLAYS WITH CONCEPTS OF WORTH AND IDENTITY AND WHAT HAVE YA.
EXACTLY!
ASSISTANT EDITOR: ELLIE PYLE
ASSOCIATE EDITOR: TOM BRENNAN
SENIOR EDITOR: STEPHEN WACKER
NICE ACCENT. STATEN ISLAND?
CLOSE. AUSTRALIAN, MATE. IN SYDNEY THEY TEACH US TO APPRECIATE HIGH ACHIEVEMENTS IN CREATIVE EXPRESSION. AND WOMEN...
SEEMS LIKE YOU'RE APPRECIATING A LITTLE FAST THERE.
ALONSO, QUESADA, LOEB, BUCKLEY, FINE – THE BOSSES
QUIT YABBERING, HAMISH, YA SHOW PONY. GRAB THE THINGO ALREADY!
WAIT, IS YOUR HAT TALKING TO YOU?

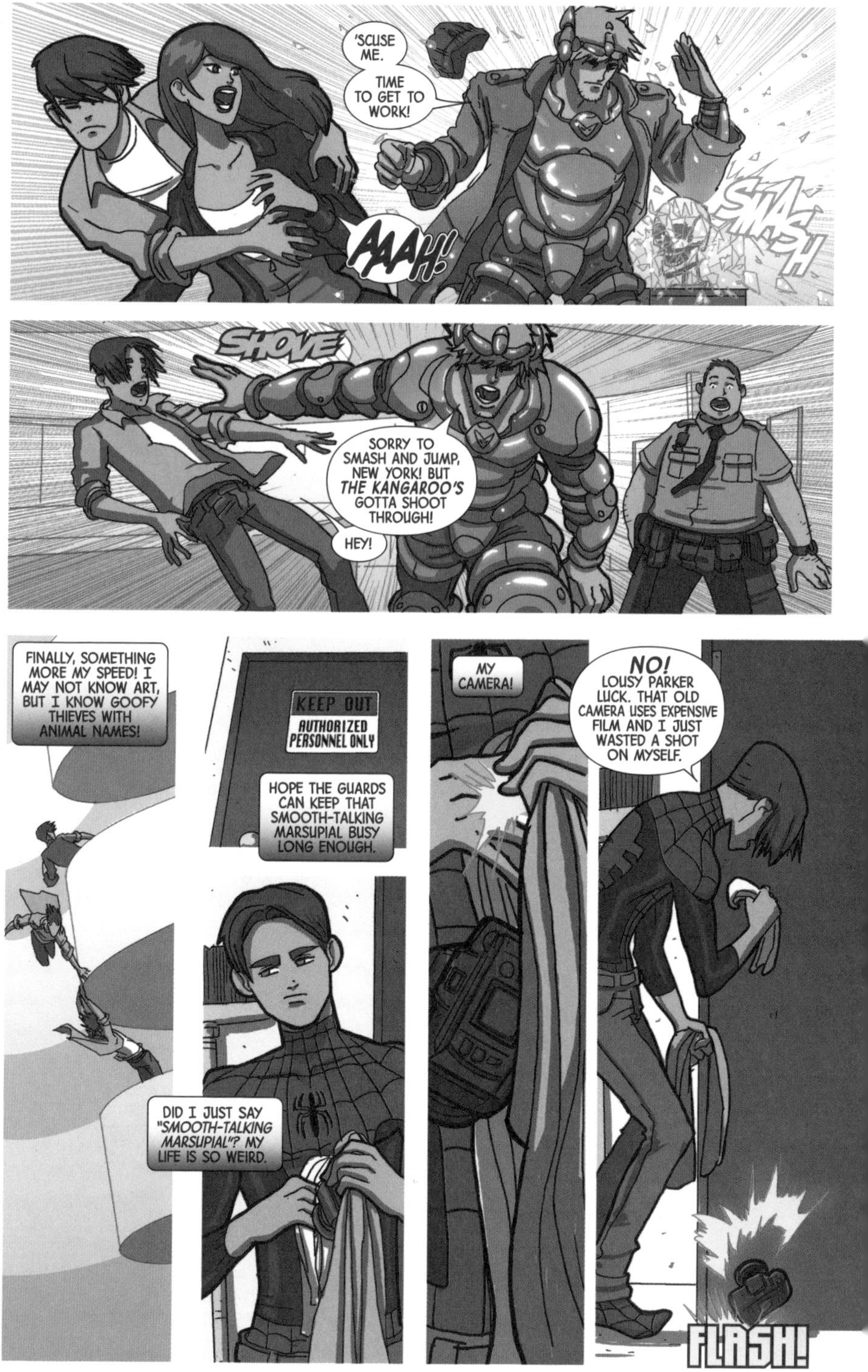
'SCUSE ME.
TIME TO GET TO WORK!
AAAH!
SMASH
SHOVE
SORRY TO SMASH AND JUMP, NEW YORK! BUT THE KANGAROO'S GOTTA SHOOT THROUGH!
HEY!
FINALLY, SOMETHING MORE MY SPEED! I MAY NOT KNOW ART, BUT I KNOW GOOFY THIEVES WITH ANIMAL NAMES!
KEEP OUT
AUTHORIZED PERSONNEL ONLY
HOPE THE GUARDS CAN KEEP THAT SMOOTH-TALKING MARSUPIAL BUSY LONG ENOUGH.
DID I JUST SAY "SMOOTH-TALKING MARSUPIAL"? MY LIFE IS SO WEIRD.
MY CAMERA!
NO! LOUSY PARKER LUCK. THAT OLD CAMERA USES EXPENSIVE FILM AND I JUST WASTED A SHOT ON MYSELF.
FLASH!

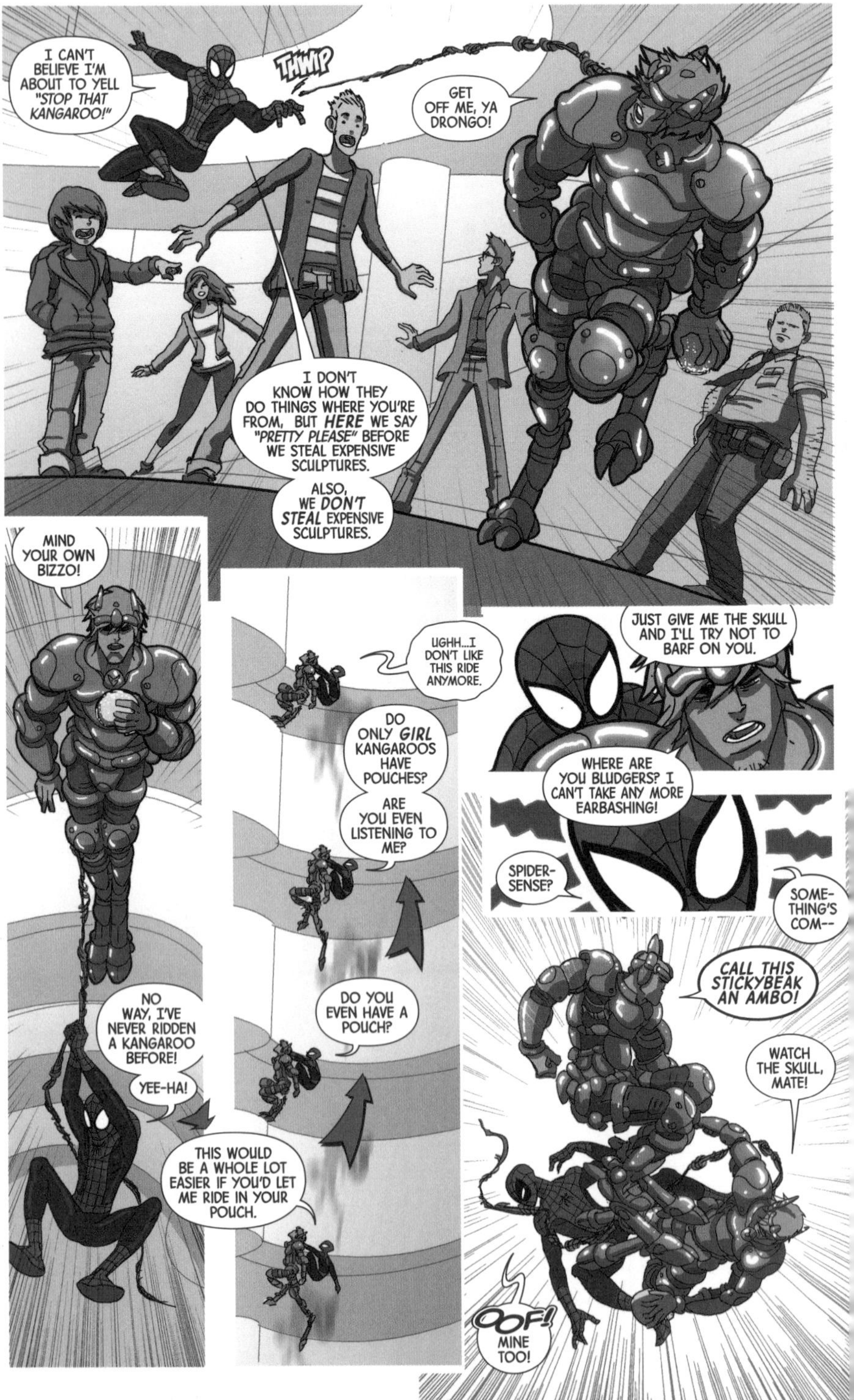

I CAN'T BELIEVE I'M ABOUT TO YELL "STOP THAT KANGAROO!"
THWIP
GET OFF ME, YA DRONGO!
I DON'T KNOW HOW THEY DO THINGS WHERE YOU'RE FROM, BUT HERE WE SAY "PRETTY PLEASE" BEFORE WE STEAL EXPENSIVE SCULPTURES.
ALSO, WE DON'T STEAL EXPENSIVE SCULPTURES.
MIND YOUR OWN BIZZO!
NO WAY, I'VE NEVER RIDDEN A KANGAROO BEFORE!
YEE-HA!
UGHH...I DON'T LIKE THIS RIDE ANYMORE.
DO ONLY GIRL KANGAROOS HAVE POUCHES?
ARE YOU EVEN LISTENING TO ME?
DO YOU EVEN HAVE A POUCH?
THIS WOULD BE A WHOLE LOT EASIER IF YOU'D LET ME RIDE IN YOUR POUCH.
JUST GIVE ME THE SKULL AND I'LL TRY NOT TO BARF ON YOU.
WHERE ARE YOU BLUDGERS? I CAN'T TAKE ANY MORE EARBASHING!
SPIDER-SENSE?
SOME-THING'S COM--
CALL THIS STICKYBEAK AN AMBO!
WATCH THE SKULL, MATE!
OOF!
MINE TOO!

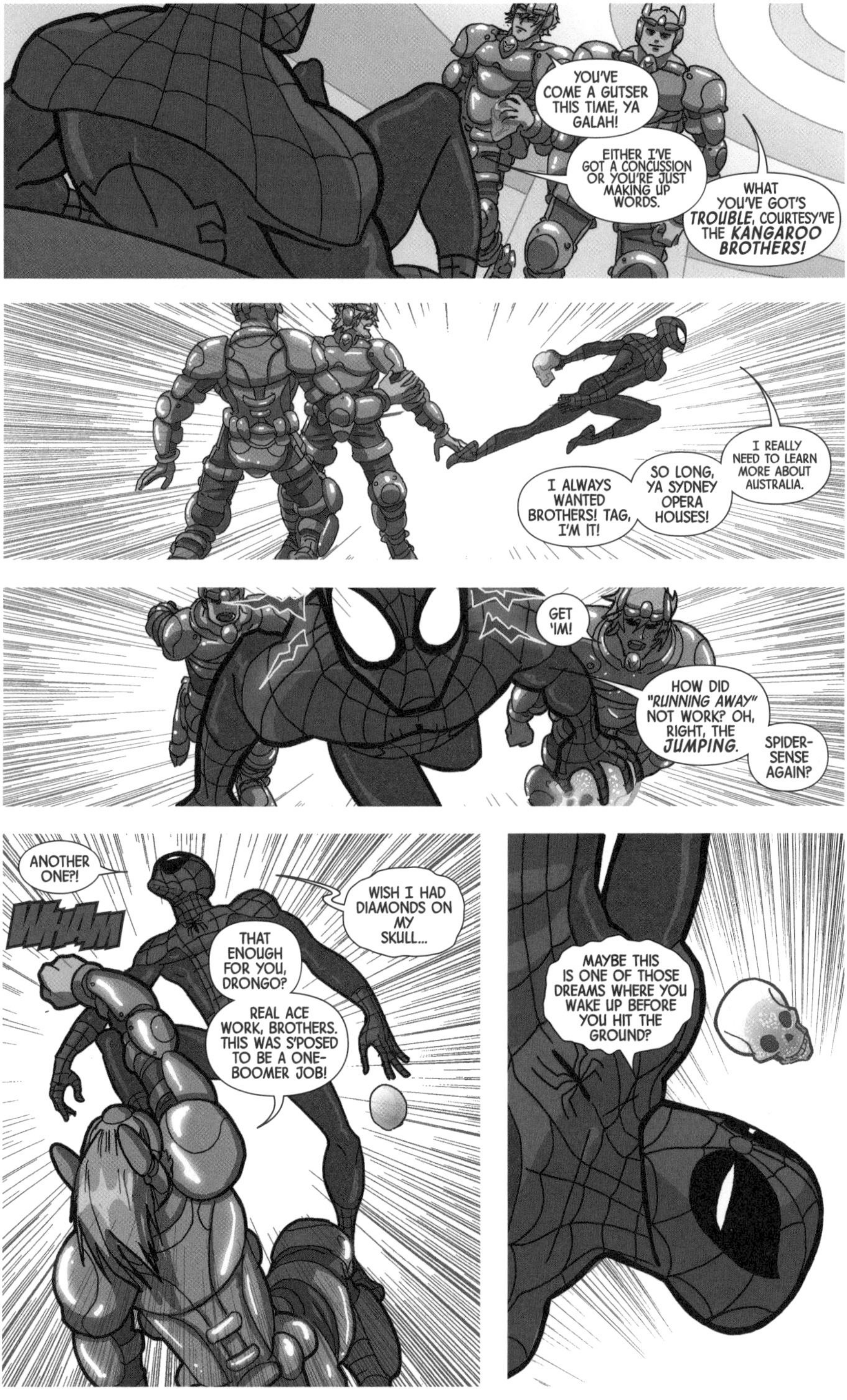
YOU'VE COME A GUTSER THIS TIME, YA GALAH!
EITHER I'VE GOT A CONCUSSION OR YOU'RE JUST MAKING UP WORDS.
WHAT YOU'VE GOT'S TROUBLE, COURTESY'VE THE KANGAROO BROTHERS!
I ALWAYS WANTED BROTHERS! TAG, I'M IT!
SO LONG, YA SYDNEY OPERA HOUSES!
I REALLY NEED TO LEARN MORE ABOUT AUSTRALIA.
GET 'IM!
HOW DID "RUNNING AWAY" NOT WORK? OH, RIGHT, THE JUMPING.
SPIDER-SENSE AGAIN?
ANOTHER ONE?!
WHAM
WISH I HAD DIAMONDS ON MY SKULL...
THAT ENOUGH FOR YOU, DRONGO?
REAL ACE WORK, BROTHERS. THIS WAS S'POSED TO BE A ONE-BOOMER JOB!
MAYBE THIS IS ONE OF THOSE DREAMS WHERE YOU WAKE UP BEFORE YOU HIT THE GROUND?

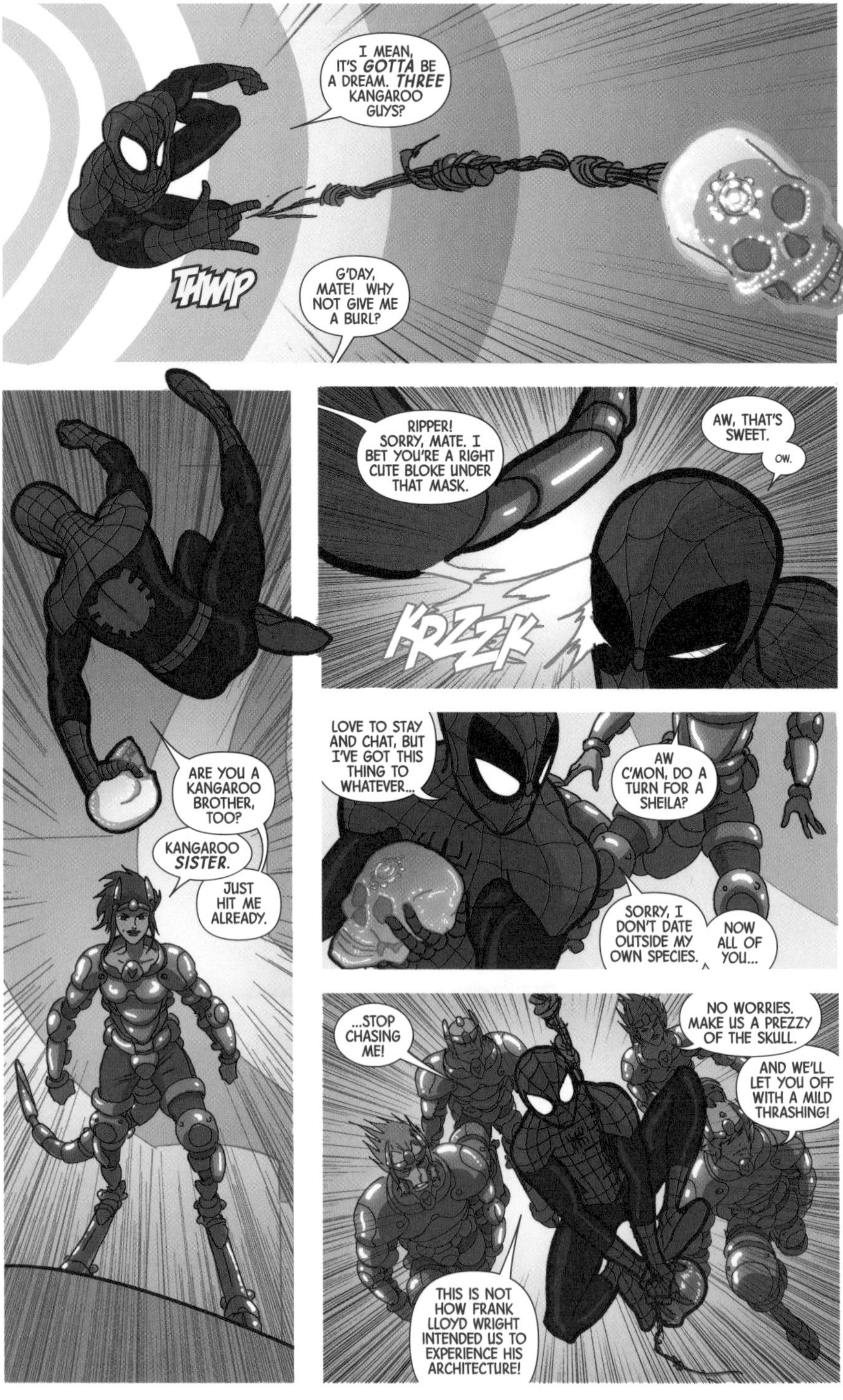

I MEAN, IT'S GOTTA BE A DREAM. THREE KANGAROO GUYS?
THWIP
G'DAY, MATE! WHY NOT GIVE ME A BURL?
ARE YOU A KANGAROO BROTHER, TOO?
KANGAROO SISTER.
JUST HIT ME ALREADY.
RIPPER! SORRY, MATE. I BET YOU'RE A RIGHT CUTE BLOKE UNDER THAT MASK.
AW, THAT'S SWEET.
OW.
KRZZK
LOVE TO STAY AND CHAT, BUT I'VE GOT THIS THING TO WHATEVER...
AW C'MON, DO A TURN FOR A SHEILA?
SORRY, I DON'T DATE OUTSIDE MY OWN SPECIES.
NOW ALL OF YOU...
...STOP CHASING ME!
NO WORRIES. MAKE US A PREZZY OF THE SKULL.
AND WE'LL LET YOU OFF WITH A MILD THRASHING!
THIS IS NOT HOW FRANK LLOYD WRIGHT INTENDED US TO EXPERIENCE HIS ARCHITECTURE!

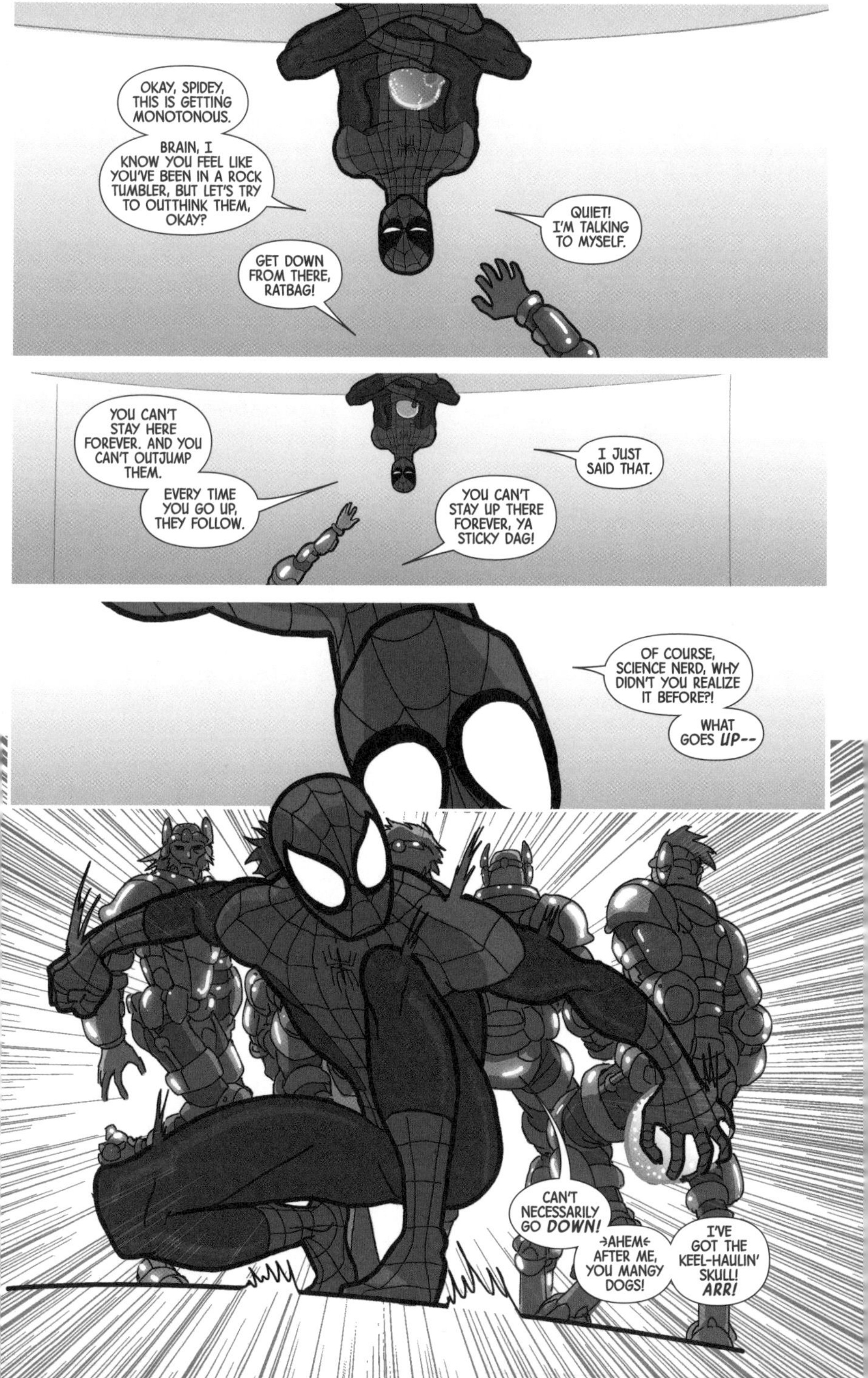
OKAY, SPIDEY, THIS IS GETTING MONOTONOUS.
BRAIN, I KNOW YOU FEEL LIKE YOU'VE BEEN IN A ROCK TUMBLER, BUT LET'S TRY TO OUTTHINK THEM, OKAY?
QUIET! I'M TALKING TO MYSELF.
GET DOWN FROM THERE, RATBAG!
YOU CAN'T STAY HERE FOREVER. AND YOU CAN'T OUTJUMP THEM.
EVERY TIME YOU GO UP, THEY FOLLOW.
I JUST SAID THAT.
YOU CAN'T STAY UP THERE FOREVER, YA STICKY DAG!
OF COURSE, SCIENCE NERD, WHY DIDN'T YOU REALIZE IT BEFORE?!
WHAT GOES UP--
CAN'T NECESSARILY GO DOWN!
→AHEM← AFTER ME, YOU MANGY DOGS!
I'VE GOT THE KEEL-HAULIN' SKULL! ARR!

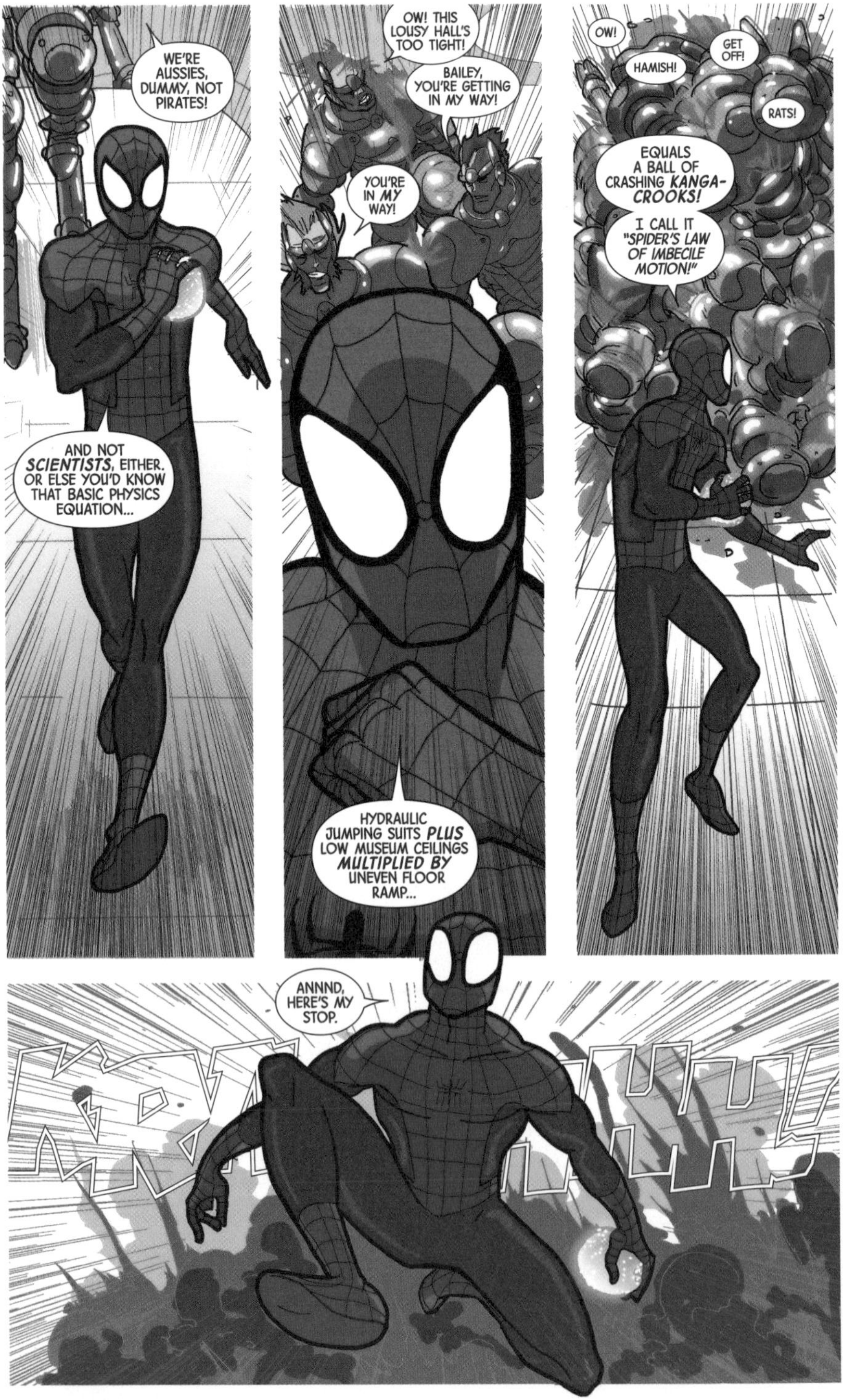
WE'RE AUSSIES, DUMMY, NOT PIRATES!
AND NOT *SCIENTISTS*, EITHER. OR ELSE YOU'D KNOW THAT BASIC PHYSICS EQUATION...
OW! THIS LOUSY HALL'S TOO TIGHT!
BAILEY, YOU'RE GETTING IN MY WAY!
YOU'RE IN *MY* WAY!
HYDRAULIC JUMPING SUITS *PLUS* LOW MUSEUM CEILINGS *MULTIPLIED BY* UNEVEN FLOOR RAMP...
OW!
HAMISH!
GET OFF!
RATS!
EQUALS A BALL OF CRASHING *KANGA-CROOKS!*
I CALL IT *"SPIDER'S LAW OF IMBECILE MOTION!"*
ANNND, HERE'S MY STOP.

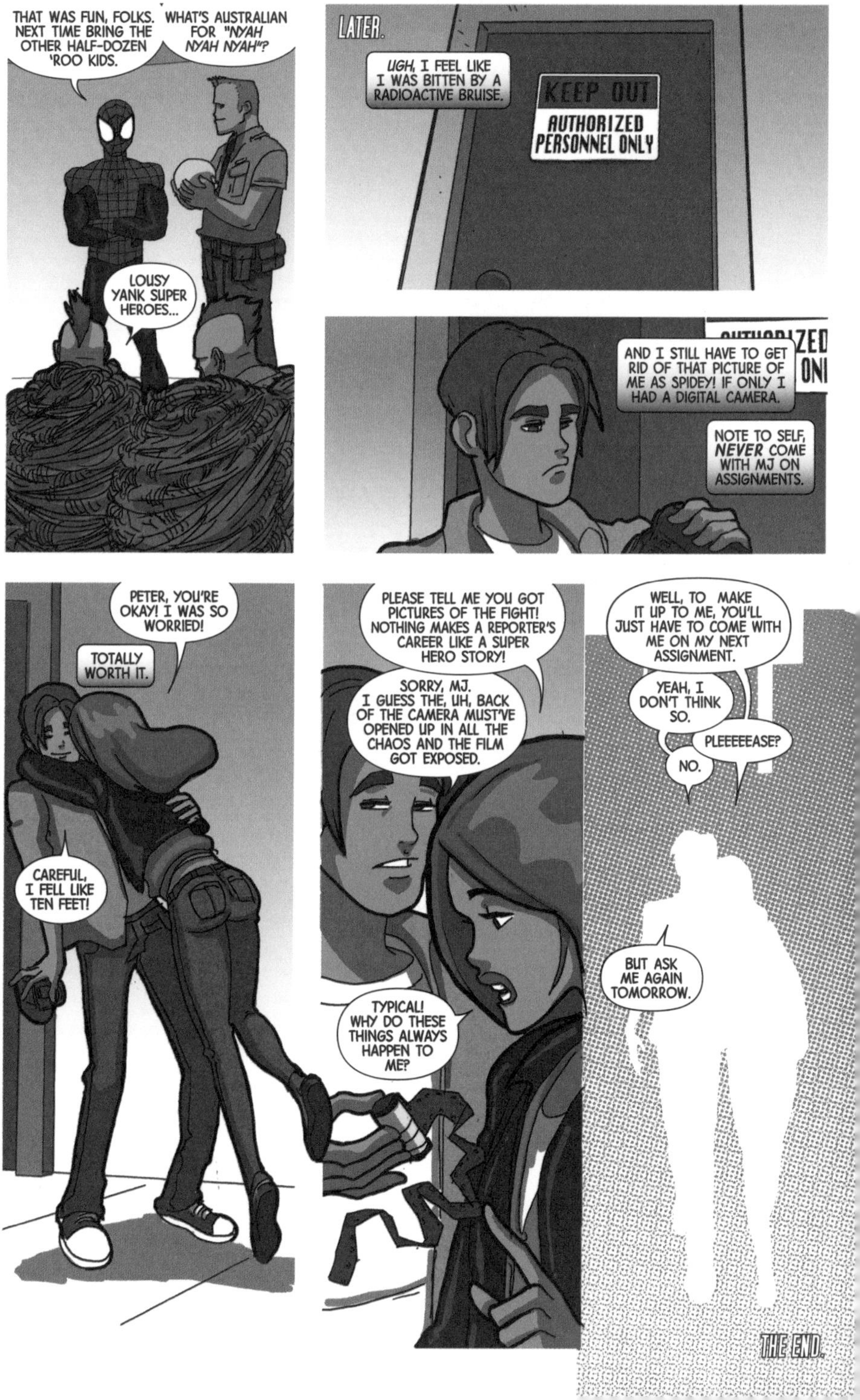
THAT WAS FUN, FOLKS. NEXT TIME BRING THE OTHER HALF-DOZEN 'ROO KIDS.
WHAT'S AUSTRALIAN FOR "NYAH NYAH NYAH"?
LOUSY YANK SUPER HEROES...
LATER.
UGH, I FEEL LIKE I WAS BITTEN BY A RADIOACTIVE BRUISE.
KEEP OUT
AUTHORIZED PERSONNEL ONLY
AND I STILL HAVE TO GET RID OF THAT PICTURE OF ME AS SPIDEY! IF ONLY I HAD A DIGITAL CAMERA.
NOTE TO SELF, NEVER COME WITH MJ ON ASSIGNMENTS.
PETER, YOU'RE OKAY! I WAS SO WORRIED!
TOTALLY WORTH IT.
CAREFUL, I FELL LIKE TEN FEET!
PLEASE TELL ME YOU GOT PICTURES OF THE FIGHT! NOTHING MAKES A REPORTER'S CAREER LIKE A SUPER HERO STORY!
SORRY, MJ. I GUESS THE, UH, BACK OF THE CAMERA MUST'VE OPENED UP IN ALL THE CHAOS AND THE FILM GOT EXPOSED.
TYPICAL! WHY DO THESE THINGS ALWAYS HAPPEN TO ME?
WELL, TO MAKE IT UP TO ME, YOU'LL JUST HAVE TO COME WITH ME ON MY NEXT ASSIGNMENT.
YEAH, I DON'T THINK SO.
PLEEEEEASE?
NO.
BUT ASK ME AGAIN TOMORROW.
THE END.

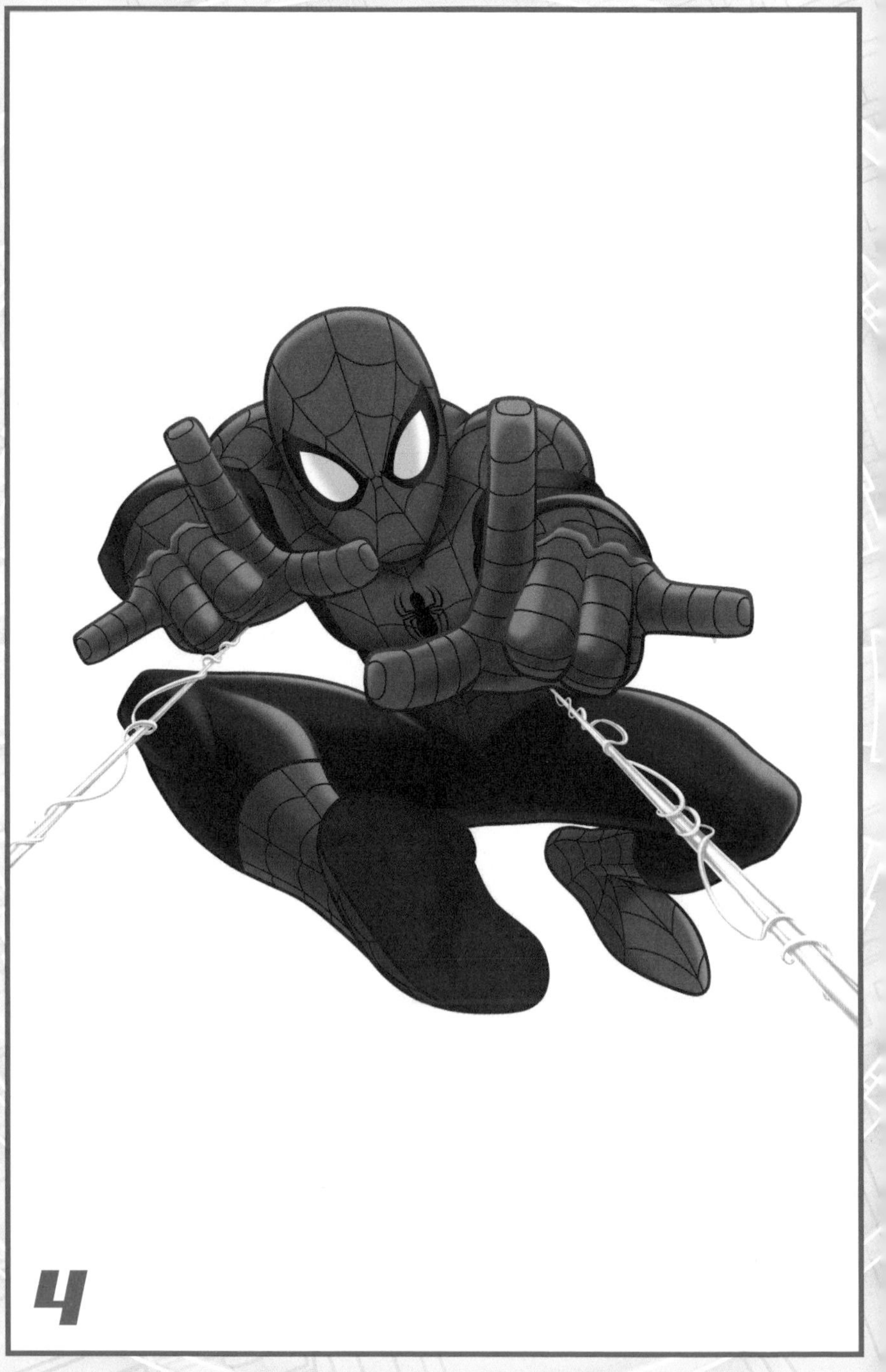

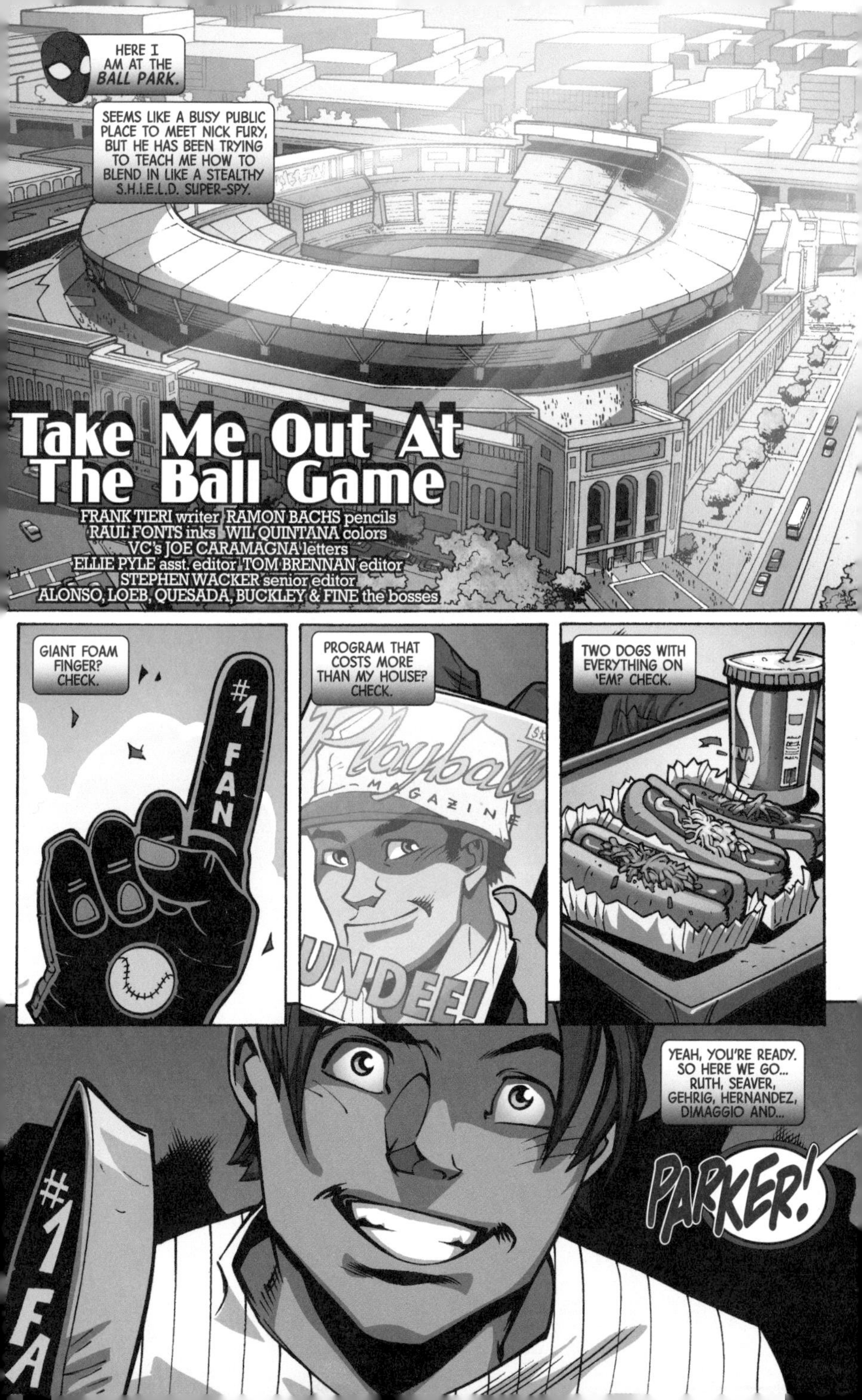
HERE I AM AT THE BALL PARK.
SEEMS LIKE A BUSY PUBLIC PLACE TO MEET NICK FURY, BUT HE HAS BEEN TRYING TO TEACH ME HOW TO BLEND IN LIKE A STEALTHY S.H.I.E.L.D. SUPER-SPY.
Take Me Out At The Ball Game
FRANK TIERI writer RAMON BACHS pencils
RAUL FONTS inks WIL QUINTANA colors
VC's JOE CARAMAGNA letters
ELLIE PYLE asst. editor TOM BRENNAN editor
STEPHEN WACKER senior editor
ALONSO, LOEB, QUESADA, BUCKLEY & FINE the bosses
GIANT FOAM FINGER? CHECK.
#1 FAN
PROGRAM THAT COSTS MORE THAN MY HOUSE? CHECK.
Playball MAGAZINE
UNDEE!
TWO DOGS WITH EVERYTHING ON 'EM? CHECK.
YEAH, YOU'RE READY. SO HERE WE GO... RUTH, SEAVER, GEHRIG, HERNANDEZ, DIMAGGIO AND...
PARKER!
#1 FA

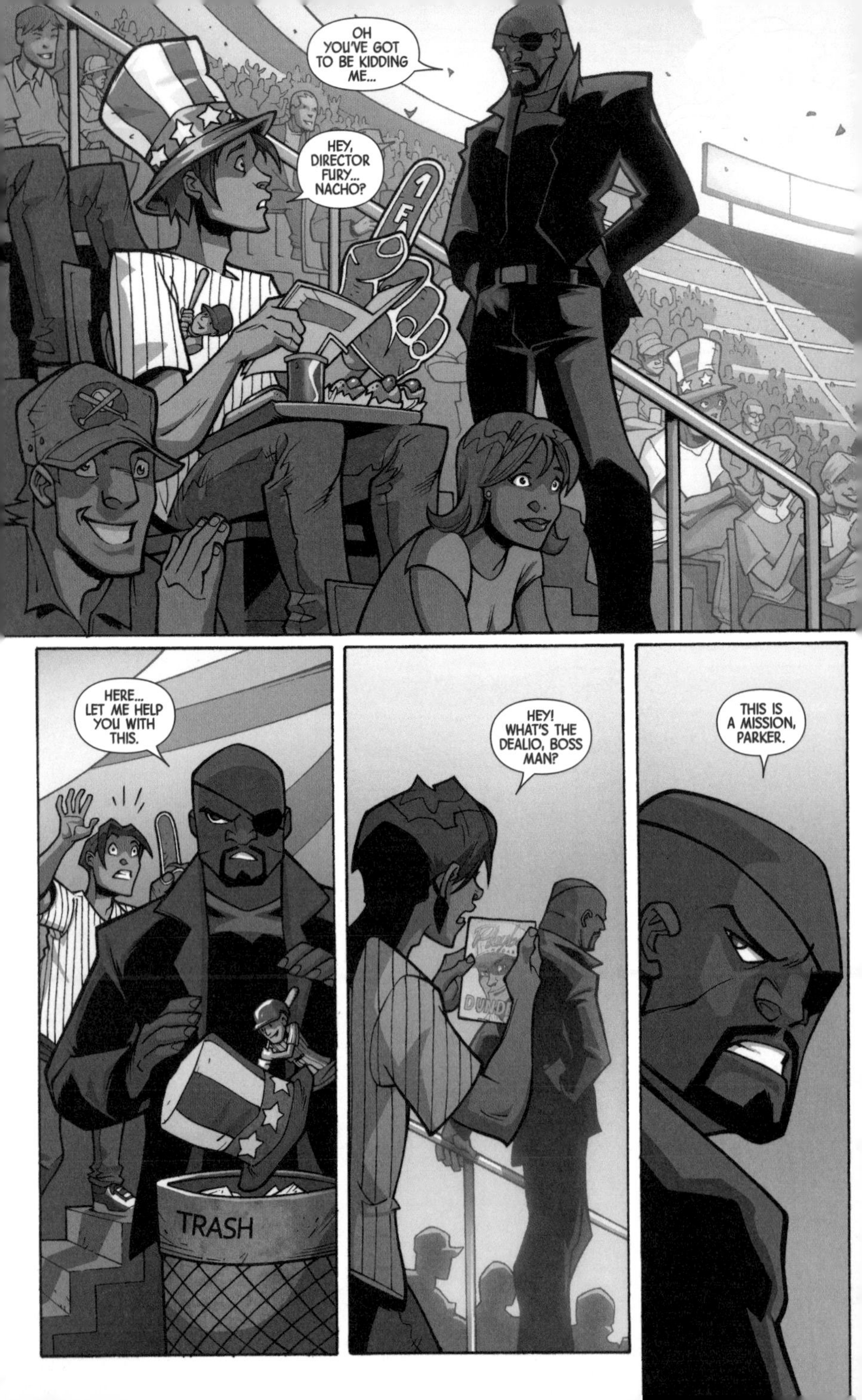
OH YOU'VE GOT TO BE KIDDING ME...
HEY, DIRECTOR FURY... NACHO?
HERE... LET ME HELP YOU WITH THIS.
TRASH
HEY! WHAT'S THE DEALIO, BOSS MAN?
THIS IS A MISSION, PARKER.

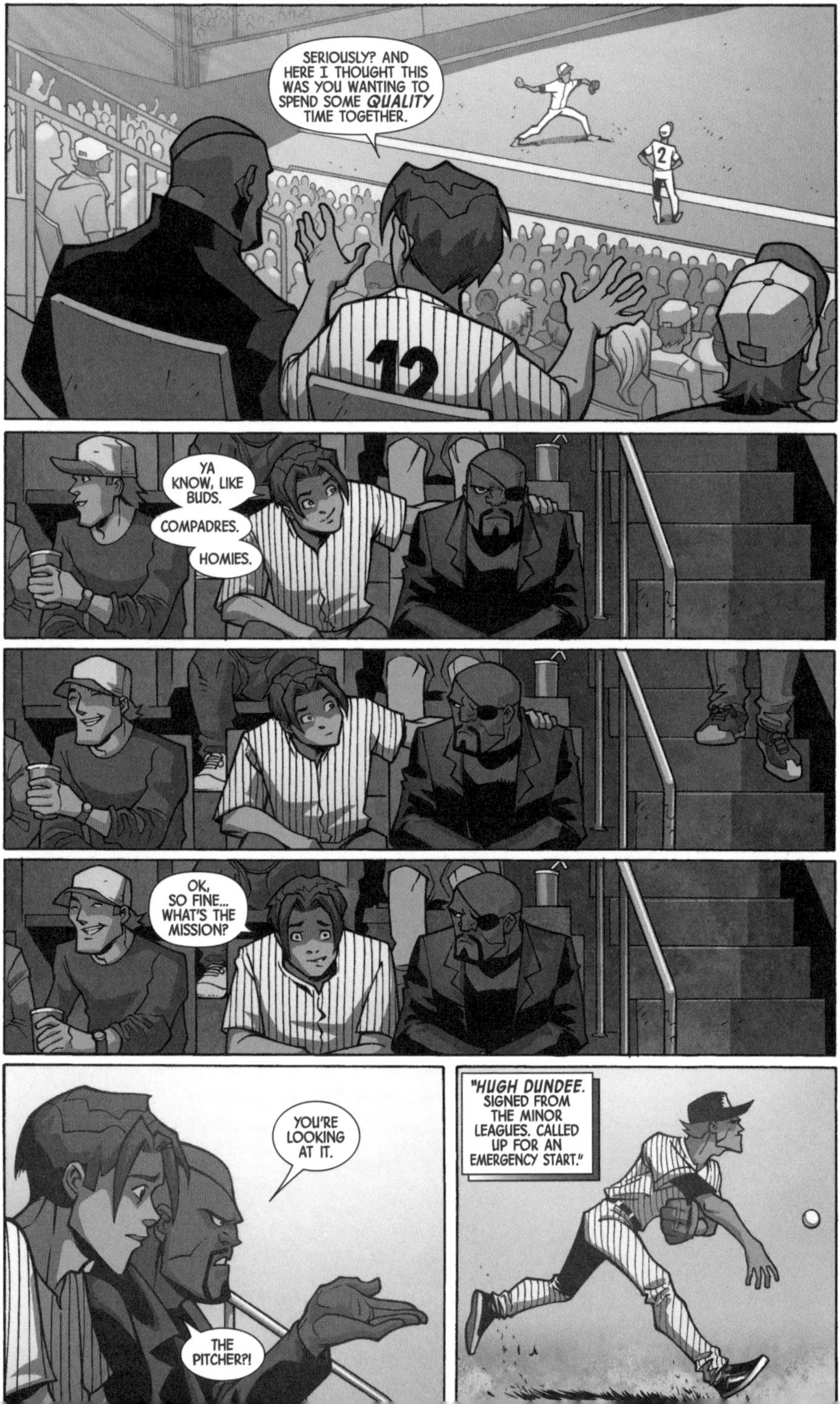
SERIOUSLY? AND HERE I THOUGHT THIS WAS YOU WANTING TO SPEND SOME *QUALITY* TIME TOGETHER.
YA KNOW, LIKE BUDS.
COMPADRES.
HOMIES.
OK, SO FINE... WHAT'S THE MISSION?
YOU'RE LOOKING AT IT.
THE PITCHER?!
"*HUGH DUNDEE.* SIGNED FROM THE MINOR LEAGUES. CALLED UP FOR AN EMERGENCY START."

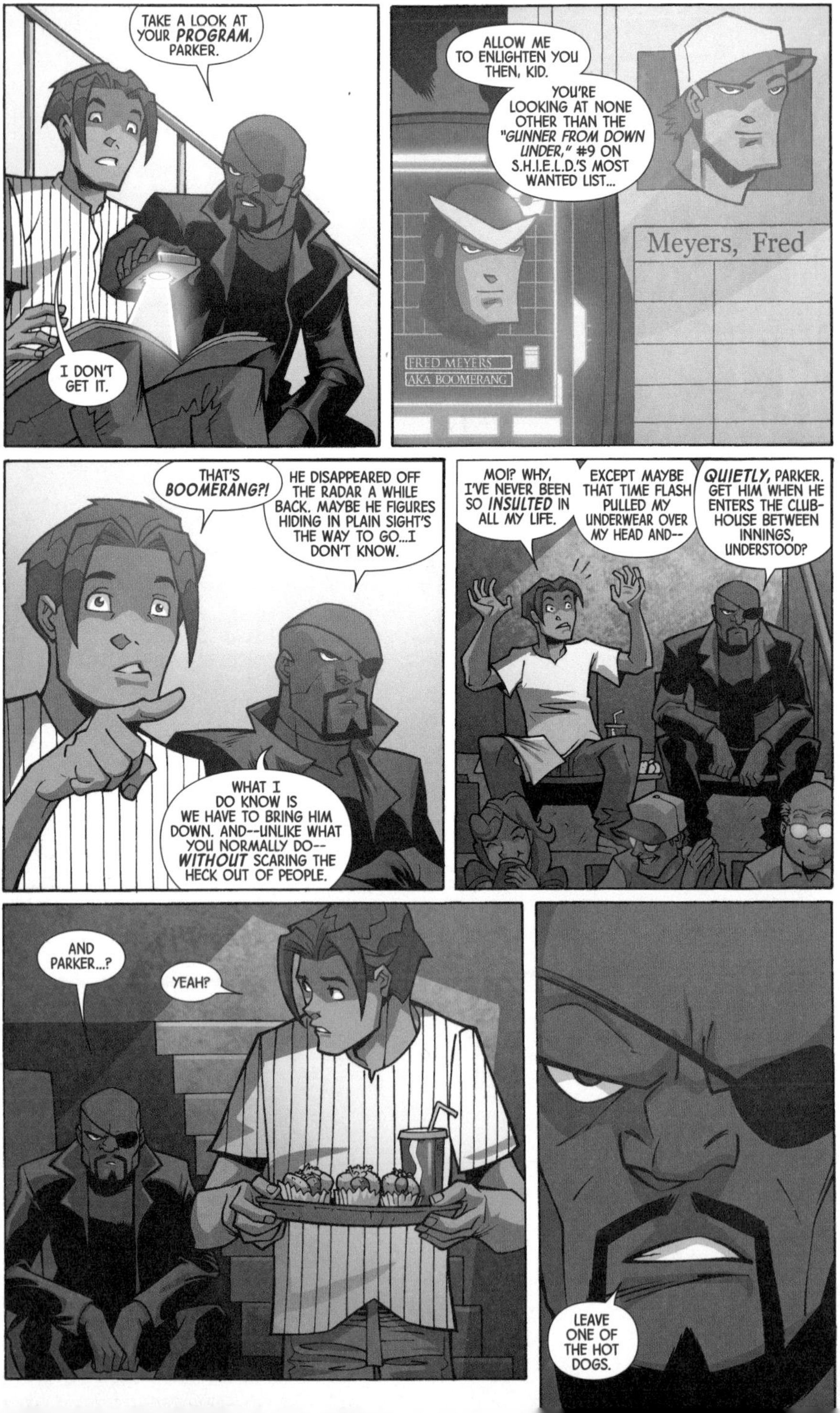
TAKE A LOOK AT YOUR PROGRAM, PARKER.
I DON'T GET IT.
ALLOW ME TO ENLIGHTEN YOU THEN, KID.
YOU'RE LOOKING AT NONE OTHER THAN THE "GUNNER FROM DOWN UNDER," #9 ON S.H.I.E.L.D.'S MOST WANTED LIST...
FRED MEYERS
AKA BOOMERANG
Meyers, Fred
THAT'S BOOMERANG?!
HE DISAPPEARED OFF THE RADAR A WHILE BACK. MAYBE HE FIGURES HIDING IN PLAIN SIGHT'S THE WAY TO GO...I DON'T KNOW.
WHAT I DO KNOW IS WE HAVE TO BRING HIM DOWN. AND--UNLIKE WHAT YOU NORMALLY DO--WITHOUT SCARING THE HECK OUT OF PEOPLE.
MOI? WHY, I'VE NEVER BEEN SO INSULTED IN ALL MY LIFE.
EXCEPT MAYBE THAT TIME FLASH PULLED MY UNDERWEAR OVER MY HEAD AND--
QUIETLY, PARKER. GET HIM WHEN HE ENTERS THE CLUB-HOUSE BETWEEN INNINGS, UNDERSTOOD?
AND PARKER...?
YEAH?
LEAVE ONE OF THE HOT DOGS.

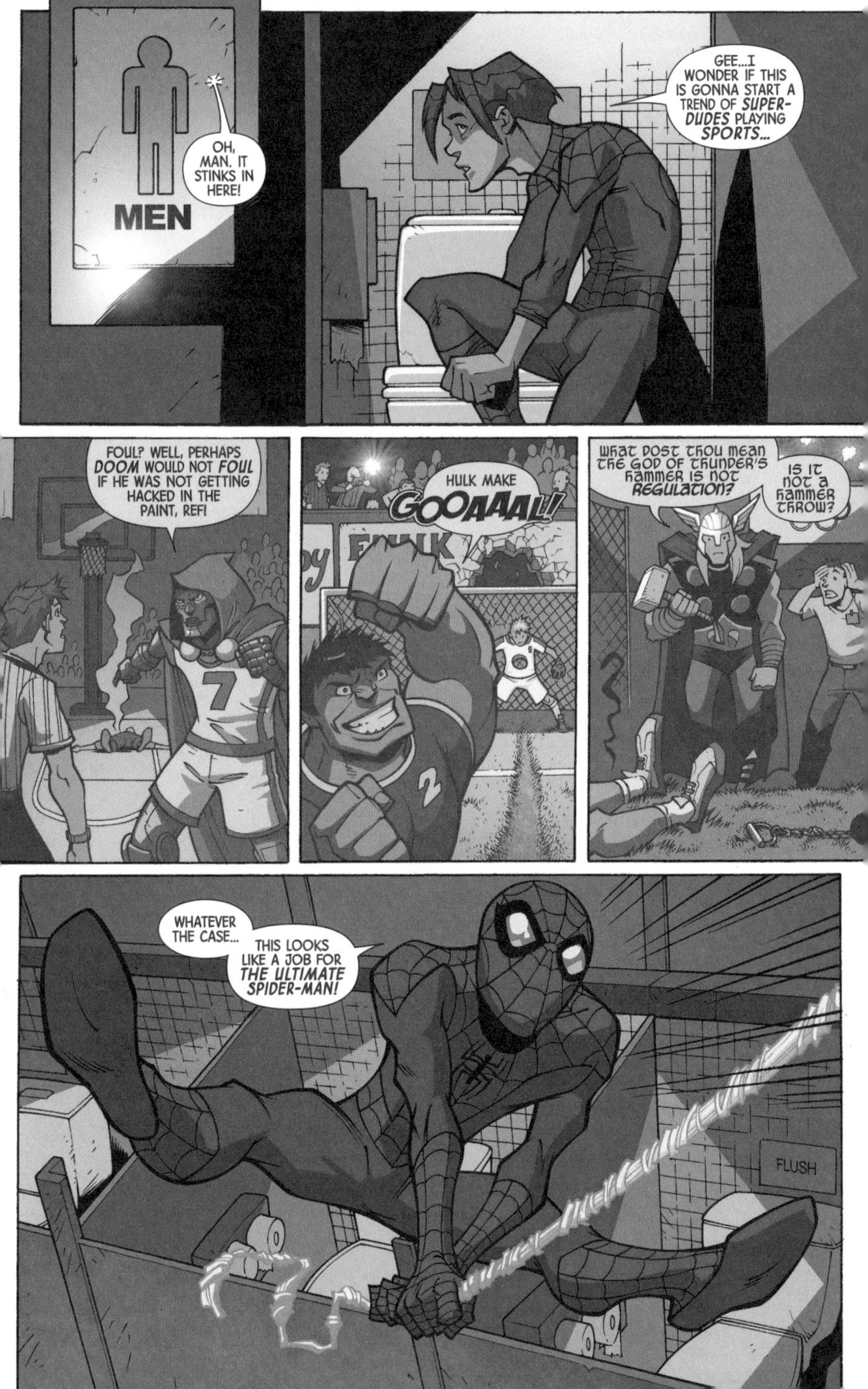
MEN
OH, MAN. IT STINKS IN HERE!
GEE...I WONDER IF THIS IS GONNA START A TREND OF SUPER-DUDES PLAYING SPORTS...
FOUL? WELL, PERHAPS DOOM WOULD NOT FOUL IF HE WAS NOT GETTING HACKED IN THE PAINT, REF!
7
HULK MAKE GOOAAAL!
2
WHAT DOST THOU MEAN THE GOD OF THUNDER'S HAMMER IS NOT REGULATION?
IS IT NOT A HAMMER THROW?
WHATEVER THE CASE...
THIS LOOKS LIKE A JOB FOR THE ULTIMATE SPIDER-MAN!
FLUSH

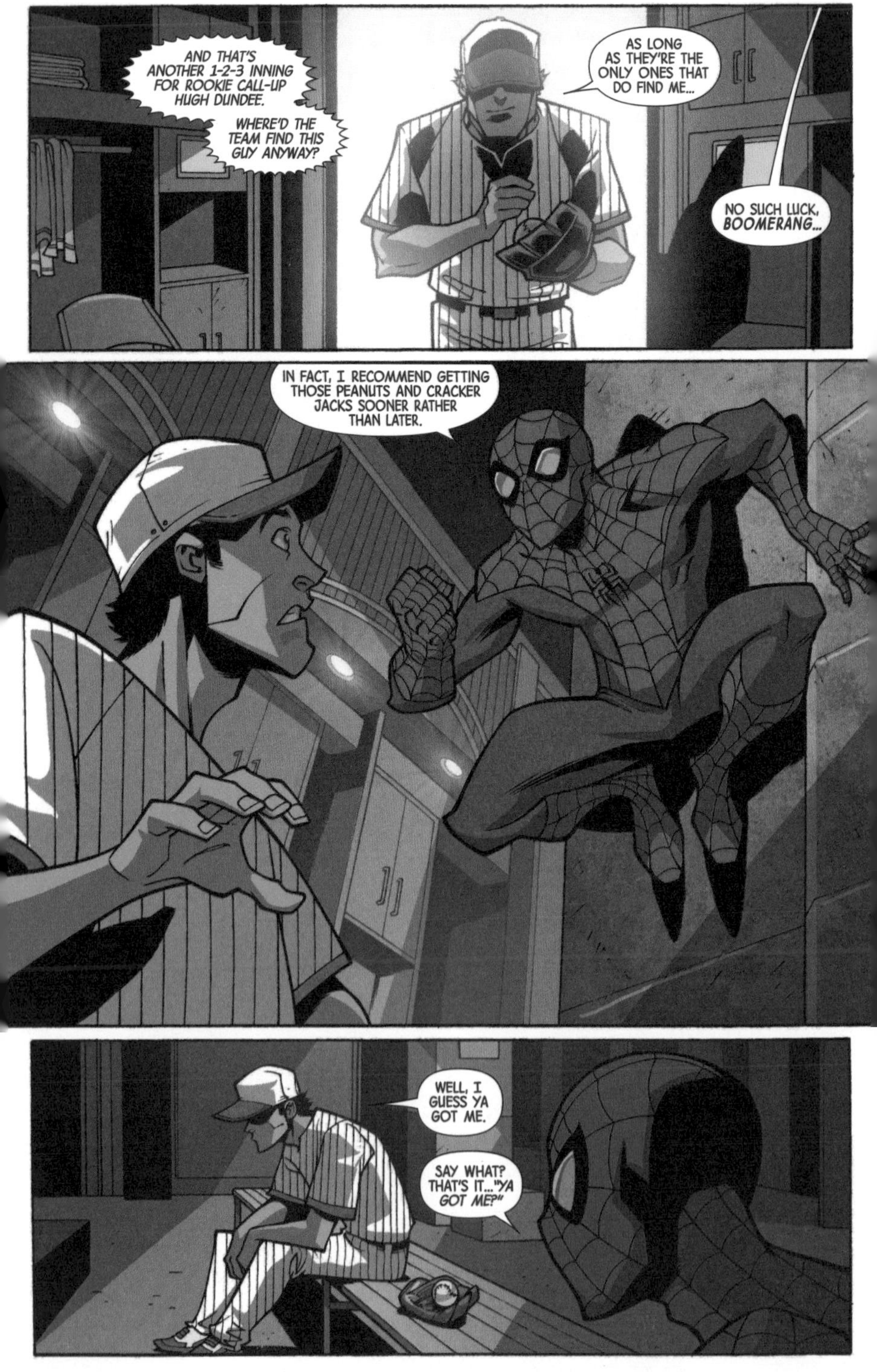
AND THAT'S ANOTHER 1-2-3 INNING FOR ROOKIE CALL-UP HUGH DUNDEE.
WHERE'D THE TEAM FIND THIS GUY ANYWAY?
AS LONG AS THEY'RE THE ONLY ONES THAT DO FIND ME...
NO SUCH LUCK, BOOMERANG...
IN FACT, I RECOMMEND GETTING THOSE PEANUTS AND CRACKER JACKS SOONER RATHER THAN LATER.
WELL, I GUESS YA GOT ME.
SAY WHAT? THAT'S IT..."YA GOT ME?"

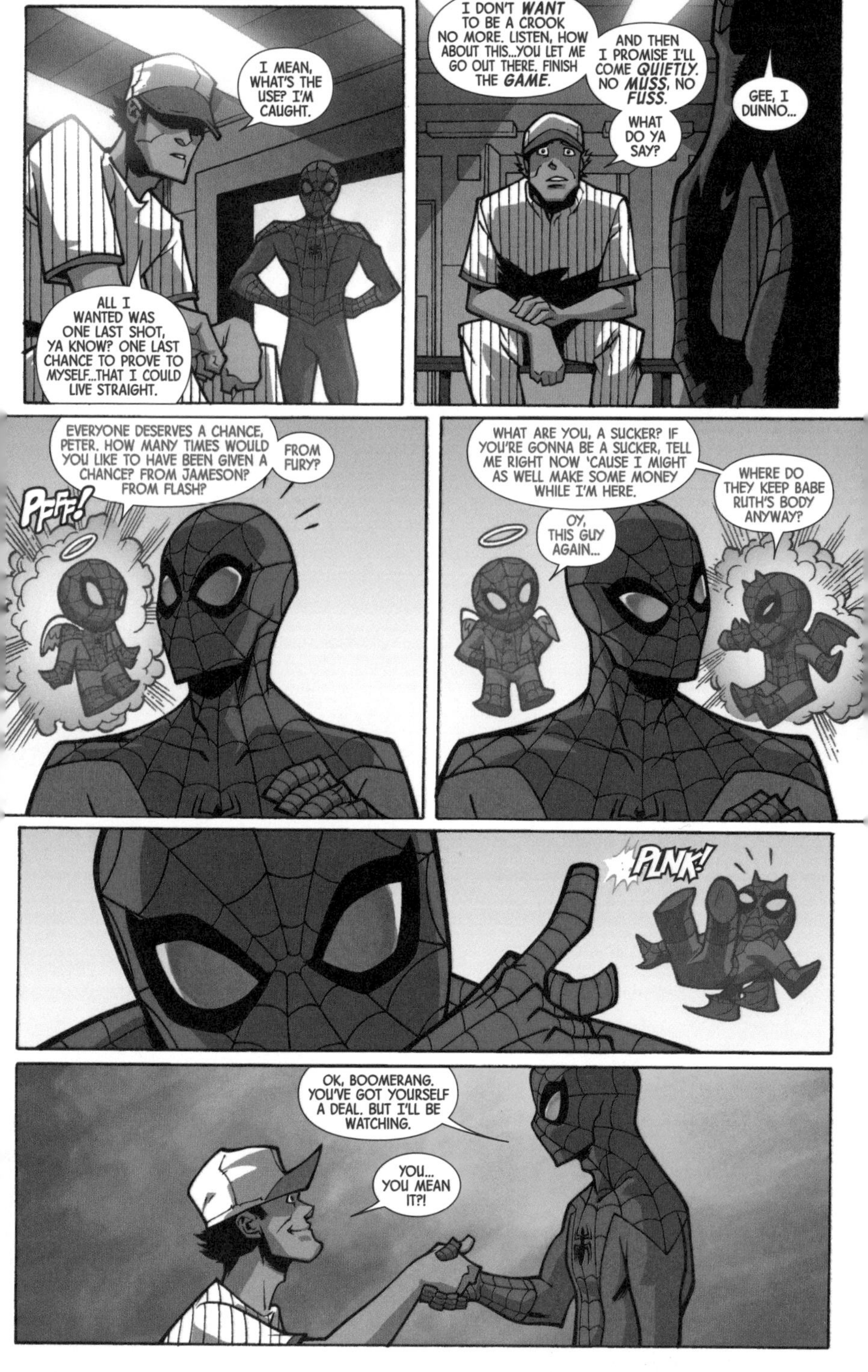
I MEAN, WHAT'S THE USE? I'M CAUGHT.
ALL I WANTED WAS ONE LAST SHOT, YA KNOW? ONE LAST CHANCE TO PROVE TO MYSELF...THAT I COULD LIVE STRAIGHT.
I DON'T WANT TO BE A CROOK NO MORE. LISTEN, HOW ABOUT THIS...YOU LET ME GO OUT THERE. FINISH THE GAME.
AND THEN I PROMISE I'LL COME QUIETLY. NO MUSS, NO FUSS.
WHAT DO YA SAY?
GEE, I DUNNO...
EVERYONE DESERVES A CHANCE, PETER. HOW MANY TIMES WOULD YOU LIKE TO HAVE BEEN GIVEN A CHANCE? FROM JAMESON? FROM FLASH?
FROM FURY?
PFFF!
WHAT ARE YOU, A SUCKER? IF YOU'RE GONNA BE A SUCKER, TELL ME RIGHT NOW 'CAUSE I MIGHT AS WELL MAKE SOME MONEY WHILE I'M HERE.
WHERE DO THEY KEEP BABE RUTH'S BODY ANYWAY?
OY, THIS GUY AGAIN...
PLNK!
OK, BOOMERANG. YOU'VE GOT YOURSELF A DEAL. BUT I'LL BE WATCHING.
YOU... YOU MEAN IT?!

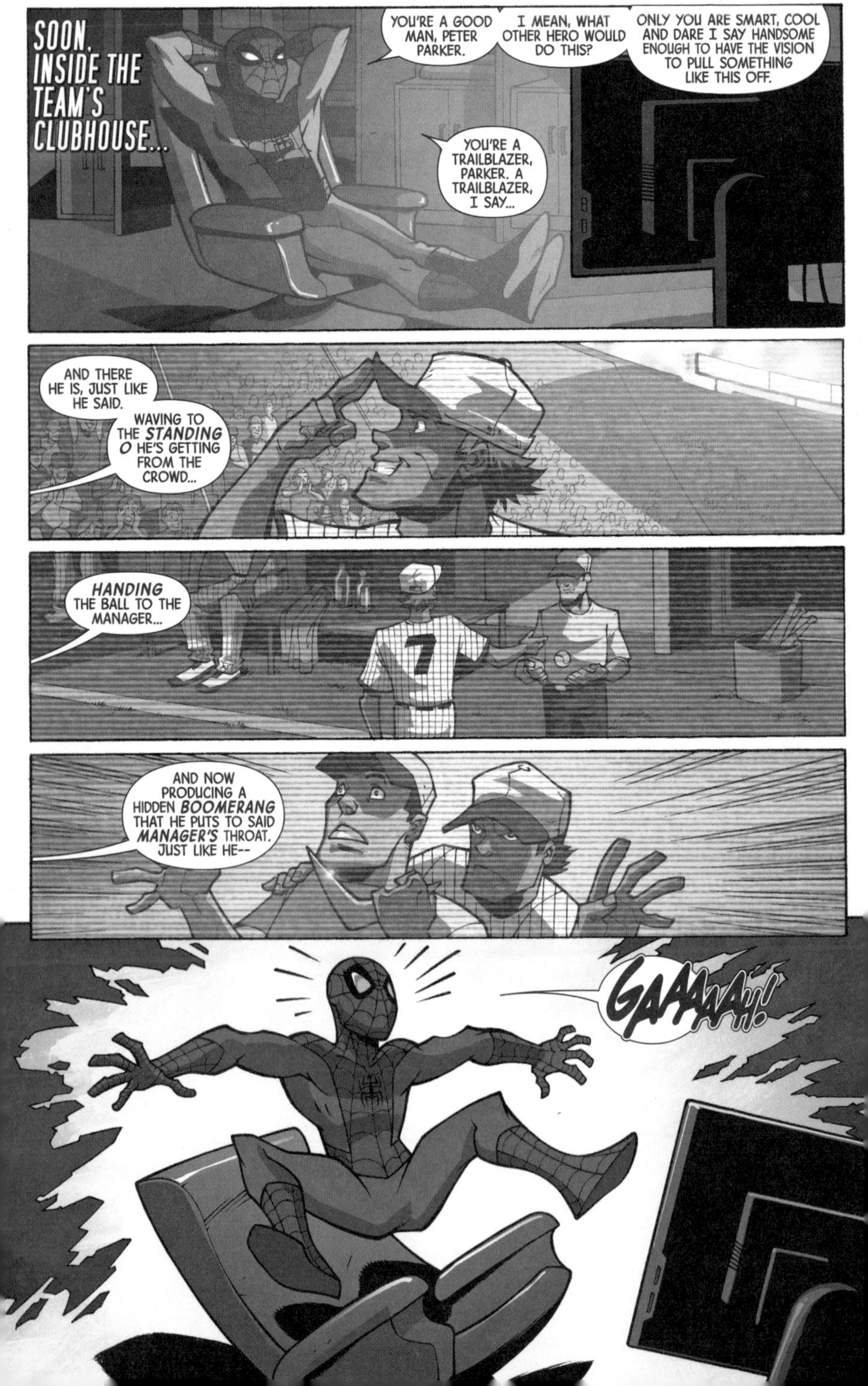
SOON, INSIDE THE TEAM'S CLUBHOUSE...
YOU'RE A GOOD MAN, PETER PARKER.
I MEAN, WHAT OTHER HERO WOULD DO THIS?
ONLY YOU ARE SMART, COOL AND DARE I SAY HANDSOME ENOUGH TO HAVE THE VISION TO PULL SOMETHING LIKE THIS OFF.
YOU'RE A TRAILBLAZER, PARKER. A TRAILBLAZER, I SAY...
AND THERE HE IS, JUST LIKE HE SAID.
WAVING TO THE STANDING O HE'S GETTING FROM THE CROWD...
HANDING THE BALL TO THE MANAGER...
AND NOW PRODUCING A HIDDEN BOOMERANG THAT HE PUTS TO SAID MANAGER'S THROAT. JUST LIKE HE--
GAAAAAH!

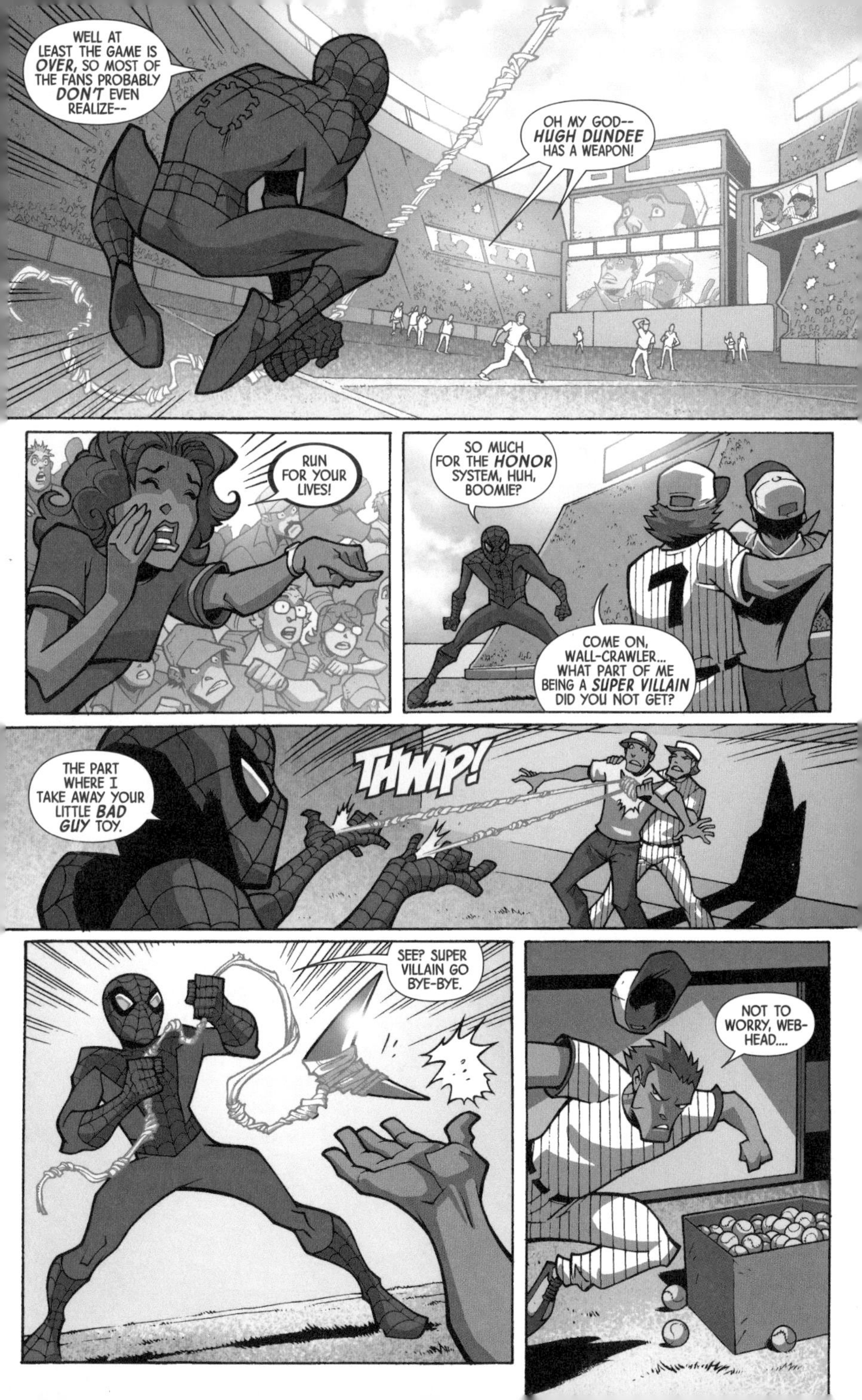
WELL AT LEAST THE GAME IS OVER, SO MOST OF THE FANS PROBABLY DON'T EVEN REALIZE--
OH MY GOD-- HUGH DUNDEE HAS A WEAPON!
RUN FOR YOUR LIVES!
SO MUCH FOR THE HONOR SYSTEM, HUH, BOOMIE?
COME ON, WALL-CRAWLER... WHAT PART OF ME BEING A SUPER VILLAIN DID YOU NOT GET?
THE PART WHERE I TAKE AWAY YOUR LITTLE BAD GUY TOY.
THWIP!
SEE? SUPER VILLAIN GO BYE-BYE.
NOT TO WORRY, WEB-HEAD....

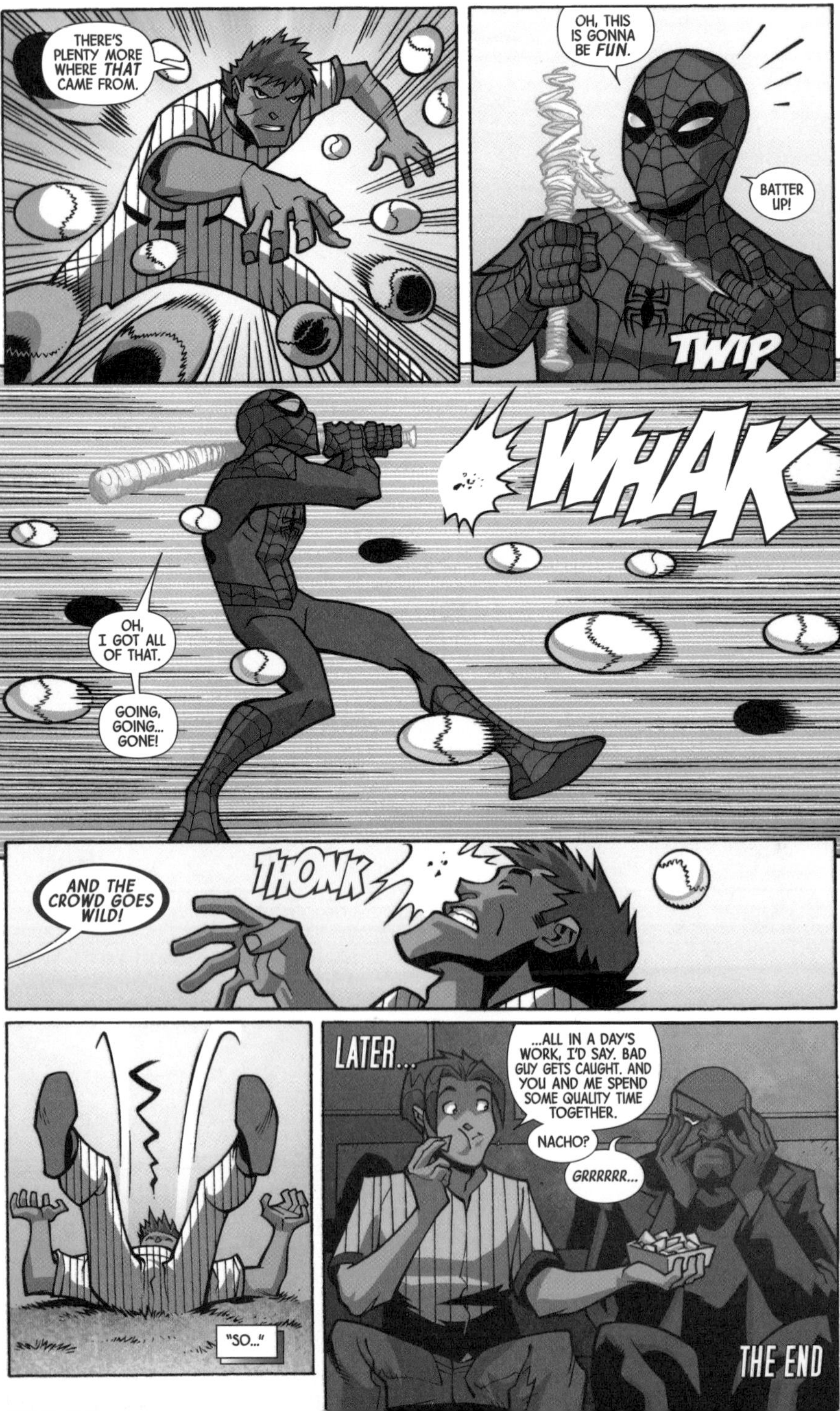
THERE'S PLENTY MORE WHERE THAT CAME FROM.
OH, THIS IS GONNA BE FUN.
BATTER UP!
TWIP
WHAK
OH, I GOT ALL OF THAT.
GOING, GOING... GONE!
THONK
AND THE CROWD GOES WILD!
"SO..."
LATER...
...ALL IN A DAY'S WORK, I'D SAY. BAD GUY GETS CAUGHT. AND YOU AND ME SPEND SOME QUALITY TIME TOGETHER.
NACHO?
GRRRRRR...
THE END

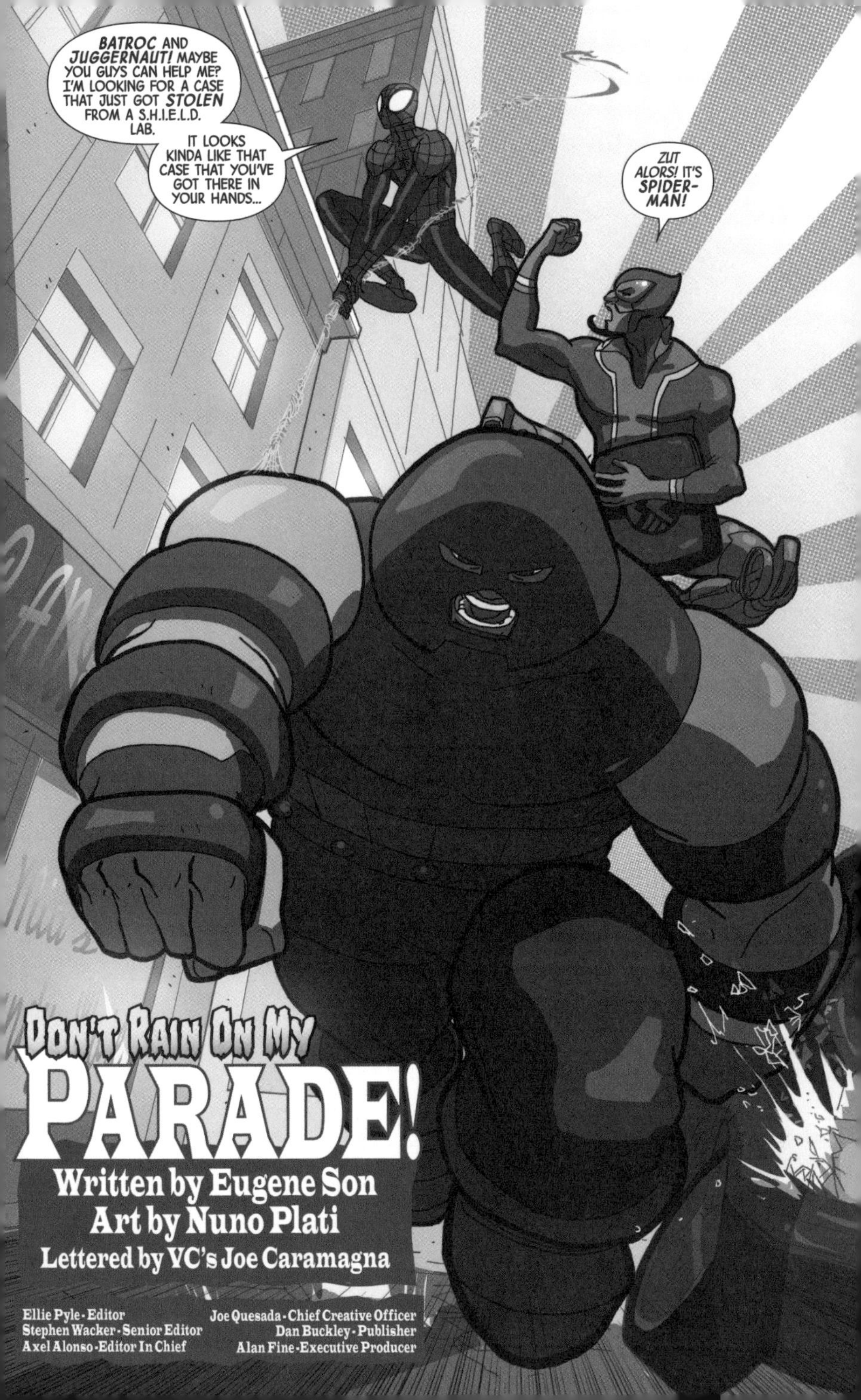
BATROC AND JUGGERNAUT! MAYBE YOU GUYS CAN HELP ME? I'M LOOKING FOR A CASE THAT JUST GOT STOLEN FROM A S.H.I.E.L.D. LAB.
IT LOOKS KINDA LIKE THAT CASE THAT YOU'VE GOT THERE IN YOUR HANDS...
ZUT ALORS! IT'S SPIDER-MAN!
DON'T RAIN ON MY PARADE!
Written by Eugene Son
Art by Nuno Plati
Lettered by VC's Joe Caramagna
Ellie Pyle - Editor
Stephen Wacker - Senior Editor
Axel Alonso - Editor In Chief
Joe Quesada - Chief Creative Officer
Dan Buckley - Publisher
Alan Fine - Executive Producer

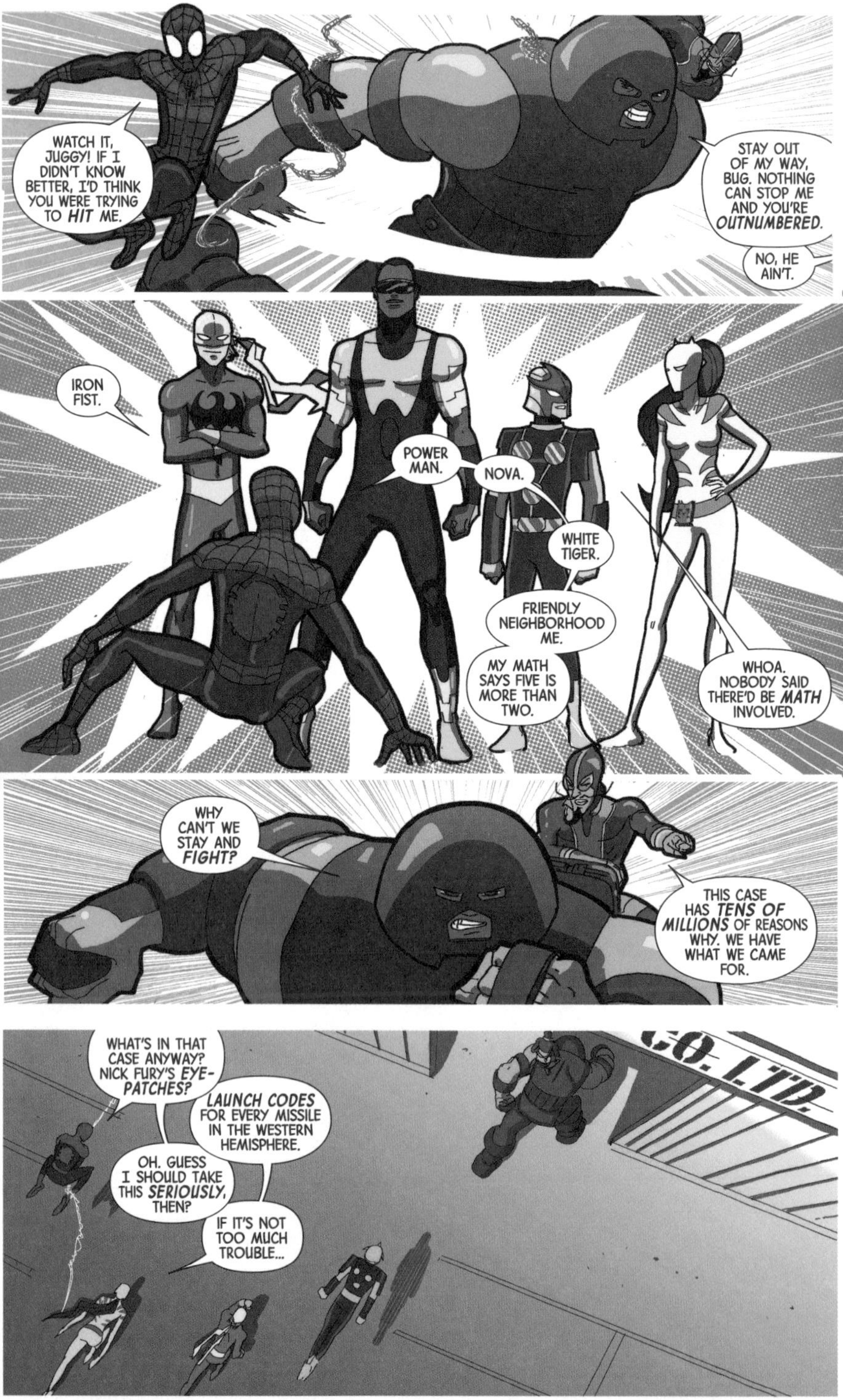
WATCH IT, JUGGY! IF I DIDN'T KNOW BETTER, I'D THINK YOU WERE TRYING TO HIT ME.
STAY OUT OF MY WAY, BUG. NOTHING CAN STOP ME AND YOU'RE OUTNUMBERED.
NO, HE AIN'T.
IRON FIST.
POWER MAN.
NOVA.
WHITE TIGER.
FRIENDLY NEIGHBORHOOD ME.
MY MATH SAYS FIVE IS MORE THAN TWO.
WHOA. NOBODY SAID THERE'D BE MATH INVOLVED.
WHY CAN'T WE STAY AND FIGHT?
THIS CASE HAS TENS OF MILLIONS OF REASONS WHY. WE HAVE WHAT WE CAME FOR.
WHAT'S IN THAT CASE ANYWAY? NICK FURY'S EYE-PATCHES?
LAUNCH CODES FOR EVERY MISSILE IN THE WESTERN HEMISPHERE.
OH. GUESS I SHOULD TAKE THIS SERIOUSLY, THEN?
IF IT'S NOT TOO MUCH TROUBLE...
CO. LTD.

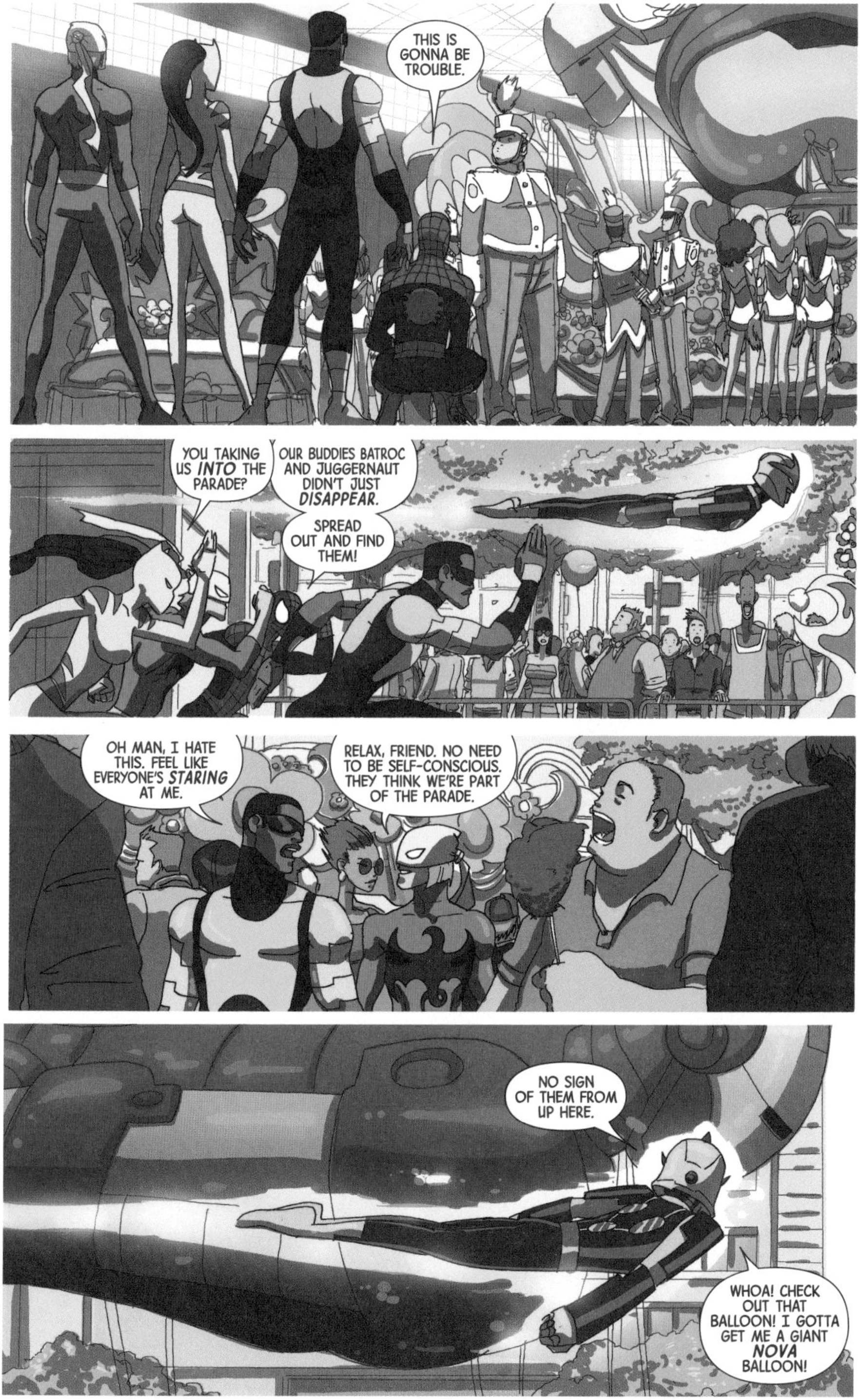
THIS IS GONNA BE TROUBLE.
YOU TAKING US INTO THE PARADE?
OUR BUDDIES BATROC AND JUGGERNAUT DIDN'T JUST DISAPPEAR.
SPREAD OUT AND FIND THEM!
OH MAN, I HATE THIS. FEEL LIKE EVERYONE'S STARING AT ME.
RELAX, FRIEND. NO NEED TO BE SELF-CONSCIOUS. THEY THINK WE'RE PART OF THE PARADE.
NO SIGN OF THEM FROM UP HERE.
WHOA! CHECK OUT THAT BALLOON! I GOTTA GET ME A GIANT NOVA BALLOON!

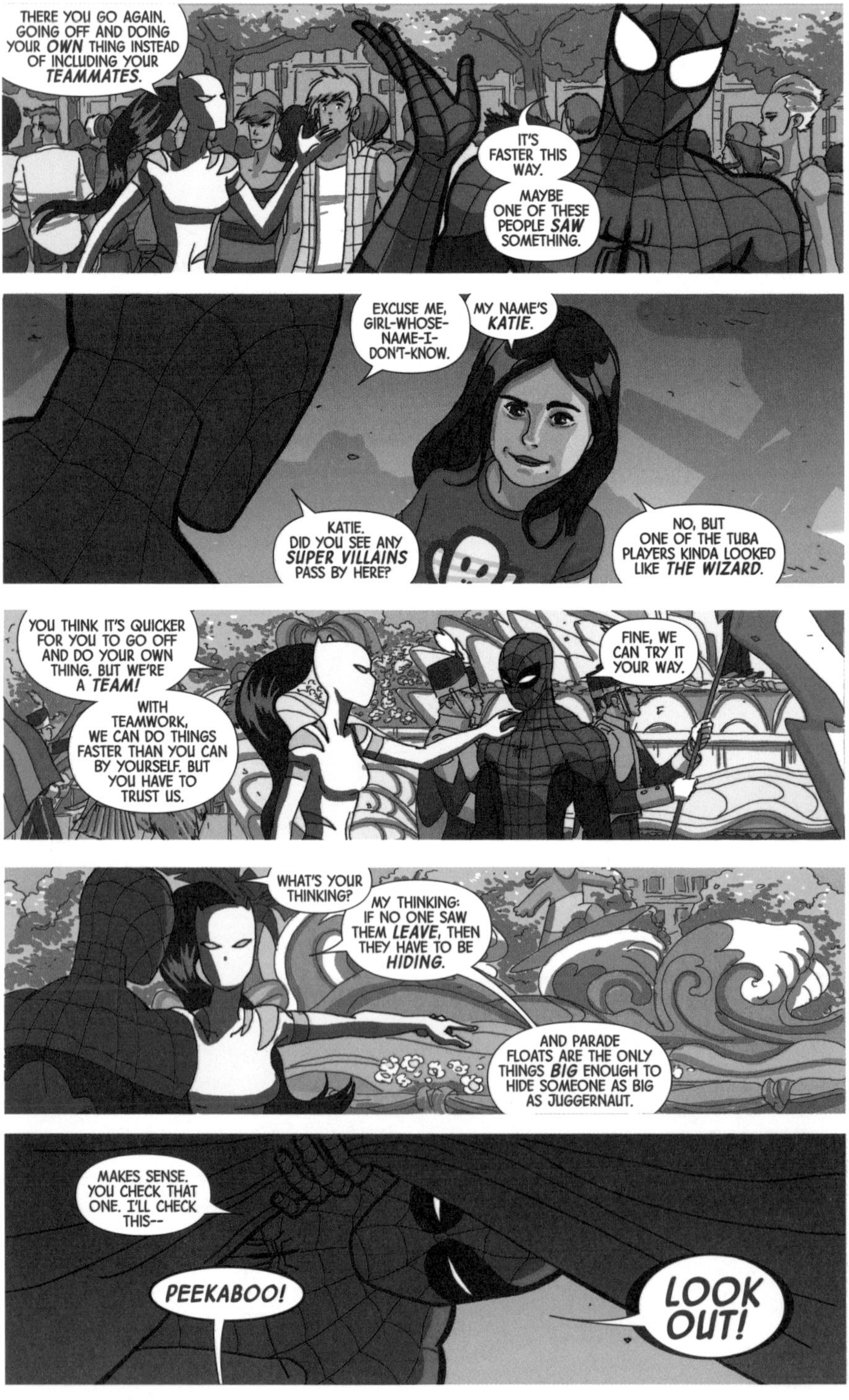
THERE YOU GO AGAIN. GOING OFF AND DOING YOUR OWN THING INSTEAD OF INCLUDING YOUR TEAMMATES.
IT'S FASTER THIS WAY.
MAYBE ONE OF THESE PEOPLE SAW SOMETHING.
EXCUSE ME, GIRL-WHOSE-NAME-I-DON'T-KNOW.
MY NAME'S KATIE.
KATIE. DID YOU SEE ANY SUPER VILLAINS PASS BY HERE?
NO, BUT ONE OF THE TUBA PLAYERS KINDA LOOKED LIKE THE WIZARD.
YOU THINK IT'S QUICKER FOR YOU TO GO OFF AND DO YOUR OWN THING. BUT WE'RE A TEAM!
WITH TEAMWORK, WE CAN DO THINGS FASTER THAN YOU CAN BY YOURSELF. BUT YOU HAVE TO TRUST US.
FINE, WE CAN TRY IT YOUR WAY.
WHAT'S YOUR THINKING?
MY THINKING: IF NO ONE SAW THEM LEAVE, THEN THEY HAVE TO BE HIDING.
AND PARADE FLOATS ARE THE ONLY THINGS BIG ENOUGH TO HIDE SOMEONE AS BIG AS JUGGERNAUT.
MAKES SENSE. YOU CHECK THAT ONE. I'LL CHECK THIS--
PEEKABOO!
LOOK OUT!

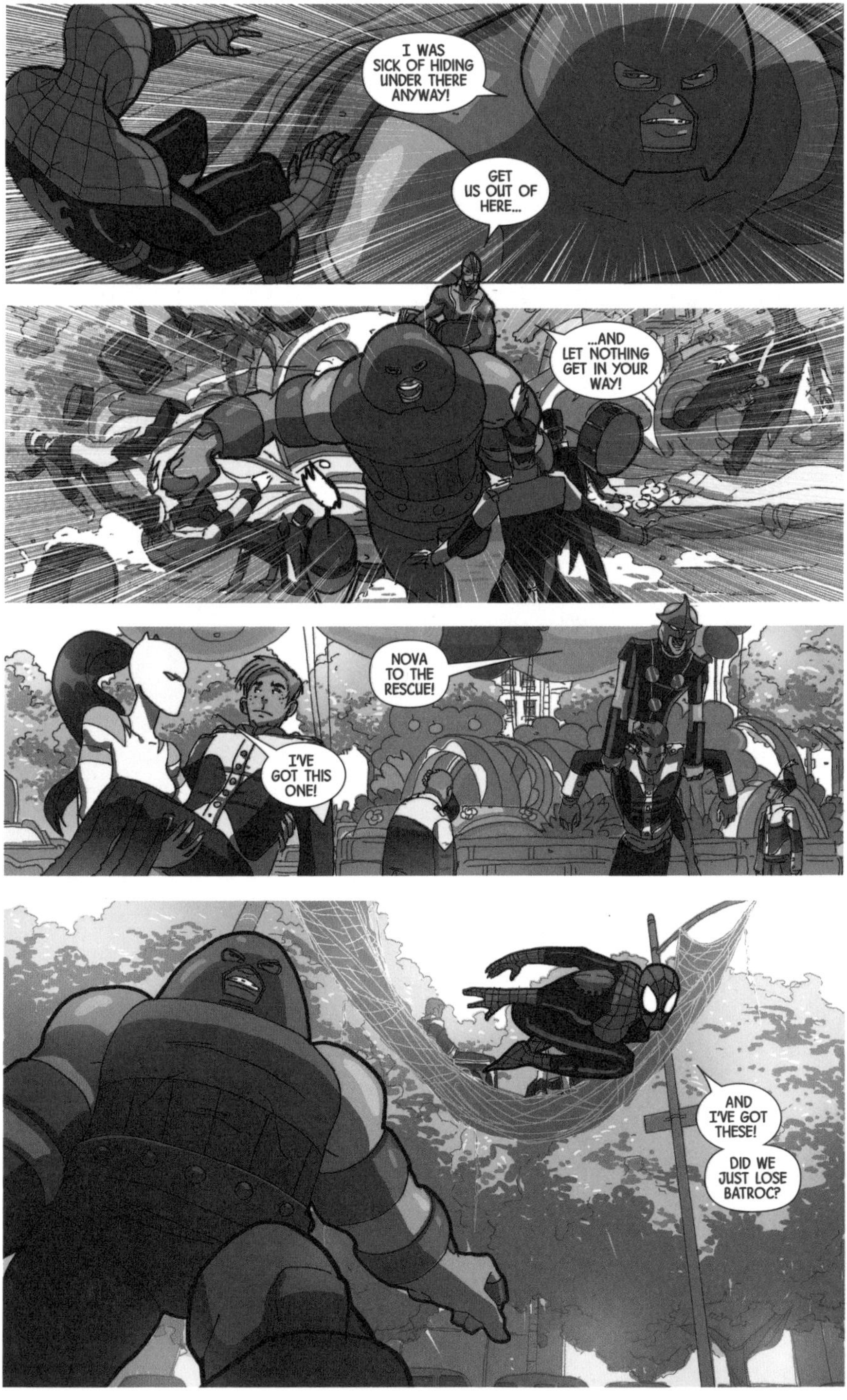
I WAS SICK OF HIDING UNDER THERE ANYWAY!
GET US OUT OF HERE...
...AND LET NOTHING GET IN YOUR WAY!
NOVA TO THE RESCUE!
I'VE GOT THIS ONE!
AND I'VE GOT THESE!
DID WE JUST LOSE BATROC?

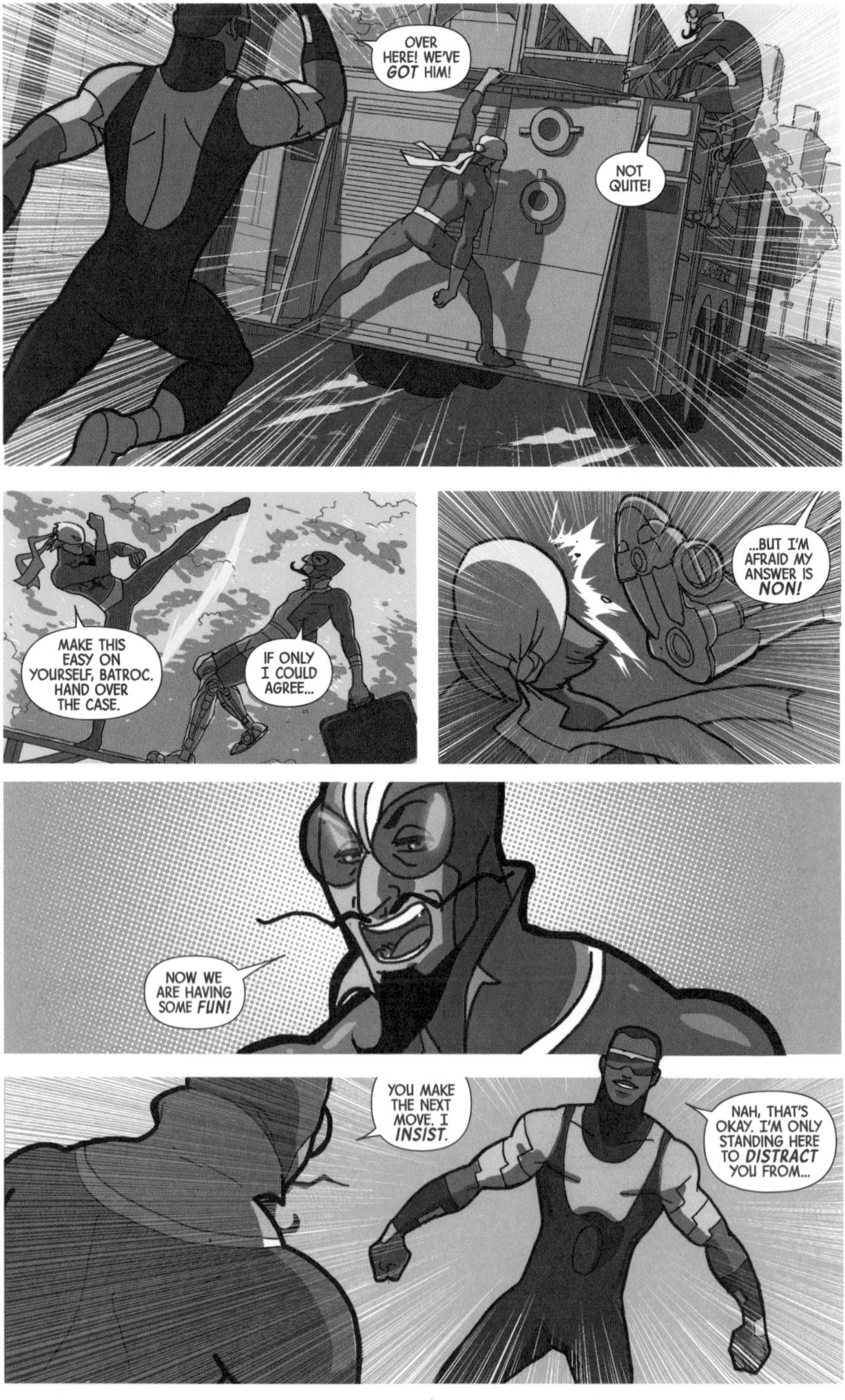
OVER HERE! WE'VE GOT HIM!
NOT QUITE!
MAKE THIS EASY ON YOURSELF, BATROC. HAND OVER THE CASE.
IF ONLY I COULD AGREE...
...BUT I'M AFRAID MY ANSWER IS NON!
NOW WE ARE HAVING SOME FUN!
YOU MAKE THE NEXT MOVE. I INSIST.
NAH, THAT'S OKAY. I'M ONLY STANDING HERE TO DISTRACT YOU FROM...

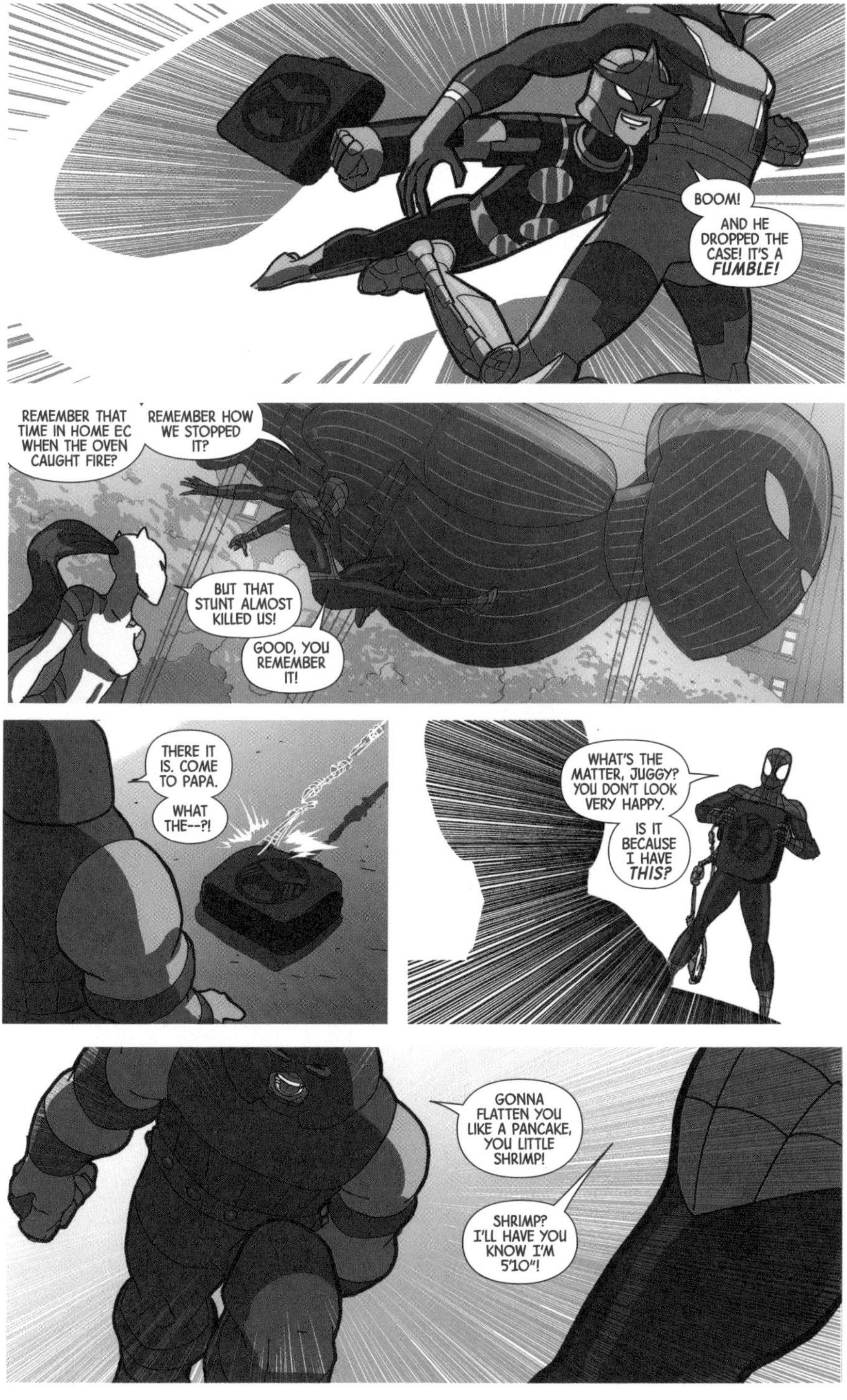
BOOM!
AND HE DROPPED THE CASE! IT'S A *FUMBLE!*
REMEMBER THAT TIME IN HOME EC WHEN THE OVEN CAUGHT FIRE?
REMEMBER HOW WE STOPPED IT?
BUT THAT STUNT ALMOST KILLED US!
GOOD, YOU REMEMBER IT!
THERE IT IS. COME TO PAPA.
WHAT THE--?!
WHAT'S THE MATTER, JUGGY? YOU DON'T LOOK VERY HAPPY.
IS IT BECAUSE I HAVE *THIS?*
GONNA FLATTEN YOU LIKE A PANCAKE, YOU LITTLE SHRIMP!
SHRIMP? I'LL HAVE YOU KNOW I'M 5'10"!

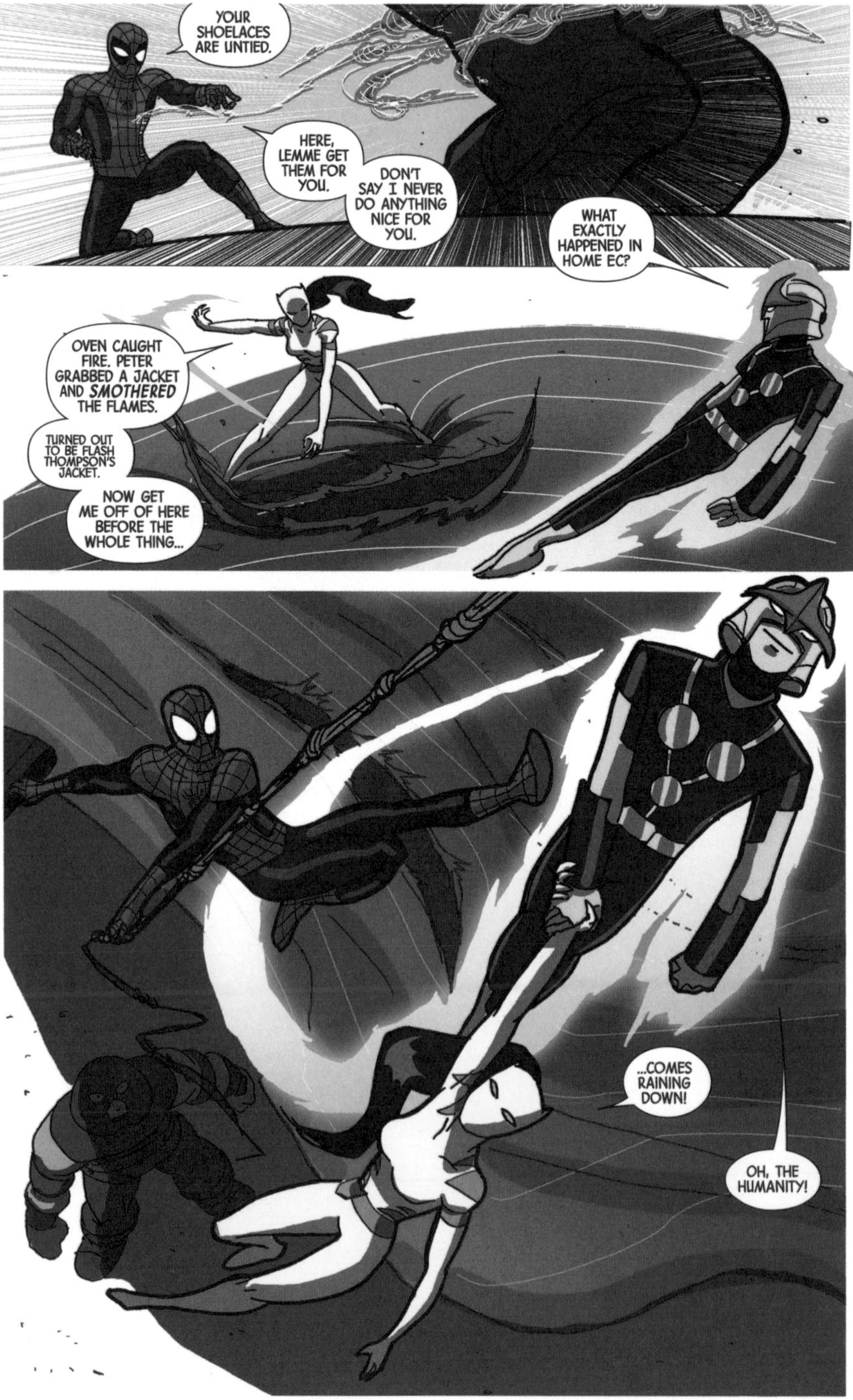
YOUR SHOELACES ARE UNTIED.
HERE, LEMME GET THEM FOR YOU.
DON'T SAY I NEVER DO ANYTHING NICE FOR YOU.
WHAT EXACTLY HAPPENED IN HOME EC?
OVEN CAUGHT FIRE. PETER GRABBED A JACKET AND SMOTHERED THE FLAMES.
TURNED OUT TO BE FLASH THOMPSON'S JACKET.
NOW GET ME OFF OF HERE BEFORE THE WHOLE THING...
...COMES RAINING DOWN!
OH, THE HUMANITY!

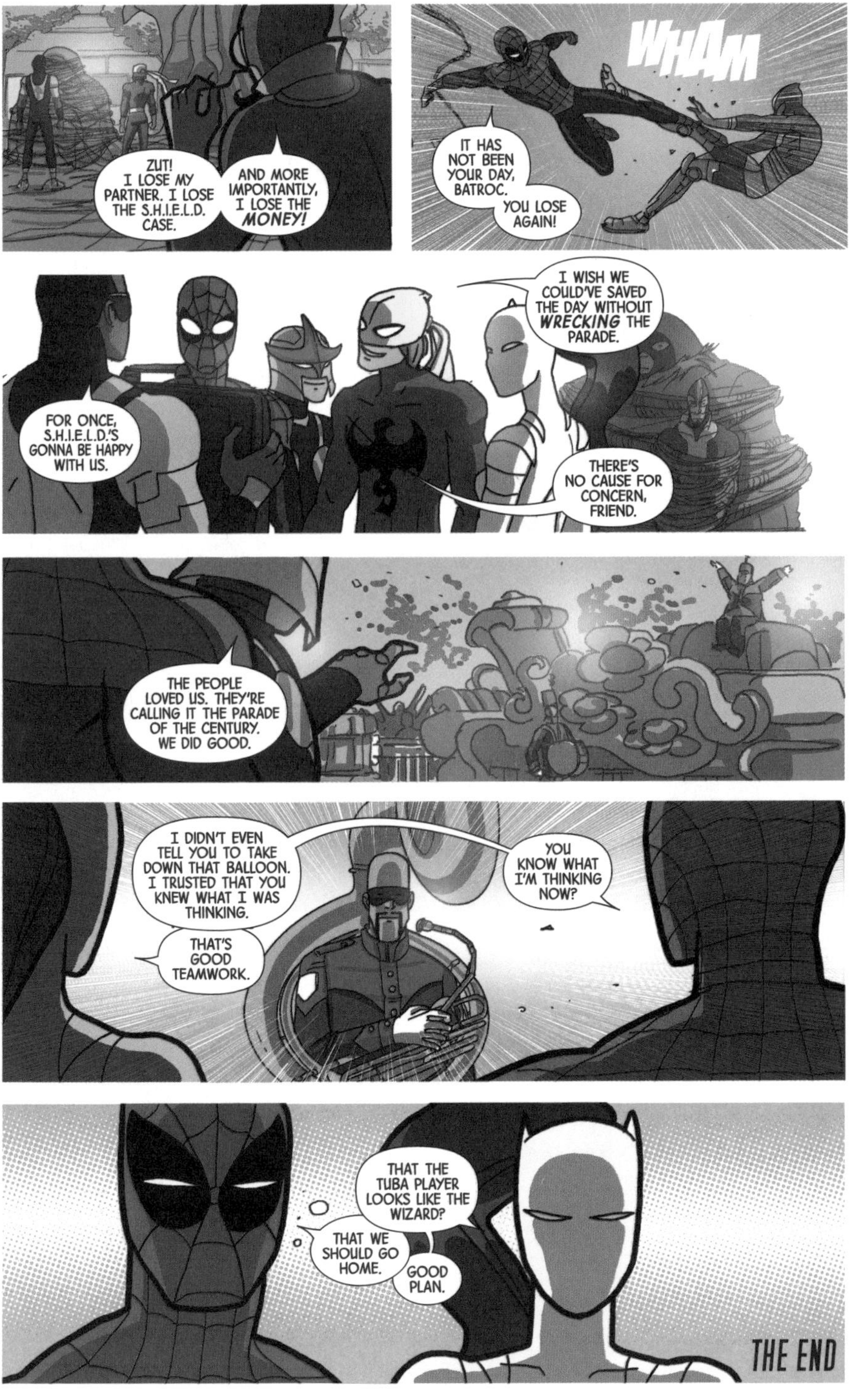
ZUT! I LOSE MY PARTNER. I LOSE THE S.H.I.E.L.D. CASE.
AND MORE IMPORTANTLY, I LOSE THE MONEY!
WHAM
IT HAS NOT BEEN YOUR DAY, BATROC.
YOU LOSE AGAIN!
I WISH WE COULD'VE SAVED THE DAY WITHOUT WRECKING THE PARADE.
FOR ONCE, S.H.I.E.L.D.'S GONNA BE HAPPY WITH US.
THERE'S NO CAUSE FOR CONCERN, FRIEND.
THE PEOPLE LOVED US. THEY'RE CALLING IT THE PARADE OF THE CENTURY. WE DID GOOD.
I DIDN'T EVEN TELL YOU TO TAKE DOWN THAT BALLOON. I TRUSTED THAT YOU KNEW WHAT I WAS THINKING.
YOU KNOW WHAT I'M THINKING NOW?
THAT'S GOOD TEAMWORK.
THAT THE TUBA PLAYER LOOKS LIKE THE WIZARD?
THAT WE SHOULD GO HOME.
GOOD PLAN.
THE END

LIVE! ON PAPER! IT'S TIME AGAIN FOR... MARVEL MASH-UP

COMICS YOU LOVE...REWRITTEN BY THE PEOPLE YOU DON'T!

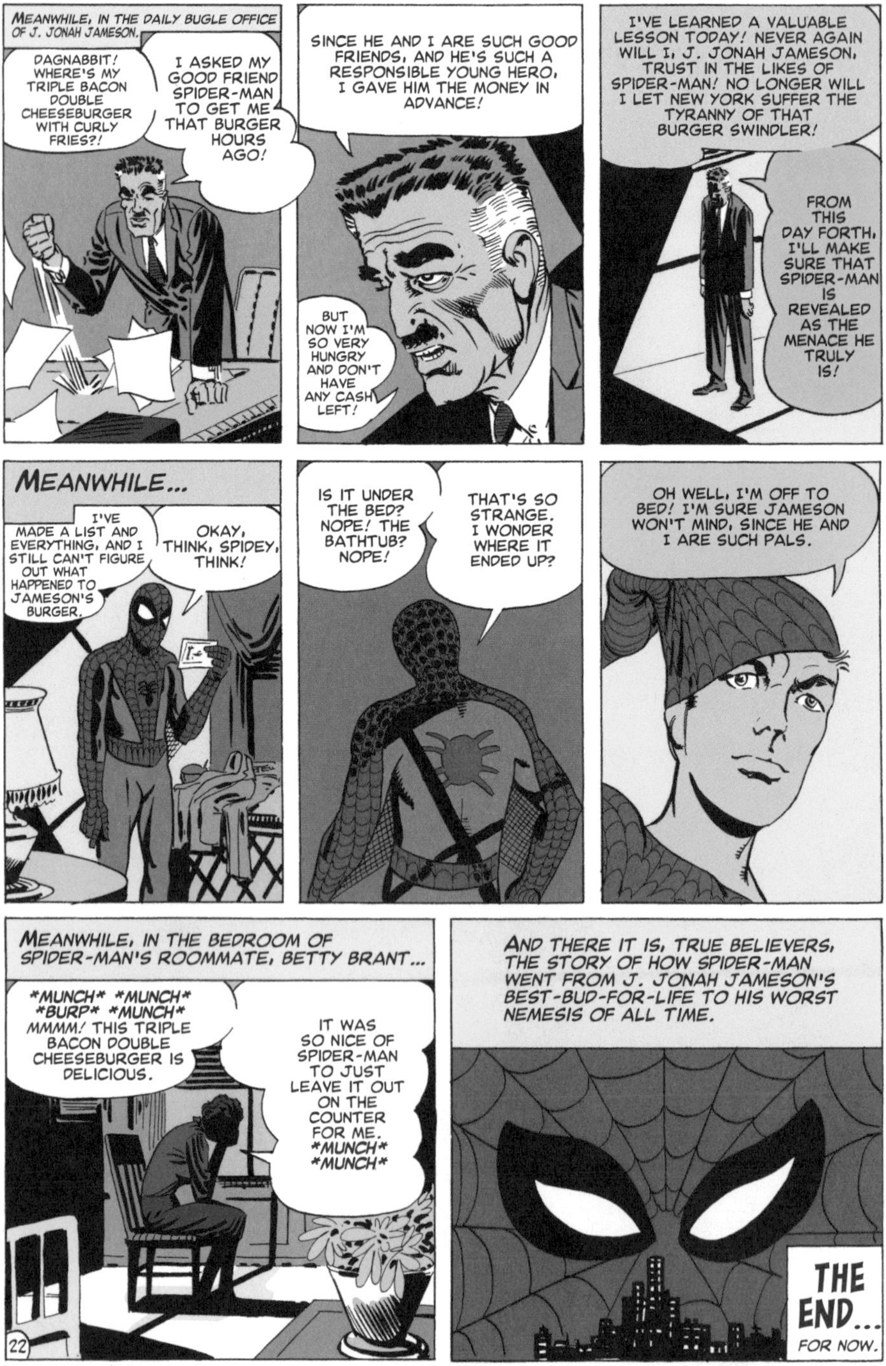
MEANWHILE, IN THE DAILY BUGLE OFFICE OF J. JONAH JAMESON.
DAGNABBIT! WHERE'S MY TRIPLE BACON DOUBLE CHEESEBURGER WITH CURLY FRIES?!
I ASKED MY GOOD FRIEND SPIDER-MAN TO GET ME THAT BURGER HOURS AGO!
SINCE HE AND I ARE SUCH GOOD FRIENDS, AND HE'S SUCH A RESPONSIBLE YOUNG HERO, I GAVE HIM THE MONEY IN ADVANCE!
BUT NOW I'M SO VERY HUNGRY AND DON'T HAVE ANY CASH LEFT!
I'VE LEARNED A VALUABLE LESSON TODAY! NEVER AGAIN WILL I, J. JONAH JAMESON, TRUST IN THE LIKES OF SPIDER-MAN! NO LONGER WILL I LET NEW YORK SUFFER THE TYRANNY OF THAT BURGER SWINDLER!
FROM THIS DAY FORTH, I'LL MAKE SURE THAT SPIDER-MAN IS REVEALED AS THE MENACE HE TRULY IS!
MEANWHILE...
I'VE MADE A LIST AND EVERYTHING, AND I STILL CAN'T FIGURE OUT WHAT HAPPENED TO JAMESON'S BURGER.
OKAY, THINK, SPIDEY, THINK!
IS IT UNDER THE BED? NOPE! THE BATHTUB? NOPE!
THAT'S SO STRANGE. I WONDER WHERE IT ENDED UP?
OH WELL, I'M OFF TO BED! I'M SURE JAMESON WON'T MIND, SINCE HE AND I ARE SUCH PALS.
MEANWHILE, IN THE BEDROOM OF SPIDER-MAN'S ROOMMATE, BETTY BRANT...
MUNCH *MUNCH* *BURP* *MUNCH* MMMM! THIS TRIPLE BACON DOUBLE CHEESEBURGER IS DELICIOUS.
IT WAS SO NICE OF SPIDER-MAN TO JUST LEAVE IT OUT ON THE COUNTER FOR ME. *MUNCH* *MUNCH*
22
AND THERE IT IS, TRUE BELIEVERS, THE STORY OF HOW SPIDER-MAN WENT FROM J. JONAH JAMESON'S BEST-BUD-FOR-LIFE TO HIS WORST NEMESIS OF ALL TIME.
THE END... FOR NOW.

ORIGINAL BY STAN LEE & STEVE DITKO

NEW DIALOGUE BY HARRISON WILCOX

LETTERED BY VC'S CLAYTON COWLES

LIVE! ON PAPER! IT'S TIME AGAIN FOR...

MARVEL MASH-UP

COMICS YOU LOVE...REWRITTEN BY THE PEOPLE YOU DON'T!

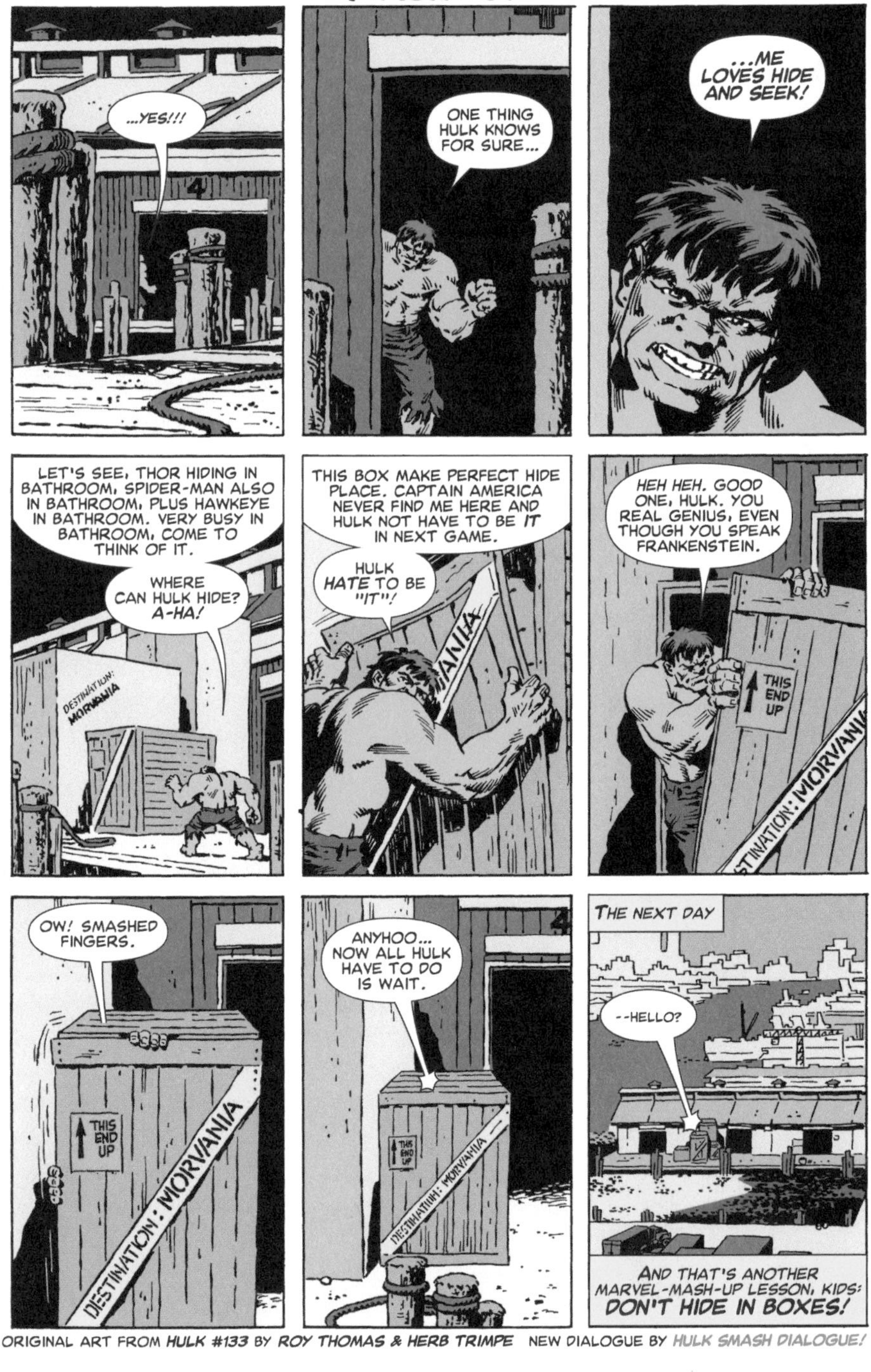

...YES!!!
ONE THING HULK KNOWS FOR SURE...
...ME LOVES HIDE AND SEEK!
LET'S SEE, THOR HIDING IN BATHROOM, SPIDER-MAN ALSO IN BATHROOM, PLUS HAWKEYE IN BATHROOM. VERY BUSY IN BATHROOM, COME TO THINK OF IT.
WHERE CAN HULK HIDE? A-HA!
DESTINATION: MORVANIA
THIS BOX MAKE PERFECT HIDE PLACE. CAPTAIN AMERICA NEVER FIND ME HERE AND HULK NOT HAVE TO BE IT IN NEXT GAME.
HULK HATE TO BE "IT"!
HEH HEH. GOOD ONE, HULK. YOU REAL GENIUS, EVEN THOUGH YOU SPEAK FRANKENSTEIN.
THIS END UP
DESTINATION: MORVANIA
OW! SMASHED FINGERS.
THIS END UP
DESTINATION: MORVANIA
ANYHOO... NOW ALL HULK HAVE TO DO IS WAIT.
DESTINATION: MORVANIA
THE NEXT DAY
--HELLO?
AND THAT'S ANOTHER MARVEL-MASH-UP LESSON, KIDS: DON'T HIDE IN BOXES!

ORIGINAL ART FROM HULK #133 BY ROY THOMAS & HERB TRIMPE NEW DIALOGUE BY HULK SMASH DIALOGUE!

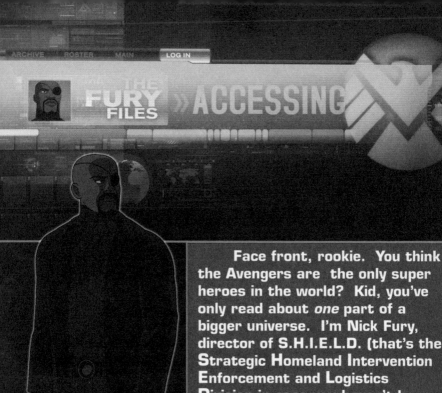

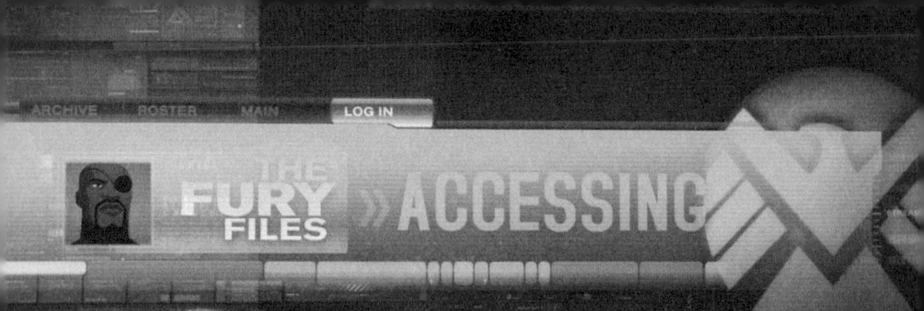
ARCHIVE
ROSTER
MAIN
LOG IN
THE FURY FILES
ACCESSING

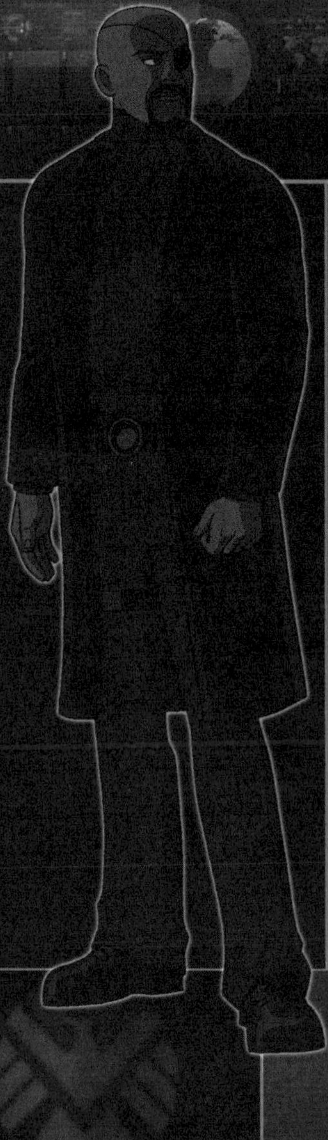

Face front, rookie. You think the Avengers are the only super heroes in the world? Kid, you've only read about *one* part of a bigger universe. I'm Nick Fury, director of S.H.I.E.L.D. (that's the Strategic Homeland Intervention Enforcement and Logistics Division in case you haven't been paying attention).

We have agents all over the planet – heck, all over the galaxy – defending us against the mightiest threats. Fortunately for you, our newest S.H.I.E.L.D. recruits, I have my extensive research files available. The best S.H.I.E.L.D. agents know everything about these super-men and super-women, so get to reading!

Adapted by Chris Eliopoulos

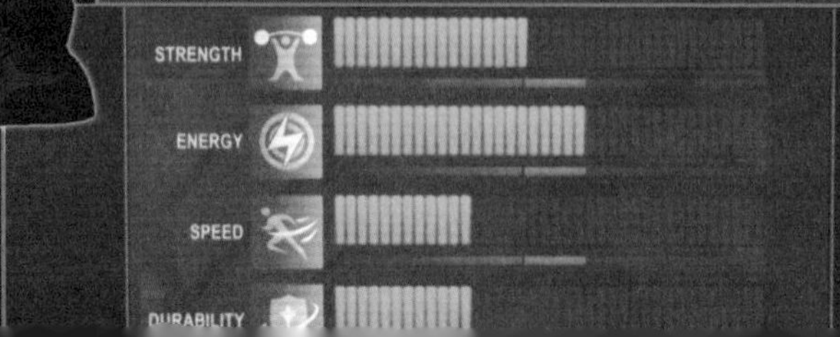
STRENGTH
ENERGY
SPEED
DURABILITY

S.H.I.E.L.D. DATA CENTER

FURY HERE. I NEED AN AGENT FOR AN *IMPORTANT* MISSION.

THE FURY FILES

ACCESSING

NOW, S.H.I.E.L.D. HAS *THOUSANDS* OF OPERATIVES STATIONED *AROUND* THE GLOBE.

EACH ONE HAS THEIR OWN *UNIQUE ABILITIES* AND *TRAINING*.

BUT, THERE'S ONLY *ONE* HERO TO DO THIS JOB...

...*IRON FIST*.

KNOCK... KNOCK.

CHOOM!

REAL NAME: *DANNY RAND*.

REAL NAME: Danny Rand

CURRENT ALIAS: Iron Fist

AFFILIATION: S.H.I.E.L.D.

PROFILE PICTURE

ACCESSING ORIGIN.

DANNY STUDIED MARTIAL ARTS IN THE MYSTICAL CITY OF *K'UN-LUN*.

THE FURY FILES

IRON FIST

HIS RIGOROUS TRAINING TAUGHT HIM THAT *EVERYONE* GETS KNOCKED DOWN, BUT *HEROES* ARE THE ONES WHO *GET BACK UP*.

AT THE END OF HIS TRAINING DANNY PROVED HIMSELF WORTHY TO HARNESS THE ANCIENT POWER OF THE IRON FIST.

THAT MEANS DANNY CAN SUMMON A *SUPERNATURAL POWER* THAT MAKES HIS *FIST* HARDER THAN...WELL...*IRON.*

ACCESSING: POWERS.

LOADING POWER GRID.

INTELLIGENCE

STRENGTH

ENERGY

SPEED

DURABILITY

FIGHTING

IRON FIST DELIVERS A PUNCH THAT TEARS THROUGH A *TANK* LIKE IT WAS *TISSUE PAPER*.

DANNY IS A *MASTER* OF K'UN-LUN'S MARTIAL ARTS, JUDO, AIKIDO, KARATE AND...

NOW THE SCREAM OF *CHAOS* WILL MEET THE *SOUL* OF IRON.

YAHHHHHHH!

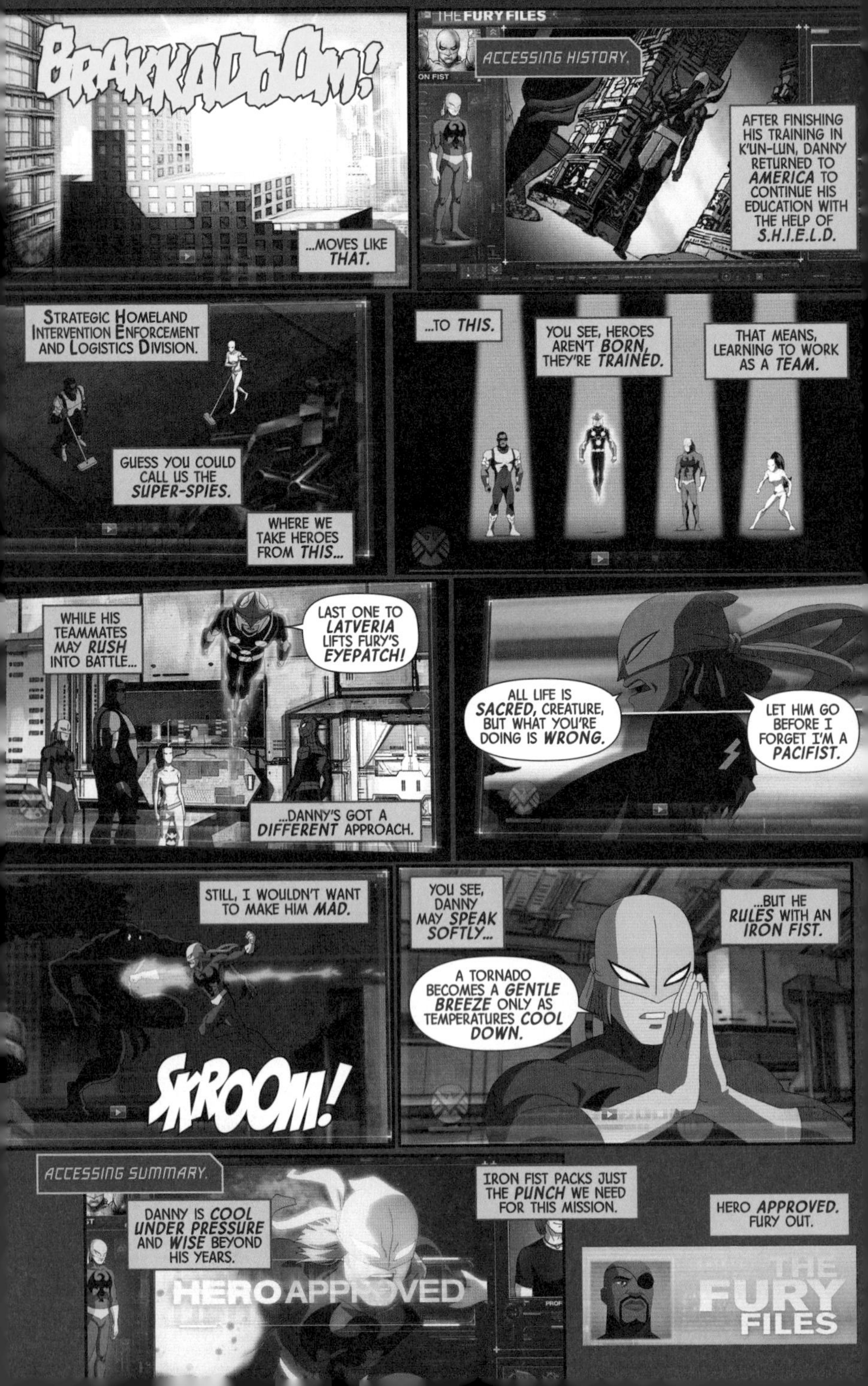
BRAKKADOOM!
...MOVES LIKE THAT.
THE FURY FILES
ACCESSING HISTORY.
ON FIST
AFTER FINISHING HIS TRAINING IN K'UN-LUN, DANNY RETURNED TO AMERICA TO CONTINUE HIS EDUCATION WITH THE HELP OF S.H.I.E.L.D.
STRATEGIC HOMELAND INTERVENTION ENFORCEMENT AND LOGISTICS DIVISION.
GUESS YOU COULD CALL US THE SUPER-SPIES.
WHERE WE TAKE HEROES FROM THIS...
...TO THIS.
YOU SEE, HEROES AREN'T BORN, THEY'RE TRAINED.
THAT MEANS, LEARNING TO WORK AS A TEAM.
WHILE HIS TEAMMATES MAY RUSH INTO BATTLE...
LAST ONE TO LATVERIA LIFTS FURY'S EYEPATCH!
...DANNY'S GOT A DIFFERENT APPROACH.
ALL LIFE IS SACRED, CREATURE, BUT WHAT YOU'RE DOING IS WRONG.
LET HIM GO BEFORE I FORGET I'M A PACIFIST.
STILL, I WOULDN'T WANT TO MAKE HIM MAD.
SKROOM!
YOU SEE, DANNY MAY SPEAK SOFTLY...
...BUT HE RULES WITH AN IRON FIST.
A TORNADO BECOMES A GENTLE BREEZE ONLY AS TEMPERATURES COOL DOWN.
ACCESSING SUMMARY.
DANNY IS COOL UNDER PRESSURE AND WISE BEYOND HIS YEARS.
HERO APPROVED
IRON FIST PACKS JUST THE PUNCH WE NEED FOR THIS MISSION.
HERO APPROVED. FURY OUT.
THE FURY FILES

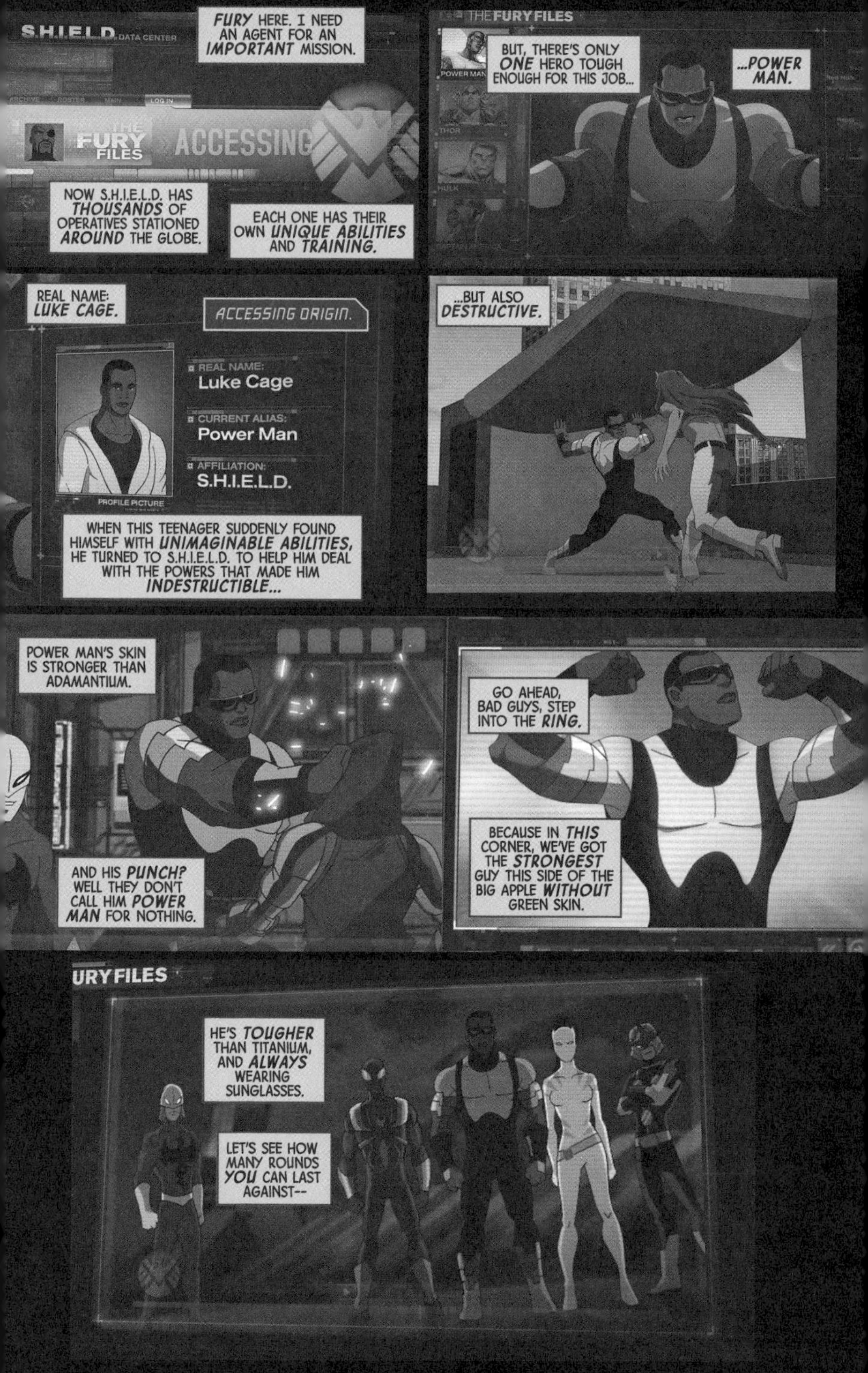
S.H.I.E.L.D. DATA CENTER
FURY HERE. I NEED AN AGENT FOR AN IMPORTANT MISSION.
THE FURY FILES
ACCESSING
NOW S.H.I.E.L.D. HAS THOUSANDS OF OPERATIVES STATIONED AROUND THE GLOBE.
EACH ONE HAS THEIR OWN UNIQUE ABILITIES AND TRAINING.
THE FURY FILES
BUT, THERE'S ONLY ONE HERO TOUGH ENOUGH FOR THIS JOB...
...POWER MAN.
REAL NAME: LUKE CAGE.
ACCESSING ORIGIN.
REAL NAME:
Luke Cage
CURRENT ALIAS:
Power Man
AFFILIATION:
S.H.I.E.L.D.
PROFILE PICTURE
WHEN THIS TEENAGER SUDDENLY FOUND HIMSELF WITH UNIMAGINABLE ABILITIES, HE TURNED TO S.H.I.E.L.D. TO HELP HIM DEAL WITH THE POWERS THAT MADE HIM INDESTRUCTIBLE...
...BUT ALSO DESTRUCTIVE.
POWER MAN'S SKIN IS STRONGER THAN ADAMANTIUM.
AND HIS PUNCH? WELL THEY DON'T CALL HIM POWER MAN FOR NOTHING.
GO AHEAD, BAD GUYS, STEP INTO THE RING.
BECAUSE IN THIS CORNER, WE'VE GOT THE STRONGEST GUY THIS SIDE OF THE BIG APPLE WITHOUT GREEN SKIN.
URY FILES
HE'S TOUGHER THAN TITANIUM, AND ALWAYS WEARING SUNGLASSES.
LET'S SEE HOW MANY ROUNDS YOU CAN LAST AGAINST--

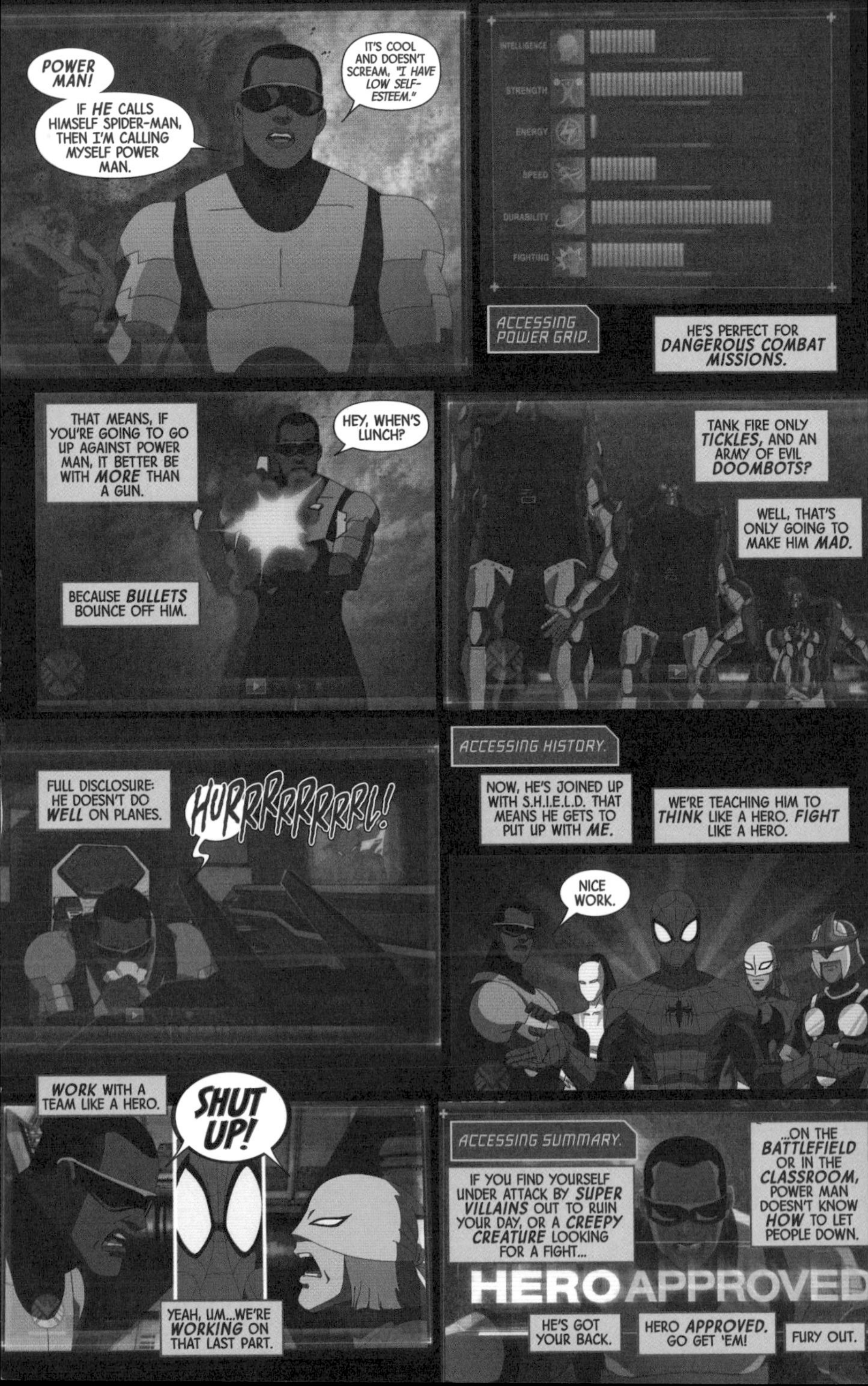

POWER MAN!
IF HE CALLS HIMSELF SPIDER-MAN, THEN I'M CALLING MYSELF POWER MAN.
IT'S COOL AND DOESN'T SCREAM, "I HAVE LOW SELF-ESTEEM."
INTELLIGENCE
STRENGTH
ENERGY
SPEED
DURABILITY
FIGHTING
ACCESSING POWER GRID.
HE'S PERFECT FOR DANGEROUS COMBAT MISSIONS.
THAT MEANS, IF YOU'RE GOING TO GO UP AGAINST POWER MAN, IT BETTER BE WITH MORE THAN A GUN.
HEY, WHEN'S LUNCH?
BECAUSE BULLETS BOUNCE OFF HIM.
TANK FIRE ONLY TICKLES, AND AN ARMY OF EVIL DOOMBOTS?
WELL, THAT'S ONLY GOING TO MAKE HIM MAD.
FULL DISCLOSURE: HE DOESN'T DO WELL ON PLANES.
HURRRRRRRRL!
ACCESSING HISTORY.
NOW, HE'S JOINED UP WITH S.H.I.E.L.D. THAT MEANS HE GETS TO PUT UP WITH ME.
WE'RE TEACHING HIM TO THINK LIKE A HERO. FIGHT LIKE A HERO.
NICE WORK.
WORK WITH A TEAM LIKE A HERO.
SHUT UP!
YEAH, UM...WE'RE WORKING ON THAT LAST PART.
ACCESSING SUMMARY.
IF YOU FIND YOURSELF UNDER ATTACK BY SUPER VILLAINS OUT TO RUIN YOUR DAY, OR A CREEPY CREATURE LOOKING FOR A FIGHT...
...ON THE BATTLEFIELD OR IN THE CLASSROOM, POWER MAN DOESN'T KNOW HOW TO LET PEOPLE DOWN.
HERO APPROVED
HE'S GOT YOUR BACK.
HERO APPROVED. GO GET 'EM!
FURY OUT.

FURY HERE.

THE FURY FILES — ACCESSING

I NEED A SPECIAL AGENT FOR A NEW MISSION. S.H.I.E.L.D. HAS THOUSANDS OF AGENTS AROUND THE GLOBE.

EACH ONE HAS *UNIQUE* ABILITIES AND TRAINING, BUT THERE'S ONLY ONE HIGH-FLYING HERO WITH THE SPEED FOR THIS MISSION...

...NOVA.

REAL NAME:
Sam Alexander

CURRENT ALIAS:
Nova

AFFILIATION:
S.H.I.E.L.D.

PROFILE PICTURE

REAL NAME, *SAM ALEXANDER.*

THIS HEADSTRONG TEEN BECAME A HIGH-FLYING SUPER HERO WHEN HE WAS CHOSEN TO WEAR A *MYSTERIOUS HELMET* MADE WITH *ALIEN TECHNOLOGY.*

FURY FILES

THIS HELMET GIVES SAM THE *AWESOME* POWERS OF NOVA!

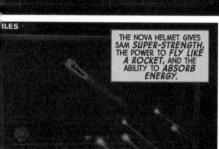

ILES

THE NOVA HELMET GIVES SAM *SUPER-STRENGTH,* THE POWER TO *FLY LIKE A ROCKET,* AND THE ABILITY TO *ABSORB ENERGY.*

I DIDN'T KNOW YOU COULD ABSORB ENERGY.

NEITHER DID I.

FURY FILES

AND HE SHOOTS FORCE BEAMS OUT OF HIS HANDS.

SAM CAN FLY AT SUPERSONIC SPEEDS, THAT MEANS HE CAN BREAK THE SOUND BARRIER.

NOT BAD FOR A KID WITHOUT A *DRIVER'S LICENSE.*

BUT THERE'S STILL *ONE* THING I DON'T UNDERSTAND...

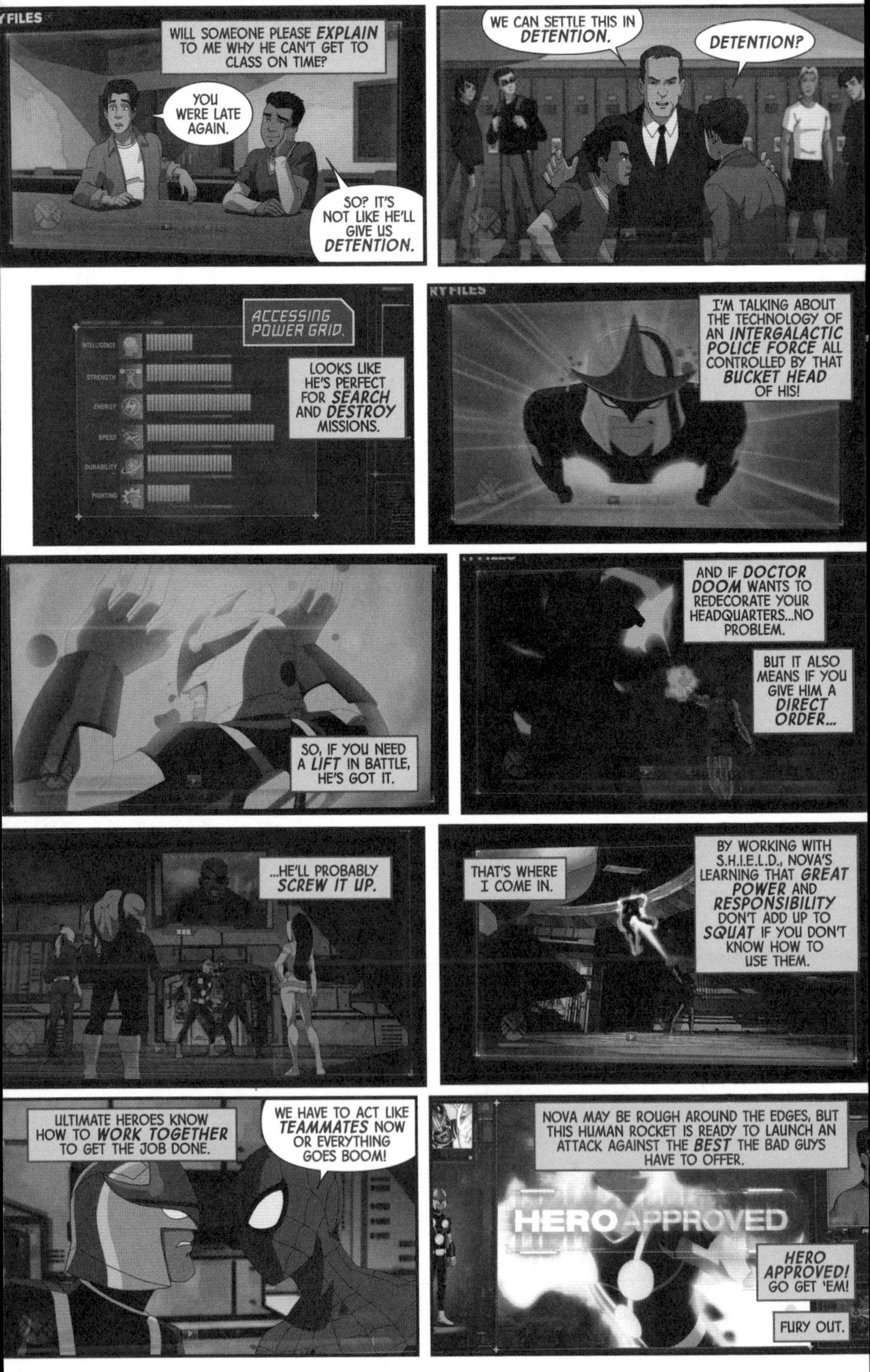
RY FILES
WILL SOMEONE PLEASE EXPLAIN TO ME WHY HE CAN'T GET TO CLASS ON TIME?
YOU WERE LATE AGAIN.
SO? IT'S NOT LIKE HE'LL GIVE US DETENTION.
WE CAN SETTLE THIS IN DETENTION.
DETENTION?
ACCESSING POWER GRID.
INTELLIGENCE
STRENGTH
ENERGY
SPEED
DURABILITY
FIGHTING
LOOKS LIKE HE'S PERFECT FOR SEARCH AND DESTROY MISSIONS.
RY FILES
I'M TALKING ABOUT THE TECHNOLOGY OF AN INTERGALACTIC POLICE FORCE ALL CONTROLLED BY THAT BUCKET HEAD OF HIS!
SO, IF YOU NEED A LIFT IN BATTLE, HE'S GOT IT.
AND IF DOCTOR DOOM WANTS TO REDECORATE YOUR HEADQUARTERS...NO PROBLEM.
BUT IT ALSO MEANS IF YOU GIVE HIM A DIRECT ORDER...
...HE'LL PROBABLY SCREW IT UP.
THAT'S WHERE I COME IN.
BY WORKING WITH S.H.I.E.L.D., NOVA'S LEARNING THAT GREAT POWER AND RESPONSIBILITY DON'T ADD UP TO SQUAT IF YOU DON'T KNOW HOW TO USE THEM.
ULTIMATE HEROES KNOW HOW TO WORK TOGETHER TO GET THE JOB DONE.
WE HAVE TO ACT LIKE TEAMMATES NOW OR EVERYTHING GOES BOOM!
NOVA MAY BE ROUGH AROUND THE EDGES, BUT THIS HUMAN ROCKET IS READY TO LAUNCH AN ATTACK AGAINST THE BEST THE BAD GUYS HAVE TO OFFER.
HERO APPROVED
HERO APPROVED! GO GET 'EM!
FURY OUT.

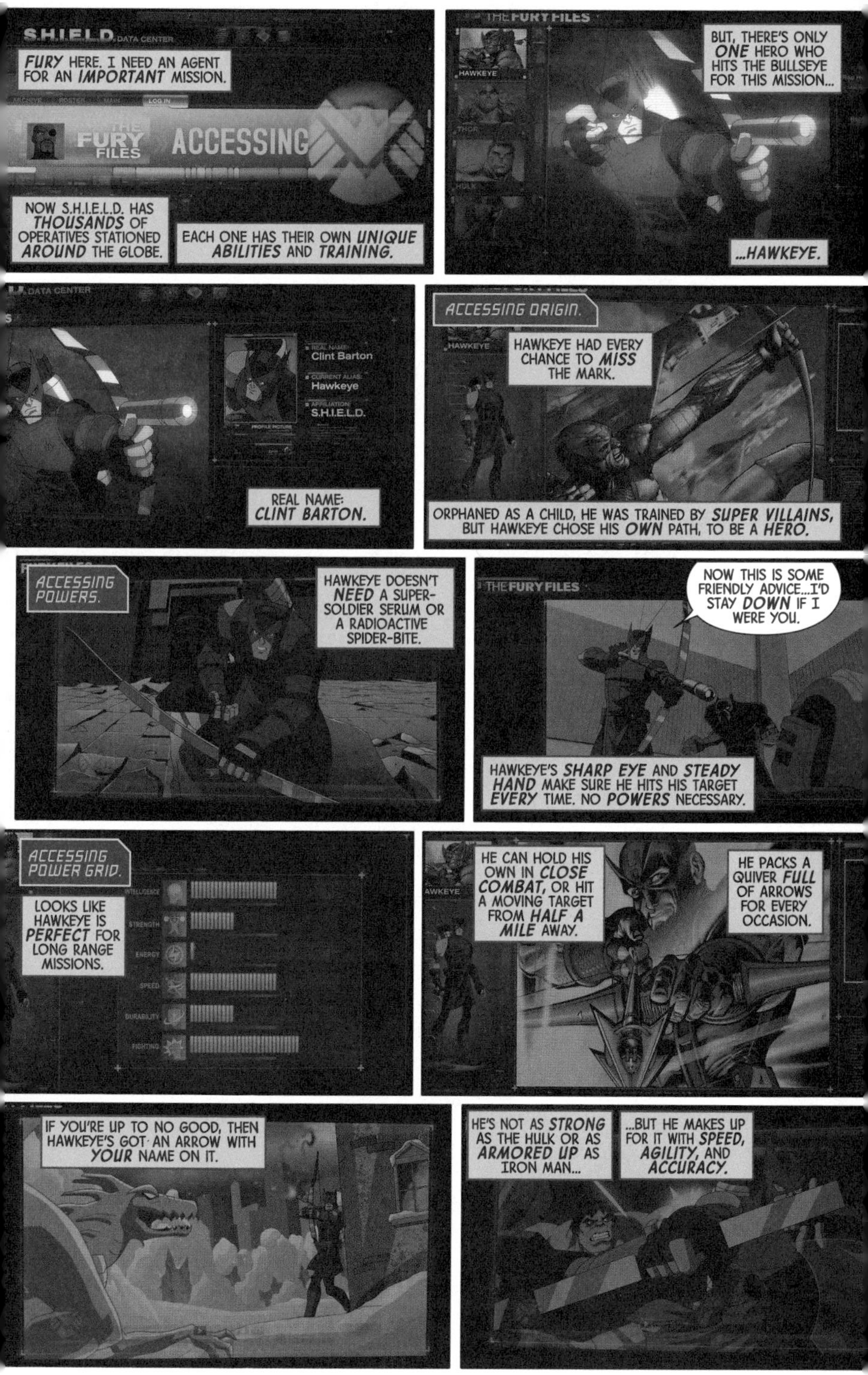
S.H.I.E.L.D. DATA CENTER
FURY HERE. I NEED AN AGENT FOR AN IMPORTANT MISSION.
THE FURY FILES
ACCESSING
NOW S.H.I.E.L.D. HAS THOUSANDS OF OPERATIVES STATIONED AROUND THE GLOBE.
EACH ONE HAS THEIR OWN UNIQUE ABILITIES AND TRAINING.
THE FURY FILES
BUT, THERE'S ONLY ONE HERO WHO HITS THE BULLSEYE FOR THIS MISSION...
HAWKEYE
THOR
HULK
...HAWKEYE.
DATA CENTER
REAL NAME: Clint Barton
CURRENT ALIAS: Hawkeye
AFFILIATION: S.H.I.E.L.D.
PROFILE PICTURE
REAL NAME: CLINT BARTON.
ACCESSING ORIGIN.
HAWKEYE
HAWKEYE HAD EVERY CHANCE TO MISS THE MARK.
ORPHANED AS A CHILD, HE WAS TRAINED BY SUPER VILLAINS, BUT HAWKEYE CHOSE HIS OWN PATH, TO BE A HERO.
ACCESSING POWERS.
HAWKEYE DOESN'T NEED A SUPER-SOLDIER SERUM OR A RADIOACTIVE SPIDER-BITE.
THE FURY FILES
NOW THIS IS SOME FRIENDLY ADVICE...I'D STAY DOWN IF I WERE YOU.
HAWKEYE'S SHARP EYE AND STEADY HAND MAKE SURE HE HITS HIS TARGET EVERY TIME. NO POWERS NECESSARY.
ACCESSING POWER GRID.
LOOKS LIKE HAWKEYE IS PERFECT FOR LONG RANGE MISSIONS.
INTELLIGENCE
STRENGTH
ENERGY
SPEED
DURABILITY
FIGHTING
HE CAN HOLD HIS OWN IN CLOSE COMBAT, OR HIT A MOVING TARGET FROM HALF A MILE AWAY.
HE PACKS A QUIVER FULL OF ARROWS FOR EVERY OCCASION.
IF YOU'RE UP TO NO GOOD, THEN HAWKEYE'S GOT AN ARROW WITH YOUR NAME ON IT.
HE'S NOT AS STRONG AS THE HULK OR AS ARMORED UP AS IRON MAN...
...BUT HE MAKES UP FOR IT WITH SPEED, AGILITY, AND ACCURACY.

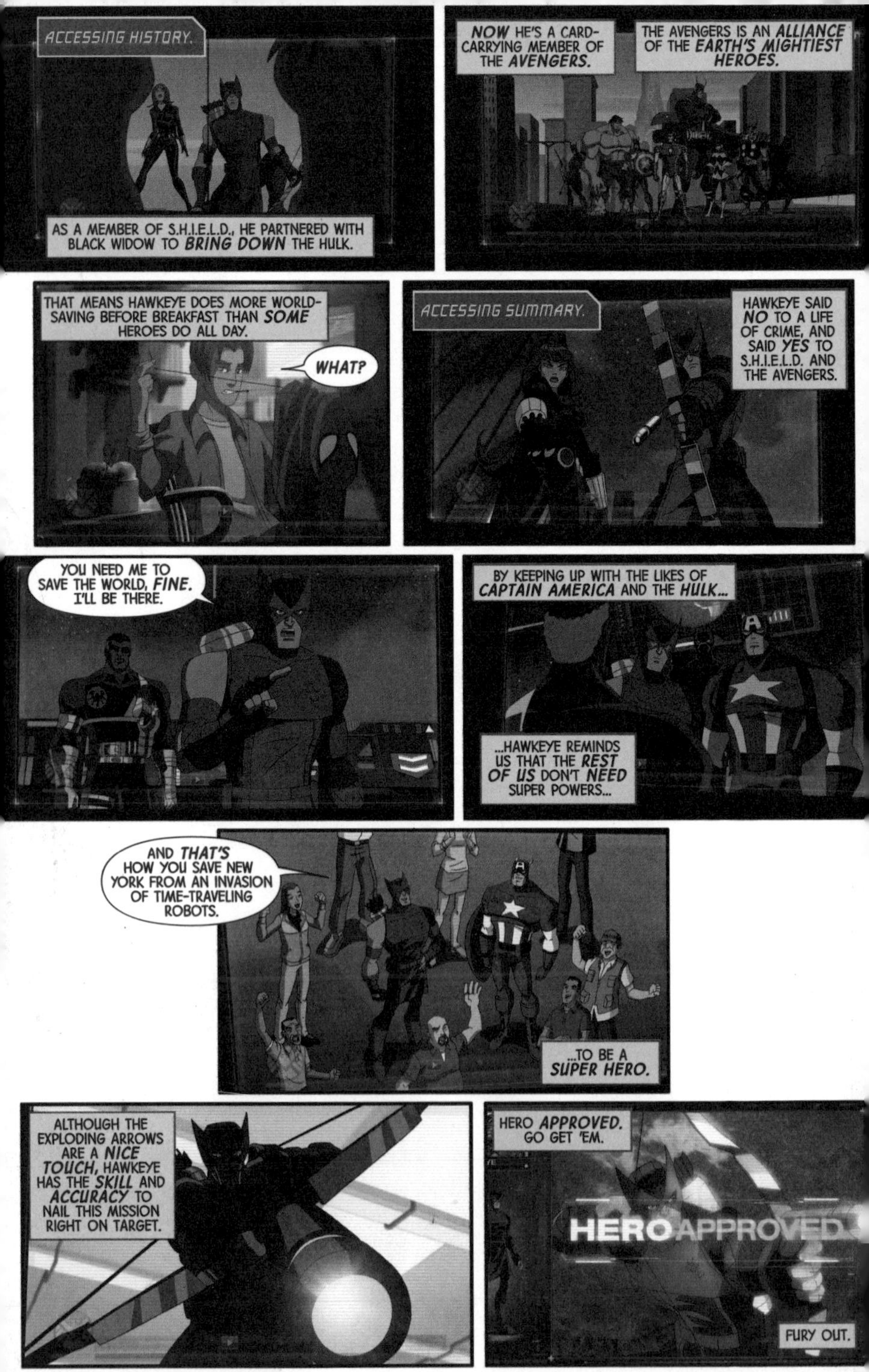
ACCESSING HISTORY.
AS A MEMBER OF S.H.I.E.L.D., HE PARTNERED WITH BLACK WIDOW TO BRING DOWN THE HULK.
NOW HE'S A CARD-CARRYING MEMBER OF THE AVENGERS.
THE AVENGERS IS AN ALLIANCE OF THE EARTH'S MIGHTIEST HEROES.
THAT MEANS HAWKEYE DOES MORE WORLD-SAVING BEFORE BREAKFAST THAN SOME HEROES DO ALL DAY.
WHAT?
ACCESSING SUMMARY.
HAWKEYE SAID NO TO A LIFE OF CRIME, AND SAID YES TO S.H.I.E.L.D. AND THE AVENGERS.
YOU NEED ME TO SAVE THE WORLD, FINE. I'LL BE THERE.
BY KEEPING UP WITH THE LIKES OF CAPTAIN AMERICA AND THE HULK...
...HAWKEYE REMINDS US THAT THE REST OF US DON'T NEED SUPER POWERS...
AND THAT'S HOW YOU SAVE NEW YORK FROM AN INVASION OF TIME-TRAVELING ROBOTS.
...TO BE A SUPER HERO.
ALTHOUGH THE EXPLODING ARROWS ARE A NICE TOUCH, HAWKEYE HAS THE SKILL AND ACCURACY TO NAIL THIS MISSION RIGHT ON TARGET.
HERO APPROVED. GO GET 'EM.
HERO APPROVED
FURY OUT.